CLASS AND PSYCHO

Does psychoanalysis have anything to say about the emotional landscapes of class? How can class-inclusive psychoanalytic projects, historic and contemporary, inform theory and practice? Class and psychoanalysis are unusual bedfellows, but this original book shows how much is to be gained by exploring their relationship. Joanna Ryan provides a comprehensively researched and challenging overview in which she holds the tension between the radical and progressive potential of psychoanalysis, in its unique understandings of the unconscious, with its status as a mainly expensive and exclusive profession.

Class and Psychoanalysis draws on existing historical scholarship, as well as on the experiences of the author and other writers in free or low-cost projects, to show what has been learned from transposing psychoanalysis into different social contexts. The book describes how class, although descriptively present, was excluded from the founding theories of psychoanalysis, leaving a problematic conceptual legacy that the book attempts to remedy. Joanna Ryan argues for an interdisciplinary approach, drawing on modern sociological and psychosocial research to understand the injuries of class, the complexities of social mobility and the defences of privilege. She brings together contemporary clinical writings with her own research about class within therapy relationships to illustrate the anxieties, ambivalences and inhibitions surrounding class, and the unconsciousness with which it may be enacted.

Class and Psychoanalysis breaks new ground in providing frameworks for a critical psychoanalysis that includes class. It will be of interest to anyone who wishes to think psychoanalytically about how we are intimately formed by class, or who is concerned with the inequalities of access to psychoanalytic therapies, or with the future of psychoanalysis.

Joanna Ryan, PhD, is a psychoanalytic psychotherapist. She has worked widely in clinical practice, teaching and supervision; in academic research; and in the politics of psychotherapy. She is co-author (with N. O'Connor) of *Wild Desires and Mistaken Identities: Lesbianism and Psychoanalysis*; co-editor (with S. Cartledge) of *Sex and Love: New Thoughts on Old Contradictions*; and author of *The Politics of Mental Handicap* and many other publications.

CLASS AND PSYCHOANALYSIS

Landscapes of Inequality

Joanna Ryan

LONDON AND NEW YORK

First published 2017
by Routledge
2 Park Square, Milton Park, Abingdon, Oxon OX14 4RN

and by Routledge
711 Third Avenue, New York, NY 10017

Routledge is an imprint of the Taylor & Francis Group, an informa business

© 2017 Joanna Ryan

The right of Joanna Ryan to be identified as author of this work has been asserted by her in accordance with sections 77 and 78 of the Copyright, Designs and Patents Act 1988.

All rights reserved. No part of this book may be reprinted or reproduced or utilised in any form or by any electronic, mechanical, or other means, now known or hereafter invented, including photocopying and recording, or in any information storage or retrieval system, without permission in writing from the publishers.

Trademark notice: Product or corporate names may be trademarks or registered trademarks, and are used only for identification and explanation without intent to infringe.

British Library Cataloguing-in-Publication Data
A catalogue record for this book is available from the British Library

Library of Congress Cataloging-in-Publication Data
A catalog record for this title has been requested

ISBN: 978-1-138-88549-3 (hbk)
ISBN: 978-1-138-88551-6 (pbk)
ISBN: 978-1-315-71540-7 (ebk)

Typeset in Bembo
by Apex CoVantage, LLC

Printed and bound by CPI Group (UK) Ltd, Croydon, CR0 4YY

CONTENTS

Acknowledgements   *vii*

1. Introduction: why class and psychoanalysis?   1
2. Asking questions of history   19
3. Elision and disavowal: the extrusion of class from psychoanalytic theory   36
4. Psychotherapy for the people? Psychoanalysis in some public sectors   57
5. Lived experiences of class: psychosocial and sociological perspectives   82
6. Class and social mobility within the psychoanalytic field   102
7. Class within therapy relationships   118
8. Contemporary psychoanalytic writings on class in the clinic   134

9 Money and some political economies of
  psychoanalytic work   159

10 Speaking class to psychoanalysis   171

Index   *189*

ACKNOWLEDGEMENTS

This book has evolved over many years of practice, discussion and engagements of various kinds. I would like to thank the participants in my research study, and all the patients and supervisees whom I have had the privilege to work with. The Tavistock Institute of Medical Psychology funded some of my research. I have benefited greatly from being a Visiting Research Fellow in the Department of Sociology', Goldsmith University of London, in 2004–08. An Honorary Research Fellowship in 2016 in the Department of Psychosocial Studies, Birkbeck, University of London, has helped me complete this book. I have gained much from my involvement with The Site for Contemporary Psychoanalysis and the critical and innovative psychoanalytic thinking that it enables.

Sheila Ernst, who died in 2015, had been a long-term companion in many of these journeys through psychoanalysis and politics, and an inspiring internal presence through the writing of it. I owe much to the stimulation and support of Vic Seidler's friendship, breadth of knowledge and critique over many years. I'm hugely grateful to Ruth Petrie for invaluable editorial input into the whole book, and for her consistent and sustaining friendship. Madelyn Brewer has read many chapters and provided thought-provoking comments, as have Sue Einhorn, Marion Gow, Julian Lousada, Allegra Madgwick, Marie Maguire, Janet Sayers and Vic Seidler. My long-standing women's group has been a constant source of support and challenge. Thanks to Marion Gow and Angela Kreeger for initiating a Laplanche study group. Casey Ryan has been invaluable in patiently helping me navigate the IT demands of the twenty-first century, as well as in his support and encouragement. Aaron Brown has been consistently concerned for my work and well-being, as have many other friends and family. Thanks also to Riccardo Steiner for his engagement and encouragement. I am immensely grateful to the NHS, and especially my GP, Dr Sanders, for their essential ministrations over the years. Margaret Mellor has done some essential copy-editing.

Excerpts from 'Extrusion and disavowal', previously published in *Sitegeist: A Journal of Psychoanalysis and Philosophy* (2009), are reprinted with kind permission of Karnac Books.

Portions of 'Class is "in" you', previously published in *British Journal of Psychotherapy* (2006), are reprinted with permission from John Wiley and Sons.

Portions of 'Class is "in" you' in *Thinking Space: Promoting Thinking About Race, Culture and Diversity in Psychotherapy and Beyond*, edited by Frank Lowe (2013), are reprinted with kind permission of Karnac Books.

Lynne Layton, Laurence Spurling, Penny Crick and Teresa Mulvena have allowed me to quote from unpublished papers.

1
INTRODUCTION
Why class and psychoanalysis?

Class can evoke extremely charged and difficult emotions. It is a determining factor in the life possibilities of many people, a source of huge inequalities or privileges that go back to our earliest experiences. Entwined with inequalities of wealth, income, education and health, class also reaches into the depths of the psyche and how we feel about ourselves in relation to others. Class can arouse feelings of shame, embarrassment, guilt, anger, contempt, envy, pleasure and pride. It can be a source of great defensiveness and inhibition, and also of solidarity and belonging. Inequality, as Richard Sennett writes in *Respect* (2003), is such a basic aspect of human experience that people are always trying to make sense of it, or, as I argue later, disavow knowledge of it. The conscious and unconscious levels at which class is lived, experienced and felt have been little explored psychoanalytically. This is in striking contrast to the very rich fictional and autobiographical literature in which class is a major theme, as well as the many plays and television series where class difference functions as a central dramatic foil. In academic work, social stratification has long been a preoccupation of sociology but there is now a growing body of sociological and psychosocial work concerning the lived experiences and emotions of class, some of it using psychoanalytic concepts, and much of it very relevant to any psychoanalytic interest in class.

This book interrogates the psychoanalytic silences around class, its hidden and yet omnipresent nature, the many disavowals involved from the earliest days of psychoanalysis until the present. Class is, however, beginning to figure within some strands of contemporary psychoanalysis, building on the recent critical interest in gender, 'race'[1] and sexuality, in ways that demand new thinking. I also address some of the many projects that have tried or are still trying to forge a more class-inclusive psychoanalytic practice, and I look at what we can learn from these. Contemporary initiatives, including my own research, suggest different ways of thinking psychoanalytically about class within clinical work. These are appraised for what they suggest about the various processes by which class can be installed in and/or structure the psyche, the ways in which, as Lynsey Hanley (2016: 227) expresses it, class builds 'walls in the head'. I also address what frameworks psychoanalysis might need in order to more fully embrace class clinically and theoretically.

Psychoanalysis is widely seen as middle class and exclusive: for the privileged classes only in its high-fee/private practice/time-consuming nature; as embodying middle-class values in its implicit norms of psychic health; and in its trainings too expensive and culturally elitist to be more inclusive. How true are these common perceptions? In this book I consider the ways in which there is an undeniable and very important reality to them, but also how the field is more complex, more diverse and in parts more socially concerned than these somewhat caricaturing statements suggest.

There have been and still are many attempts to challenge and remedy the exclusivity of psychoanalysis, by the establishment of free or low-cost accessible community clinics, by its historic development within the public health system of the UK National Health Service (NHS), and in the community mental health movements of the USA. Often these community projects are or were fuelled by intense passions, by concerns for social justice or revolutionary change, and by convictions about the value of psychoanalytic therapy. These historical and contemporary initiatives have received relatively little recognition as regards what they might contribute to the mainstream of psychoanalytic thinking, what issues arise when psychoanalysis is practised in different contexts from its usual one and what might be learned psychoanalytically about the psychic impacts of class. Looking at the historic clinics in Chapter 2, and more contemporary ones in Chapter 4, I consider the scattered information about these diverse projects, the different motivations, ideologies and psychoanalytic theories involved in attempts to widen the economic and class basis of psychoanalysis. However, more inclusive access is only part of the story. Cultural and social aspects of psychoanalysis are often salient, and class can enter and inflect therapy relationships in important ways, as Chapters 7 and 8 show.

Working-class lives are barely represented in the annals of psychoanalysis, despite the much greater occurrence of life events and circumstances likely to cause psychological harm. Many studies have shown that within mental health systems working-class patients are less likely to be referred for psychoanalytic or psychodynamic therapies, and more likely to be offered pharmacological or behavioural treatments. This bias continues to the present: a recent study of psychotherapists' responses to intending patients showed substantial discrimination against working-class and black inquirers (Kugelmass, 2016).

The silence of psychoanalysis about class extends beyond its origins and location in high-fee private practice. Psychoanalysts do not readily have the language or the concepts to integrate matters of class into their systems of thought and theories, and this applies as much to middle- and upper-class positionings as to working-class ones. At issue here is more than the well-worn conceptual gap or caesura common to most of the 'psy' disciplines, between ways of thinking about the individual and about society, the psyche and the social, although that is relevant. Rather, as I argue in Chapter 3, the extrusion of class from psychoanalytic theorising and from consideration in individual analyses took place in its originating theories and case studies, with long-lasting consequences in the unavailability of language and concepts with which to think about class psychoanalytically. The rich contemporary psychosocial and sociological research on class as it is lived and experienced affectively, some of which is outlined in Chapter 5, could address these gaps, just as psychoanalytic concepts already do inform some of this work. I thus explore how the languages of class and of psychoanalysis can be brought into relation with each other, reading them alongside, together with or against each other, in many different contexts and practices.

This book comes out of my experience over decades as a psychoanalytic psychotherapist, patient and clinical supervisor, hugely appreciative of the power of psychoanalysis to illuminate aspects of subjectivity that other psychologies do not remotely reach, and its potential to enable positive change in individual lives. My varied experience also as an academic, a researcher and a sometime political activist has contributed to my taking a view of the psychoanalytic field from outside as well as inside, in its historical, economic and institutional locations, at the same time as holding on to the central importance of its extensive theorising of the intra-psychic, and its intimate, highly nuanced clinical practice. Here I identify my starting points, assumptions, definitions and aims.

Definitions

In this book I widen the field beyond the strict but contested definition of what counts as psychoanalysis to include psychoanalytic psychotherapy and some forms of psychodynamic or psychoanalytic counselling. I encompass all these practices under the generic term of *psychoanalytic therapy*, while also mindful of their differences, and using other terms as appropriate to context. Historically, there has been extensive debate within the profession in both the UK and the USA as to these definitions,[2] the criteria for distinction, and who has the right to legitimate certain professional labels, a debate intensified by the evolution of the regulatory functions of the main umbrella organisations. I argue in Chapter 4 that this debate has the hallmarks of the operation of symbolic power, the conferring of recognition and status underpinned by the access that economic and cultural capital provide. I suggest that the forces driving these distinctions, and those between 'pure' and 'applied' clinical work, are part of the hierarchy whereby work outside long-term intensive private practice is seen as lesser, a form of symbolic violence that perpetuates internal class divisions. British psychoanalyst Harvey Taylor, in his far-reaching discussion and critique, argues that in the interests of a new dispensation for psychoanalysis, any institutions and individuals using psychoanalytic theory should be encompassed under the term *psychoanalytic community* (Taylor, 2013). This represents a desire, as yet mainly unrealised, but echoed by Gary Fereday, current CEO of the British Psychoanalytic Council (BPC), to critique some of the exclusivity and the hierarchy, and reach outwards to kindred forms of psychoanalytic therapy (Fereday, 2015). In choosing the term 'psychoanalytic therapy' I am emphasising the commonalities of thought and practice, striving towards an inclusivity that is necessary if we are to seriously contest the inequalities embedded in the field.

It is also necessary to locate psychoanalysis in its institutional and educational practices. These embody aspects of the power, social and economic capitals involved in the production of contemporary psychoanalytic practitioners. In the UK there is a schism in the field between those psychoanalytic organisations that belong to the BPC and those that belong to the United Kingdom Council for Psychotherapy (UKCP). A third, larger body, the British Association for Counselling and Psychotherapy (BACP), also regulates many psychodynamic counsellors and psychotherapists.[3] The resources needed to undertake all such trainings, predominantly in private or in charitable organisations, are considerable, itself a major class issue, as Chapter 9 discusses. The cultural milieux encountered on trainings may also embody socially coded values, as I explore in Chapter 6.[4]

Despite these organisational divides there is considerable overlap among many psychoanalytic therapists, whatever their institutional affiliation, in the use of basic psychoanalytic theory and modes of practice. Theoretical affiliations (e.g. between object-relations therapists, Lacanians or Jungians) may represent significant differences in approach and understanding, but these mainly cut across the main organisational divides, with some exceptions. The field of clinical psychoanalysis is thus large, differentiated and theoretically diverse, if not fragmented. For present purposes I am including any psychotherapeutic practice that makes use of psychoanalytic theory and core psychoanalytic concepts, such as those of unconscious fantasy, transference, repression and defence, free association and non-directive listening, and interpretation.

Any mention of class issues readily provokes the question: what do you mean by class? There is an extensive sociological literature on issues of definition and demarcation, and also on class identities. Historically and officially, class has been stratified by occupational status. Recently, there have been attempts to broaden the economic bases of categorisation, to include modern research on the multidimensionality of class, embracing social and cultural distinctions (Savage, 2015). However, as Beverley Skeggs forcefully argues, class categorisation is itself an activity that is imbued with various class interests and moral evaluations, unacknowledged in dominant systems of stratification (Skeggs, 2015), but reflecting historical judgements of social value. In my research I have used participants' own definitions of their class status; indeed, the criteria and language they used, as well as the emotions evoked, were part of the study. The common parlance of 'working class' and 'middle class' is not so tightly specified as in the categorisations of sociology, but still has great applicability, as a recent national survey on class identities and class awareness found (Evans and Mellon, 2015). My usage here will depend very much on context, recognising that such ascriptions are themselves hybrid and heterogeneous in important ways, and subject to social change. Further, in including both UK and US literature, I am aware that definitions of class can be different between these two countries.

Class works in and through other aspects of people's lives, such as place, history, gender, 'race', ethnicity, age, sexuality and disability. The uncertainty and ambivalence often surrounding the use of class terms is a topic in its own right (see Chapters 5 and 6). They indicate the emotional and other complexities of drawing these distinctions, not that the social realities they pertain to do not exist as powerful factors. Class, as both Skeggs (2015) and Tyler (2015) argue, is centrally an identifier of inequality. It has a double aspect in its attribution of location within a social hierarchy and as a name for struggles against the far-reaching effects of such positionings.

The sociological frameworks I have found most useful here are those which invoke the notions of distinction and relationality.[5] Much of the contemporary sociological work on class as it is lived and experienced sees class in terms of processes and practices, existing 'not . . . as something given but *something to be done*' (Bourdieu, 1998: 12, italics in original). Pierre Bourdieu's work, especially his depiction of different kinds of capital – economic, cultural, social and symbolic – operating in social space, is of great relevance in understanding the classed dynamics of the psychoanalytic field, and also as a framework for exploring the subjective, emotional and unconscious aspects of class, as Chapter 5 illustrates. However, the material and economic circumstances which characterise different social positions and which play such a powerful part in driving inequalities cannot be reduced to matters only of distinction and culture, even though they importantly involve them. This is the ever-present danger of and challenge to any investigation of the subjective and affective aspects of class. The problem this poses is how to relate and integrate the material and the psychological, the social and the psychic, an issue that has a well-trodden history in Freudo-Marxist theorising. Here, while I do adopt some of the arguments of such thinkers, I mainly eschew large-scale theorising in favour of smaller-scale explorations in the practices of psychoanalysis as a clinical and intellectual discipline and as a socially located activity.

Class, politics and therapy

My starting point is that class matters. It matters because it is a major source and consequence of inequality, often transmitted intergenerationally. This is so even in the face of individual social mobility, as some of the psychoanalytic explorations in this book will show. Class is a prime example of the past operating in the present, and thus could be of great psychoanalytic interest as to how it constructs and endures within the psyche, even with huge changes in social circumstances, as I argue in Chapter 6. *The Hidden Injuries of Class* (Sennett and Cobb, 1972) amply illustrates this, but the full import of this classic work has only recently been developed. The title itself points to two fundamental dimensions of class, themes which continue into the present, and which have great psychoanalytic resonance.

Class, it is widely acknowledged, disappeared from political and academic discourse in the recent past, with the supposed era of the classless society, where class could not be named as such, but was rendered only as social exclusion, if at all. The demise of Marxist thinking, the influence of postmodernism and the privileging of identity politics, all led to a focus on other forms of difference and diversity, while generally ignoring class.

Neo-liberalism has become hegemonic in economics and politics, and permeates the mental health field too. It has led to a falsely but powerfully individualising attitude to social issues and a marketisation of health care, even as structural inequalities intensify. Concomitant with all this has been the lessening of collective forms of organising, as trade unions have been weakened by restrictive legislation and the increasing globalisation of capital, so that the bargaining power of labour has been progressively reduced since the 1970s.

However, as Richard Hoggart said: 'Each decade we shiftily declare we have buried class, yet each decade the coffin remains empty' (Hoggart, 1989, cited in Hanley, 2016: xiv). We are now faced with the evidence of extreme inequality between rich and poor within many societies, not least those of the UK and USA. Inequality has risen up the political agenda nationally and globally, with many different ways of measuring its extent, and a correspondingly burgeoning literature.[6] Economic inequality and socioeconomic class are not synonymous but are highly correlated; other factors such as gender, ethnicity, disability and age are also important (National Equality Panel, 2010). This latter research charts how the disparities in wealth and income between different socioeconomic sections of society in the UK have grown since the 1980s and how initial disadvantages in terms of socioeconomic status tend to accumulate over a lifetime. These are also correlated with life expectancy. The Social Mobility and Child Poverty Commission (2014) describes how partial economic recovery since the 2007–08 recession has not been matched by social recovery, with average earnings continuing to fall and Britain remaining a deeply divided and elitist society, with social mobility flatlining. Their report envisages that these stark inequalities will worsen unless progressive social policies are put in place. In the UK, the hard-won achievements of the welfare state are being cut back, fragmented and undermined by underfunding, outsourcing and privatisation, all changes which negatively affect the provision of psychodynamic and psychoanalytic therapy within the NHS, and also the funding of those third-sector organisations which provide low-cost therapy. At the present time we are witnessing the political fall-out from this disempowerment, neglect and pauperisation of sections of the working classes.

The effects of neo-liberal ideologies and of government policies have been to increasingly blame the poor for their poverty (an old historical trope), and to attribute their lack of social advancement to various habits, behaviours and other psychological characteristics, while denying the effects of exploitation and structural inequalities. Poor families are now renamed 'troubled', measures of child poverty no longer include income as one criterion, and proposals to make counselling compulsory in job centres have been put forward (and withdrawn after being energetically contested by the psychotherapy umbrella organisations). At the same time, the 'happiness agenda' of the current drive for cognitive behavioural therapy (CBT) has advanced a notion of individuals as entrepreneurs in their own lives, free of social context.

Valerie Walkerdine (2015) argues that the history of blame and pathologisation of the poor has blocked understanding of complex histories of suffering. Both social history and forms of psychoanalysis are needed to encompass the ways in which specific histories of exploitation, oppression and insecurity are transmitted through generations in embodied patterns of feeling, as Walkerdine and Jimenez's (2012) work on the effects of deindustrialisation on people's emotions and relationships shows.

Concomitant with this, psychoanalysis has been facing its own crises, in challenges to its popularity, legitimacy, viability and applicability as a practice, much commented on in some of the professional literature of the last decades. This has partly come from the growth of less expensive forms of psychoanalytic psychotherapy and counselling, and also the official adoption of CBT as the psychological treatment of choice within the NHS, something which is now being contested by various writers and organisations.[7] Further, demands for a more widely recognised evidence base for psychoanalysis have marginalised many practitioners. However, there are now a growing number of psychoanalytic researchers devising innovative research methods that both satisfy the demand for specifiable criteria and are appropriate to the nature of psychoanalysis (e.g. Leuzinger-Borleber and Target, 2002; De Livan, 2014; Fonagy et al., 2015). Some of these emphasise the importance of improving the quality of clinical observation, of specifying criteria for transformative change, and the necessity for triangulated forms of evaluation and validation.

The declining popularity of psychoanalysis in its more expensive and exclusive forms also derives from its weakness and tardiness in adjusting to contemporary social changes and mores, most notoriously in the case of homosexuality. In the wake of sustained and energetic challenges, this has now altered considerably. Furthermore, some of the accrediting organisations are now requiring that training courses address diversity and discrimination, a growing recognition that the social world needs to have more of a place within psychoanalytic and psychodynamic education.

Some challenges to psychoanalysis have come from various groups which have been either excluded or misrepresented; this has meant that the issues of gender, sexuality and race/ethnicity have been the source of much new creative psychoanalytic thinking and practice, although their integration into the mainstream has been slow. The common charge has been that psychoanalysis has not been able to encompass a sufficiently social understanding of its clientele, nor of itself. It thus often mistakes for inherent psychological attributes or pathologies what are in fact complex social constructions, albeit lived personally. The quest for a more social psychoanalysis goes back to the earliest days of the left social democratic and Marxist Freudians, and their attempts at a more class-inclusive practice, as Chapter 2 illustrates. It resurfaced in the many radical projects of the 1970s and '80s, some of which are discussed in Chapter 4. I consider the long-running tensions and debates around just this historic question: how can psychoanalysis become more social in its understandings and practices without losing or flattening its depth, complexity and richness as to the workings of the unconscious, which is its hallmark, and for which it is invaluable?

Class and (my) biography

I have claimed that class matters, and framed this in moral terms – its fundamentally inequitable and injurious nature. How did it come to matter to me, and why, as a psychoanalytic psychotherapist, am I interested in it? As a child in the 1940s and '50s I daily witnessed class deference and class contempt in that supposedly most intimate of spaces, the family. I felt torn apart, worried and confused, long before I could have named anything in class terms, by the imbalance of power and status, and by the stilted, unaffectionate but charged relationship between the two most significant adults in my life. As the child of an upper middle-class mother, I was mainly looked after, loved and nurtured by a working-class woman of limited education. She had previously started in service at the age of fourteen as a kitchen maid, and without any formal training she had managed to become a nanny. From birth to age three, until the end of World War II, I lived exclusively with her. She thus became my primary figure, a mother yet not my mother; and she continued to work for and live with my family, a part of it and yet not, until long after I had left home. From her, I absorbed in vivid detail what it was like to have grown up in rural poverty, sometimes going hungry, to leave school at thirteen with very little possibility of any social power, yet still have a zest for life and love.

I developed a split maternal figure, where the split was characterised by a profound class difference, as well as other polarised attributes. The Marxist oral historian, Ronald Fraser, also describes such a split configuration arising from class hierarchy, using his own psychoanalysis to illuminate this (Fraser, 1984). To me it felt agonising, and I became hyper-aware of our nanny's vulnerabilities and social weakness, her disempowered status as a domestic employee, the poverty in which many of her relatives still lived and from which she had come. And yet, as an adolescent I came to identify much more with my parents' status and values and, like my mother, to disdain her limitations and to reject some of her values, while remaining strongly and guiltily attached. Not surprisingly, such internal paralysing conflicts became part of the material of my later explorations in psychoanalytic therapy. Helpful as this has been, I have always felt there to be a lack of interest or a degree of incomprehension about the specifically class aspects – a shortcoming that several therapists in my research also reported in their own analyses (see Chapter 6).

Such a formation, the delegation of intimate childcare to working-class employees, was and still is common, one of the ways in which class intrudes and leaves its marks in the bourgeois family. Using the time and labour of others in the making of one's life is part of class exploitation and class relations, as Skeggs (2015) points out, noting the present-day, now increasingly globalised, ubiquity of servants for the rich. Domestic labourers have on the whole not been seen as part of working-class political struggle, and for a long time were ignored by trade unions. Further, little is written about the experiences and emotional conflicts of these working-class employees themselves, from their point of view as subjects in their own right. It is often extraordinarily difficult to trace even basic information about their lives, as Alison Light's book on Virginia Woolf's servants shows, let alone obtain much sense of their feelings and relationships (Light, 2007). Nonetheless, they represent important ways in which the functioning of many families depends on class. Further, the dependency of middle- or upper-class employers on the labour of such employees to carry out the tasks they do not wish to perform themselves, is often denied, and sometimes projected into the supposed dependency of the working classes.

Importantly for present purposes, such domestic relationships figure in several of Freud's case studies, and in his own childhood. In Chapter 3, I argue that class and cross-class relationships are often descriptively present in the significant information that Freud presents about his patients, but are omitted from the theory and from much clinical interpretation. This is a form of disciplinary disavowal that has had profound consequences for the extrusion of class from psychoanalytic theory. Domestic class relationships are, of course, only one of the myriad ways in which class may be lived and experienced. Class as experienced through work, or as poverty and disenfranchisement, seldom figures in clinical accounts, with some exceptions (see Chapters 4 and 8), although other aspects, especially social mobility, are present in some contemporary work.

As an adult, I revisited much of this territory, when in the 1970s I joined a libertarian socialist group, Big Flame, living and organising in East London, UK. Although I had always broadly subscribed to social democratic ideas of social justice, I now embraced a much more radical version of social change, and also garnered, through study groups and discussions, some understanding of the structures and operations of capitalism and of class struggle. Unlike most other left groups at that time, and much influenced by feminism, we saw the importance of personal life as an aspect of class oppression and class struggle, and we tried to develop forms of political activity that embraced that. One of our projects was a food co-op on a local estate, jointly organised with the working-class women who lived there (Big Flame, 2014). This food co-op achieved many things, but it also revived my sense of awkwardness and inhibition in the face of class difference, and the paralysing effects for me personally of the huge disparities in class and life opportunities with the women from the estate. I can see retrospectively how my lack of spontaneity hid a longing for an unconstrained connection, across gulfs of class, that I was unable to make.

Towards a more social psychoanalysis – some frameworks

Class and therapy

These political concerns also led to creating a radical self-help therapy group, Red Therapy (Ernst and Goodison, 1981; Big Flame, 2014), influenced by our understanding of how capitalism creates forms of personal suffering, and by Wilhelm Reich's ideas about combining political activity and psychoanalysis. Such ideas became widely read and influential in the ferment of the social movements of the 1960s and 1970s. We critiqued the ideological biases and socially conservative values of much psychoanalysis but we also used fundamental psychoanalytic understandings and taught ourselves many therapy skills and techniques. This led to my working in a socialist psychoanalytic therapy centre (see Chapter 4) and subsequently training as a psychoanalytic psychotherapist.

More recently, I have become aware of how much implicit information there can be about class embedded in clinical work, if appropriate questions are asked. As a psychotherapist in private practice, I was privileged to hear many stories of upward mobility, all different but each involving enormous pain, conflict and struggle with the psychic effects of class and class transition. However, it took me several years to realise the tenacity and complexity of these class histories, something which has important implications as to how we understand the impress of class, as I explore in several chapters. I also became aware of my own inhibitions and resistances in addressing class within the transference, similar to some of the middle-class therapists of Chapter 7.

As a supervisor in various community clinics, I was struck by the relief many therapists expressed once a discussion about class was initiated, and what a wealth of unarticulated knowledge could be tapped. There was, though, a lack of appropriate frameworks for articulating thoughts and experiences about class within clinical contexts, an issue of central concern to this book, as well as anxiety that it might be 'unanalytic' to do so. I also became aware, in subsequent investigations, of how difficult it is for many people to talk about class personally and interpersonally, how inhibited yet charged many attempted group discussions become, especially where there are obvious class differences. The sources of this anxiety and inhibition are prime topics for psychoanalytic enquiry, something which this book elaborates, especially in Chapter 10.

My enduring concern, like that of many others, has been how to work psychoanalytically in a way that includes a greater recognition than is usual of the social world, without losing the complexities and nuances of psychoanalysis, in its focus on unconscious processes. There are and have been many applications of psychoanalysis *to* aspects of cultural and social life, where psychoanalysis is the unexamined master discourse. Here, rather, I am concerned with how sociological and political understandings can be brought *into* psychoanalysis, to recognise the ways the social world can manifest itself within the practices and workings of the clinic, and in how class has its effects in and through the workings of the psyche, as this is understood by psychoanalysis. Chapter 8, in appraising contemporary clinical writings, addresses whether this requires new psychoanalytic concepts and practices, or elaborations of old ones.

Pluralism and critique

Class is a massive, complex and often elusive subject, and can be approached through a host of different frameworks. It is also a highly contested subject, involving fundamental issues of inequality, ethics and justice. Class spreads out into many areas of life and experience; it intertwines with or dissolves into other issues – there but not there. It can span many disciplinary boundaries. Because there has been so relatively little that reads class and psychoanalysis together or alongside each other, I have at times chosen to abstract class from its multifarious interconnections with other aspects of life and practice, despite the reductiveness this may risk.

My approach is pluralistic in the commitment to a multiplicity of voices from different class backgrounds, and the inclusion of different theoretical positions. This is an exploratory project, mapping and ground-clearing, making links and drawing on a wide diversity of sources. I am not aiming to evolve a single overarching theory or definitive perspective into which all phenomena of interest can be subsumed; this is neither a plausible nor a desirable aim. Indeed, I argue (in Chapter 3) that the universalising tendencies of psychoanalysis have contributed to the obscuring of class. I am more concerned to map out the different intersections of class and psychoanalysis from many perspectives: economic, historical, theoretical, clinical, sociological, psychosocial, political/professional. I aim to open up dialogue and debate that could be taken further in many different ways, including understanding the intersections of class with other vital factors.

This book is also critical, by which I mean critical of the status quo, in which wealth, privilege, and many other life goods, including psychoanalysis, are so unequally distributed. I argue that we need a critical psychoanalysis, one that engages with the conditions in which people live in the social world, conditions which contribute to mental distress of many kinds. Recent initiatives to formulate the terms of a critical psychotherapy[8] address the impact of austerity policies on people's lives and on the provision of mental health services. Here I hope to make a contribution to the evolution of a critical psychoanalysis by opening up the manifold issues that we need to confront in thinking about class and psychoanalysis together.

I also start from the assumption that any such exploration has to take account of the class basis of psychoanalysis itself, its material and ideological practices. Such a reflexive position would be unexceptional within the social sciences but is much less common within psychological disciplines. The book therefore situates accounts of relevant clinical material, found mainly in Chapters 7 and 8, alongside the experiences of therapists as classed and economic subjects and the political economies of psychoanalysis, in Chapters 6 and 9. Psychoanalytic projects that embrace greater class inclusivity also underline the necessity for some reflexive social understandings of the discipline, as well as of the social and historical circumstances of their clientele, as Chapters 2 and 4 illustrate.

Hybridity and heterogeneity

The kinds of life stories that abound about class and some of the relevant sociological and clinical work all indicate the hybridity and heterogeneity of class. Some people's class positions may be relatively homogeneous and stretch back over generations of a family in the same class, whereas those of others may be much more mixed, with parents or significant others from different class backgrounds, or with significant social mobility. Within any given class ascription there will also be different strata and groupings. The specifics of place, history, 'race', culture, age and gender and other factors all intersect in complex ways with class. This intersectionality, and the plurality and multiplicity of voices, need to be kept in a productive tension with a sense of social structure and position going beyond the givens of experience.

Psyche/social

The study of the subjective, affective and unconscious aspects of class raises questions of psychosocial thinking, especially those of the old individual/society and agency/structure dichotomies, and the more contemporary ones concerning the theorisation of the psychosocial. Class is above all a psychosocial topic – but what does this mean? The ways in which we are both subject to the workings of power and of society, and also experience and see ourselves as subjects (albeit divided ones) with desires and agency, is central to the concerns of this book. One challenge for a more social or critical psychoanalysis is to keep these two aspects in productive tension rather than sidelining one in favour of the other. Frosh and Baraitser (2008: 346) argue for a type of psychoanalytic subject 'that is both social and psychological, which is constituted in and through its social formations, yet is still granted agency and internality'. I have found contemporary psychosocial research, especially that using psychoanalytic ideas, helpful in furthering this aim in relation to class, as I explore in Chapter 5. The challenge is how to make this clinically relevant and meaningful, as I address in Chapters 7 and 8.

One current debate is whether psychosocial theorising aims to create links and bridges between two discrete sets of phenomena – the social and the psychological – and to specify the terms of interaction, or whether a more radical re-theorising is required. The latter aims to transcend the split by seeing the social and the psychological as inseparably constitutive of each other, understanding the ideological presuppositions that sustain this dichotomy, as Adorno (1967) advocated, and, as Judith Butler argues: 'thinking the theory of power together with a theory of the psyche' (Butler, 1997: 3).[9] These positions have implications for theorising clinical work, especially as to how social and cultural factors are seen as working on, in and through the psyche, and whether a psyche outside power is envisaged, as I address in Chapters 8 and 10. Lynne Layton, a contemporary psychoanalyst foremost in writing about class, has identified processes of unlinking as a way in which the social and the psychic world become divorced from each other within psychoanalysis and in wider society, often enacted in therapy encounters (Layton, 2006).

This psychosocial terrain abounds with different terms and concepts. Key terms for this book are 'subjectivity' and 'psyche'. To use the term 'subject' – relatively unusual within psychoanalysis – is to retain the dual aspects of subjecthood, to give more weight than the term 'individual' does to how we are formed within structures of power. 'Subjectivity' encompasses the material and discursive processes whereby particular forms of subjectivity are produced and maintained, including the range of experiences, self-constructions, emotions, relationships and practices that may constitute us as subjects. This has allowed much to be understood about the ways in which power and ideology shape experiences, including emotions and self-conceptions, and how identities are formed. 'Subjectivity' is thus more than an awkward bridging concept between the dualisms of individual and society, but rather, in some usages, is a genuinely psychosocial concept. Its limitations are that it tends to have a relatively superficial rendering of selfhood and does not, with some notable exceptions, include the intra-psychic, or notions of depth, interiority, repression and unconsciousness. Indeed some versions may eschew such terms. However, as Chapter 5 argues, some work emanating from this tradition on the subjective and affective aspects of class provides knowledge very relevant to psychoanalytic concerns.

Within psychoanalysis, the notion of an individual, albeit always divided and not unitary, is used self-evidently, in its assumed distinction from what is construed as social. I am using 'psyche' to denote the psychical reality of the psychoanalytic subject with its accompanying intra-psychic processes and unconscious mechanisms. This is close to but exceeds what is also called the inner or internal world in much psychoanalytic writing. These terms are problematic in the absoluteness of the dualisms they depend on, for example, internal and external worlds, and in the ascription of ontological certainty to these. Nonetheless, most psychoanalysis is premised on these terms; they are the productive and enabling concepts, constructions and metaphors on which most psychoanalysis is built.

The psyche is thus different from the subject, and the languages of the disciplines that investigate each are also different. The production of the distinct domain of the psyche – psychoanalysis's territory – is itself a historical and social production and this applies both at a disciplinary level and in terms of individuals. This poses a problem in bringing together necessary insights from each sphere. Within psychoanalysis the psyche is seen as having a radical autonomy from the social or external world, although the extent of this is increasingly being called into question. This presupposition of autonomy, along with practices that hive off the external world to ensure the efficacy of therapy, has undoubtedly allowed the huge edifices and subtleties of psychoanalytic thinking and clinical work to emerge and continue. However, it has produced many problematic questions as to how then issues of power, culture and oppression, including class, can be addressed. It reinforces what some have described as the glass cage of psychoanalysis. I thus attempt to elucidate how the psyche/social interface with respect to class has been conceptualised in relevant sociological and psychoanalytic writings.

Class, as this chapter suggests, is everywhere in the economic basis of psychoanalysis, and in some of its cultural assumptions, but (almost) nowhere in its explicit discourses. It is this absent presence that I address throughout the book. I trace a roughly historical path from the earliest days of progressive psychoanalytic concerns with class inclusivity, through modern and contemporary ones; from the extrusions and disavowals of some founding texts to recent conceptualisations of class within clinical work; through experiential accounts and other writings regarding the formations of class identities; to the institutions of psychoanalysis, its internal class structures and its political economies.

Notes

1 My use of inverted commas with 'race' is to indicate the problematic and contested nature of this category. Where possible I prefer to use the terms racialisation and racism to denote the realities of the processes involved.
2 A debate which is mainly inconclusive, to judge by Hinshelwood (2001). The use of the term 'psychoanalyst' by individuals qualified in organisations outside those accredited by the International Association of Psychoanalysts (IPA) has not only stirred up considerable controversy, but more importantly raises questions as to the locus and basis of legitimating authority within the whole field.

3 The websites of the different umbrella bodies contain information about which therapy organisations each recognises and accredits.
4 UKCP has consistently aimed for inclusivity and diversity, in formulating equal opportunity policies and social responsibility initiatives. Both it and BACP have clear statements of commitment to diversity and difference.
5 'Distinction' pertains to the manifold processes by which people differentiate themselves from those perceived to be of a different class, or feel differentiated themselves by these others. In contemporary literature it mainly refers to the many cultural forms of taste, style, manners, bodily presentations, etc., that are taken to distinguish classes. 'Relationality' refers to the ways in which class location and experience are frequently experienced in relation to other classes, real or imagined, and to the social world from which we are derived and in which we are implicated.
6 UK inequality was a major factor in the outcome of the 2016 EU referendum.
7 UKCP, for example, have succeeded in getting NICE to reconsider their prejudice in recommending only CBT for treatment of depression and other symptoms. See also the 2016 joint submission of UKCP and BPC to the Public Accounts Committee, regarding the current state of IAPT therapies, available on the BPC website.
8 For example, a Freud Museum conference on critical psychotherapy and a PCSR conference on austerity politics and therapy, both in 2015. See also *The Psychoanalyst Activist*, newsletter of Section IX, Division 39 of the APA.
9 Positions in the debate are often signalled by whether the two terms are hyphenated, as psycho-social, or joined together as psychosocial.

References

Adorno, T. (1967) 'Sociology and psychology (Part I)', *New Left Review* 1(46): 67–80.
Big Flame (2014) 'Food Co-Op'. Available at: www.eastlondonbigflame.org.uk. Accessed July 2015.
Bourdieu, P. (1998) *Practical Reason*. Cambridge: Polity Routledge.
Butler, J. (1997) *The Psychic Life of Power*. Stanford: Stanford University Press.
De Livan, M. (ed) (2014) *Time for Change: Tracking Transformations in Psychoanalysis*. London: Karnac.
Ernst, S. and Goodison, L. (1981) *In Our Own Hands*. London: Women's Press.
Evans, G. and Mellon, J. (2015) 'Social class'. In *British Social Attitudes*, vol. 33: 1–19. London: NatCen Social Research.
Fereday, G. (2015) 'Response to "long-term strategy for the profession" by Nigel Burch', *British Journal of Psychotherapy* 31: 134–5.
Fonagy, P., Rost, F., Carlyle, J., McPherson, S., Thomas, R., Fearon, R., Goldberg, D. and Taylot, D. (2015) 'The Tavistock adult depression study', *World Psychiatry* 14: 312–21.
Fraser, R. (1984) *In Search of Place*. London: Verso.
Frosh, S. and Baraitser, L. (2008) 'Psychoanalysis and psychosocial studies', *Psychoanalysis, Culture and Society* 13: 346–65.
Hanley, L. (2016) *Respectable: The Experience of Class*. London: Allen Lane.
Hinshelwood, R. (2001) 'Surveying the maze'. In Frisch, S., Hinshelwood, R. and Gauthier, J. M. (eds) *Psychoanalysis and Psychotherapy: The Controversies and the Future*. London: Karnac.
Hoggart, R. (1989) 'Introduction'. In Orwell, G. *The Road to Wigan Pier*, Harmondsworth: Penguin.
Kugelmass, H. (2016) 'Sorry, I'm not accepting new patients', *Journal of Health and Social Behavior* 57(2): 168–83.

Layton, L. (2006) 'Attacks on linking'. In Layton, L., Hollander, N. and Gutwill, S. (eds) *Psychoanalysis, Class and Politics: Encounters in the Clinical Setting*. London: Routledge.

Leuzinger-Borleber, M. and Target, M. (eds) (2002) *Outcomes of Psychoanalytic Treatment*. London: Routledge.

Light, A. (2007) *Mrs Woolf and the Servants*. London: Fig Tree.

National Equality Panel (2010) *An Anatomy of Economic Inequality in the UK: Report of the National Equality Panel*. London: Centre for Analysis of Social Exclusion. Available at: http://sticerd.lse.ac.uk/dps/case/cr/CASEreport60.pdf. Accessed July 2016.

Savage, M. (2015) *Social Class in the 21st Century*. London: Penguin Random House.

Sennett, R. (2003) *Respect*. London: Allen Lane.

Sennett, R. and Cobb, J. (1972) *The Hidden Injuries of Class*. New York: Knopf.

Skeggs, B. (2015) 'Introduction: Stratification or exploitation, domination, dispossession and devaluation?', *The Sociological Review* 63: 205–22.

Social Mobility & Child Poverty Commission (2014) *State of the Nation 2014: Social Mobility and Child Poverty in Great Britain*. London: HMSO.

Taylor, H. (2013) 'UK psychoanalysis: Mistaking the part for the whole', British Psychoanalytic Council Discussion Paper, June: 1–17.

Tyler, I. (2015) 'Classificatory struggles: Class, culture and inequality in neoliberal times', *The Sociological Review* 63: 493–511.

Walkerdine, V. (2015) 'Transmitting class across generations', *Theory & Psychology* 25: 167–83.

Walkerdine, V. and Jimenez, L. (2012) *Gender, Work and Community after De-Industrialisation: A Psycho-Social Approach to Affect*. Basingstoke: Palgrave Macmillan.

2
ASKING QUESTIONS OF HISTORY

The detailed history of the Berlin and Vienna free clinics remained largely unknown[1] until Elisabeth Danto's comprehensive work, *Freud's Free Clinics: Psychoanalysis and Social Justice 1918–1938*. In it she claims: 'Between 1918 and 1938 psychoanalysis was neither inaccessible for working people, nor rigidly structured, nor luxurious in length' (Danto, 2005: 2). Here we can learn how the clinics were set up and run, about the motivations and ideologies of their founders and the issues they faced. It is extraordinary, given the size and creativity of these clinics, that this became such a forgotten history, ignored even in those accounts of psychoanalysis sympathetic to the aims of a more class-inclusive practice. Russell Jacoby's *The Repression of Psychoanalysis* (Jacoby, 1983) is the main exception, but he does not discuss the Vienna clinic. This neglect reflects how divorced from mainstream concerns the enterprise of free and low-cost psychoanalysis became and still is, a theme taken up in Chapter 4 and elsewhere.

There is however much that we can learn from the passion and creativity of the founders of these clinics and their commitment to developing a more class-inclusive psychoanalysis, a key theme for this book, and one which could inform the present challenges facing psychoanalysis, something David Fisher (2007) also suggests. Danto's work is contested in some quarters, as exaggerating the importance and radical nature of the clinics; in many more others it has been welcomed and endorsed.[2] Here I outline some of the specifics of how these clinics were founded, their detailed workings and the ideas of their leading figures; attention to the materiality of these inclusive projects is important in understanding what is at stake in the interface of psychoanalysis with various social realities. I am approaching the wealth of information available, not to give any kind of condensed history, but rather to identify the theoretical and practical issues in these early transpositions of psychoanalysis into working-class contexts. Many of these themes resurface in subsequent class-inclusive projects, and in the wider considerations of this book.

Social and political contexts

The Berlin Polyclinic was established in 1920, and the Vienna Ambulatorium opened in 1922. Both offered free and low-cost psychoanalysis. They were notable for the number and social diversity of their patients, recorded in published reports. They were followed by shorter-lived clinics in Budapest and Frankfurt, and by a smaller London Clinic. Their founders and staff were variously motivated by socialist, revolutionary or social democratic beliefs. They assumed without question the universal applicability and value of psychoanalysis. Otto Fenichel, for example, wrote retrospectively that 'many analysts . . . have analysed proletarians, and have established that the scientific laws of man's inner life which psychoanalytic research has revealed are generally valid irrespective of class distinctions' (Fenichel, 1967: 310). This continues to be debated and contested (e.g. Fanon, 1952); Fenichel himself was more equivocal than this statement suggests (see p. 32).

These left psychoanalysts also assumed the importance of psychoanalysis for social reform and progress: it would help transform civil society; and it represented human liberation, social empowerment and freedom from bourgeois conventions. They also, and Freud as well, recognised that extending the reach of psychoanalysis to the poorer sections of the population was essential to the future of psychoanalysis and its acceptance by the general public, a vital argument that has renewed relevance now. Alert to the 'immense neurotic misery of the masses' (Fenichel, 1967: 310), they devoted considerable energy to popularising psychoanalysis, writing accessible articles and doing outreach work of various kinds. Danto argues that psychoanalysis gained an acceptance and popularity that it has seldom enjoyed since.

The founding of these clinics was framed by the impact of the 1917 Russian revolution, and the experience and aftermath of World War I. The war ended the dominant imperial regimes of Austro-Hungary and Germany; it produced enormous social upheavals, economic collapse and poverty, and led to attempted Communist revolutions in several countries. Post-war Vienna was governed by a Social Democratic council which initiated many social welfare reforms of a far-reaching nature, in housing, education and women's and children's health, forming the context for the Ambulatorium. The Weimar Republic in Germany was a time of huge modernist innovation in art, architecture, literature, theatre and music. The earlier youth movements were radicalising influences in the lives of many analysts, such as Fenichel, Siegfried Bernfeld, Wilhelm Reich and Annie Reich. These organised movements challenged conformist and restrictive values and demanded a more informed and less moralistic approach to sexuality, which psychoanalysis was able to provide. The power of psychoanalysis to illuminate sexuality has often been part of socially critical movements.

Danto also attributes the rise of these clinics to Freud's far-reaching speech to the first psychoanalytic congress after the war. In 'Lines of Advance in Psychoanalytic Psychotherapy', Freud makes the much quoted claim: '[I]t is possible to foresee that . . . the conscience of society will awake and remind it that the poor man should have just as much right to assistance for his mind as he now has to the life-saving help offered by surgery . . .' (Freud, 1918: 167). He predicted that institutions and outpatient clinics would be started where treatment would be free. This appears to have acted as a challenge and as encouragement to a younger generation of analysts to set up these clinics. Freud also foresaw that the establishment of free clinics would involve clinical research and standardised training programmes, the bases for which were provided by the clinics. Reviewing progress a decade later, he wrote how the Berlin Poliklinik 'endeavors to make our therapy accessible to the great multitude who suffer under their neuroses no less than the wealthy but who are not in a position to meet the cost of their treatment' (Freud, 1930: 257).

Here I address how these clinics were set up and funded, the difficulties and resistances they faced externally, the innovations and debates they gave rise to, as well as how they were run and organised internally. There are however few published case histories attributed to work at the clinics. Fenichel claimed that 'a great many case reports of proletarians have been published by analysts' but does not give details (Fenichel, 1967: 308). There is a modern resonance in how little is written about clinical work in similar contemporary projects. However, the work of these clinics does represent a time when the political and clinical passions of a substantial number of psychoanalysts were at their most conjoined, and when these were much closer to the mainstream of psychoanalysis than ever since. Many saw themselves working towards a social or Marxist psychoanalysis, and wrestled with theory accordingly. How the social world can be represented within psychoanalytic work is an abiding debate, as well as a central concern of this book. Other left psychoanalysts subscribed to more social democratic beliefs, with the main aim of increasing access to psychoanalysis for those excluded by money, a concern that also continues in many forms today.

The Berlin and Vienna clinics were different in many respects, although there was considerable exchange of ideas and movement of staff between them, mostly from Vienna to Berlin, which was seen as allowing more adventurous thought and practice, and which established a training institute somewhat earlier.

The Berlin Poliklinik

The Berlin clinic was initiated by Ernst Simmel and Max Eitingon. Simmel, a socialist, had been a doctor during the war and was convinced of the usefulness of psychoanalysis in treating traumatised soldiers. Such experiences were important in demonstrating that psychoanalysis could be applied in different contexts. For Simmel, depriving poor people of psychoanalysis, which he saw as an instrument of personal enhancement for the rich, was for him as much part of their class oppression as were their material deprivations. Eitingon, also a war doctor and independently wealthy, provided most of the funding for the clinic, which meant that the core staff could be paid small salaries. Reporting on the first years of the clinic, Eitingon emphasises the urgent need for such provision: neurotic distress had greatly increased, there was great public demand for psychoanalysis, and, he says: 'we were more confident' (Eitingon, 1923). It was a 'favourable moment', psychoanalysis having had no part in the old illusions, which had now perished. They, together with Karl Abraham, formed the initial staff of the clinic.

Freud's architect son Ernst designed the layout and furnishings of the clinic in a modernist style, with the whole environment planned to convey a sense of community as well as confidentiality. There was a reading room where psychoanalytic literature could be read by patients and staff, all very different from the traditional, impersonal doctor's office and planned to dispel fear about beginning analysis. The waiting room was seen as a place where patients could realise they were not alone, neither in their suffering nor in their feelings for their analyst. Such attention to the total environment and the messages it may convey to intending patients has now become part of analytic practice for many clinics.

The clinic was flooded with applications for free treatment. Patients were accepted entirely on diagnostic grounds, and then asked what they could contribute in fees, if anything. In the first two and a half years they received 600–700 applications and conducted 130 analyses (Eitingon, 1923), impressive by any standards. The occupational categories recorded demonstrate conclusively how socially inclusive the Poliklinik was. Danto (2005: 115) suggests that the large lower-class patient population resulted in part from Simmel's social activism, an indication of how politics and psychoanalysis may need to be conjoined in the interests of inclusivity.

All analysts of the Berlin Psychoanalytic Society were obliged to donate either free time or a financial equivalent. So novel was the idea of free treatment that Eitingon found it necessary to write defending its use, dispelling the notion that it would increase resistance (still a preoccupation of some), and pointing out how it allowed for greater flexibility and experimentation on the part of the analyst. He acknowledged that fees or free treatment could become clinical and transferential issues, but came to believe that payment was more significant for the therapist than for the patient, an issue rehashed many times in the history of the discipline, and which I revisit in Chapter 9.

Eitingon and Fenichel saw the importance of empirical data in proving the clinic's worth and the value of psychoanalytic treatment. They devised sophisticated schemes of record keeping. Eitingon (1923) used the clinic figures to prove how effective it was, with roughly two-thirds considered cured or improved, most of the rest still in progress, and only a small number discontinued. Unfortunately, it is not clear how these assessments were made. Patients were seen between three and four times a week, and the length of analyses was short by modern standards, but usual then. The most common length was six months or under, although some lasted longer. No arbitrary limit was set. According to Danto, debates about appropriate lengths of treatment were carried on in many clinical discussions, with the notion of 'fractionary analysis' advocated as a specific curative technique, whereby unavoidable interruptions to analyses, because of the conditions of life of some patients, could allow for consolidation and re-evaluation of the treatment. Danto suggests that while they experimented extensively with the parameters of treatment, they condemned as 'useless . . . the copper of direct suggestion' that Freud had advocated for work in the free clinics. Rather they adhered closely to the fundamentals of psychoanalytic processes (Danto, 2005: 179). Whether psychoanalytic work under the more constrained conditions of free or low-cost work counts as 'real' psychoanalysis is a debate that continues to haunt the field, as Chapter 4 illustrates. The founders of the free clinics, however, never doubted they were practising psychoanalysis, despite the constraints, and were widely seen as doing so.

Initial diagnoses covered a very wide range of conditions, as did the patients' occupations. At the outset half came from manual occupations, or the unemployed. Eitingon records that the 'authentic proletarian' proportion got less with time, with more impoverished intelligentsia and professionals attending, which he bemoaned. By 1927, the clinic had grown so much that it moved to new quarters. By 1930, a total of 721 analyses had been carried out (Danto, 2005: 202).

In 1927, after much fundraising, Simmel opened an inpatient facility, the Schloss Tegel Sanatorium. Simmel's own account of the sanatorium contains considerable clinical detail but does not specifically address social issues (Simmel, 1929). It is remarkable for the boldness and creativity of his ideas; in many ways the clinic prefigured family therapy, and the insights of modern therapeutic communities.

The Poliklinik was closely connected to the Berlin training institute, and by 1922 Berlin was regarded as the leading centre of psychoanalysis. With Melanie Klein's involvement it also became one of the pioneers of child analysis. Danto describes the avant-garde and convivial atmosphere surrounding the clinic and the institute, as does Alix Strachey, who was in analysis with Abraham and involved with her husband in translating Freud into English. Veronika Fuechtner's research shows the extensive contacts and activities that members of the Berlin Institute had with the cultural modernism and social activism of the society around them (Fuechtner, 2011). Strachey's letters vividly convey their hectic and intense lives, their passionate commitments to psychoanalysis, but she makes scant reference to the Poliklinik, other than as the place where she attended lectures and seminars. However, she does, in the course of remarking on the feeling of 'the solid reality of the unconscious mind' engendered by reading Freud's Wolf Man case, bemoan the fact that there must be a hundred unwritten records at the Poliklinik which 'would set psychoanalysis on its feet' (Meisel and Kendrick, 1985: 199). Strachey supposes that no one there had the time, interest and talent to write such case histories. This does suggest that there were indeed few in-depth clinical accounts stemming from the Poliklinik. It also indicates the losses to psychoanalysis as a whole of all class-inclusive projects not having the resources for writing clinical accounts of their work.

Radical theorising about the relationship between socialism and psychoanalysis was also developing in Berlin; in 1924 Fenichel and his colleagues formed themselves into a group, known as the 'Children's Seminar'.[3] Operating outside of the main Institute curriculum, it included a diversity of left-wing political views, and met regularly until 1933. Its central topic of discussion was 'the social factor' in psychoanalysis. The seminar then evolved into Fenichel's *Rundbriefe*, the secret distribution of which kept these left-wing analysts in touch in exile. Some of these analysts were drawn towards the Social Democrats, and others, including Fenichel and Reich, towards the Communists. The debates of the Children's Seminar also stimulated Simmel's interest in a burgeoning interdisciplinary group of intellectuals, who later formed the Frankfurt Institute for Social Research and Critical Theory. Erich Fromm, who (according to Jacoby) participated in the Berlin discussions, helped establish a small outpatient clinic in Frankfurt in 1929, alongside the academic institute. The Frankfurt group became the pre-eminent thinkers of Marxist Freudian synthesis. In both cities, there was a fertile period of intense psychoeducational activity, with psychoanalysts much in demand for teaching and outreach work with other professions. All these and many other developments illustrate the immense fertility of thought and practice that flowed from the openness of these psychoanalysts to wider social, cultural and political issues, and their refusal to encase psychoanalysis within narrow social parameters.

The subsequent history of the Berlin Poliklinik in the hands of the Nazis, and the flight of the Jewish analysts has been well told elsewhere (Jacoby, 1983; Steiner, 2000; Frosh, 2009). As the debates of the secret *Rundbriefe* show, the ideas of these left analysts lived on for some years, even though the practical project of free clinics largely did not. Post-war psychoanalysis largely 'forgot' its radical potential and social openness in the increasing conservatism and professional marking out of territories of much American and British practice, legacies which are still with us.

The Vienna Ambulatorium

The Vienna clinic had more of a struggle to establish itself than the Berlin one, but faced similar issues. Danto places it firmly in the context of the post-war social democracy of 'Red Vienna', the widespread poverty, and the ferment of revolutionary and activist thought. She names this 'an exceptional nexus of ideology and practice' (Danto, 2005: 31). The new city government promoted municipal welfare facilities of many kinds: child guidance clinics, sanitation, community health centres, educational reform, housing and leisure facilities. Many young prospective analysts, radicalised by the political context, were keen to learn and apply psychoanalysis to progressive social causes. Among these were Reich and Fenichel who attended the weekly meetings of the Vienna Psychoanalytic Society. Despite the favourable political climate, there was much resistance to the proposal for a free psychoanalytic clinic from the conservative medical and psychiatric establishment who distrusted psychoanalysis as a method of treatment, a recurrent issue throughout the history of psychoanalysis. Freud was much more ambivalent about the prospective Vienna clinic than the Berlin one, fearing that it would depend too heavily on himself and his name, distrusting anyone to run it well, and also wanting to keep psychoanalysis politically neutral (Danto, 2005: 65).

Finally, after two years of persistent petitioning, Eduard Hitschmann, a friend and colleague of Freud's, obtained a licence for the clinic by promising that it would not compete for patients with the psychiatrists, illustrating the economic forces at work. He also agreed that only medically qualified analysts would work in it, an issue that was to dominate psychoanalytic societies in many countries. Even so, there was a subsequent attempt to close it down. The clinic opened with a staff that included many of the younger generation of left analysts. Between 200 and 250 patients per year registered with the clinic, a demand in excess of what could be met. Hitschmann (1932) records that over ten years 750 patients were analysed, with 40–50 analyses in progress at any one time, again an impressive figure. Hitschmann's table for the multiple diagnostic categories used shows that sexual impotence, anxiety hysteria, obsessional neurosis and shyness were the most common. Rules for the clinic meant that only very poor non-paying patients could be treated, and the occupational figures Hitschmann gives support this. Every member of the Vienna Psychoanalytic Society donated either time or money to the clinic.

At the outset a separate unit was founded for work with children. Many of the analysts participated in outreach work in various progressive educational projects and youth services,[4] again illustrating the desire for engaging psychoanalysis with the social world. In 1929, a new department was founded for patients with borderline and psychotic diagnoses, many of whom were treated psychoanalytically, sometimes with modifications of method. It is striking that at both clinics, widening access to psychoanalysis led to the recognition that different forms of psychoanalytic treatment were needed for the more disturbed patients, leading to many innovations.

Although the Ambulatorium had to battle for its survival, nonetheless it gave rise to many fertile clinical discussions and innovations, as part of its weekly meetings. It was where Reich especially pioneered ideas and practices that still endure. The clinic and the training institute, founded in 1924, were closely connected, but separate enough to allow the training of non-medical analysts. Helene Deutsch (1932) records how under the pressure of the number of applicants to the clinic, the need to train more analysts grew ever greater. Grete Bibring-Lehner describes the transition from the earlier informal and ad hoc discussions to the introduction of a regular group seminar on therapy and technique, as well as yearly reviews (Bibring-Lehner, 1932). The need for such a seminar also arose from how clinic work confronted analysts with many challenges to established practice, with various difficulties in treatment and different patterns of distress (Diercks, 2002). This is a familiar consequence of widening access.

Reich, who was deputy director of the Ambulatorium from 1924 to 1930, and in charge of the technical seminar, thought that it was important to learn from difficulties and failures in clinical work, and to create a forum where analysts felt able to discuss these, an innovation at that time. He describes in *Character Analysis* (Reich, 1945) how patients who came to the clinic often did not suffer from the classic neurotic symptoms, did not realise they were ill, and often did not follow the analyst's invitation to freely associate. Reich described antisocial, uninhibited and instinct-driven men, whose ego he saw as remaining infantile and fragmentary, very different from the repressed middle-class neurotics of previous case histories. He also argued that analysts, despite their theoretical knowledge to the contrary, considered resistance simply unwelcome, and would try to challenge or subvert it, rather than understanding how the neurosis is contained in the resistance and needs to be brought into the analysis. Negative transferences were common, and great skill was needed in the timing of interpretations; the established analytic rules about interpreting all material whenever it surfaced had to be adapted to what the patient was able to make use of at any given point in the analysis. Reich also argued against too much analytic passivity and silence. Such need for adaptability in approach, for a wider understanding of the sources of distrust, fear and resistance, is a common, if sometimes disputed, feature of most contemporary projects attempting to widen access to psychoanalysis.

The Vienna Ambulatorium survived until 1938 when Austria was occupied by Nazi Germany and most of the remaining analysts fled. Unlike the Berlin Poliklinik, which was aryanised and which offered Nazi-approved therapy, the Vienna clinic closed completely. Recently, however, the Ambulatorium has been reopened and continues, with some state funding, to offer free and low-cost psychoanalytic psychotherapy (Diercks, 2002).

Danto records how some of the analysts who went to the USA did establish free clinics in two places (Chicago and Topeka), but that largely the project of a more class-inclusive psychoanalysis was not continued. Instead, in the more conservative post-war period, the notion that working-class people were not suitable for psychoanalysis took increasing hold, in both the USA and the UK, and they were mainly offered physical and pharmacological treatments. Some of the original ideas and activities, especially the outreach ones, persisted: in the Hampstead nurseries in London, for example, and within progressive education generally, and also, as Danto suggests, in psychoanalytically informed social work. It was only with the social movements of the 1960s and '70s that accessible free or low-cost community clinics arose again, in a great variety of forms.

However, low-cost clinics attached to training institutes and providing patients for trainees did become and are now common, as the history of the London Clinic, founded in 1926 and continuing today, exemplifies (Crick, 2016). For some years this clinic did take some patients funded by the NHS, although the British Society had previously decided not to become part of the medical organisation of health care. Crick describes the long-running tensions between the needs of the clinic to provide suitable patients for analysis for unpaid trainees and the needs of intending patients, many of whom may not fit the selection criteria. Social obligation has to some extent inspired the clinic, and many low-cost analyses have been carried out, but the priorities of the training have been primary.

The ideas that informed and that were generated from the original clinics do however continue to be debated. Reich and Fenichel are of particular importance in articulating class in relation to psychoanalysis and the quest for a more social form of psychoanalysis. There exists a large and mainly theoretical literature of and about Freudo-Marxism; the purpose here is not to attempt an evaluation of this, which has been done many times, but rather to focus on the ideas of these two analysts whose practice was firmly rooted in the free clinics. Fenichel indeed argued that the schism between culture and instinct (drive) had to be seen as existing dialectically, and could be merged only in practice, as at the free clinics (Danto, 2005: 284), an argument that has informed much of this book.

Reich

Reich's innovations as regards technique, based on his work in the Ambulatorium, became part of many analytic trainings, although insufficiently credited to him. His political commitments and activities earned him dismissal in 1933 from the Berlin clinic (where he had moved in 1930) and the International Psychoanalytic Association, at the same time as he was expelled from the Communist party for his psychoanalytic interests.[5] It would be a mistake to split the clinical Reich from the political one, as is often done. His energetic engagement with the intricacies of psychoanalytic work in the clinic were part of his passion for the value of psychoanalysis in understanding the structure of individual misery within society and in informing political struggle. Reich is often rightly criticised for the direction he took in making orgasmic sexual activity so central to his notions of psychic health, and for the biologistic nature of his theorising, which led him and his followers to privilege naturalistic ideas of heterosexuality and gender. Despite this, there is much that can be learned from Reich's earlier writings on the intersection between psychoanalysis, class and politics. His ideas emerged from within a social context of great poverty, huge moralistic disapproval of young people's sexual curiosity and desires, widespread sexual ignorance and repression, and little availability of contraception, abortion or privacy. In both the Berlin and Vienna clinics, impotence was one of the most common presenting symptoms (Eitingon, 1923; Hitschmann, 1932), indicative of the widespread nature of sexual repression and anxieties.

Reich argued that any political party or campaign had to start from the everyday concerns of ordinary life, including personal and sexual matters, and also housing and leisure. Reich saw psychoanalysis as able to illuminate the kinds of struggles people grappled with to live fulfilling lives, where both external conditions and internal repression could conspire to keep people afraid, confused and subject to mystifying ideologies, such as religion and 'tradition'. He, along with many of his contemporaries sought to understand why the German Communist revolution had failed, when the conditions had looked promising, and also, later, why national socialism and fascism were able to attract so much popular support. The notion of basing political analysis and activity on people's everyday concerns brought Reich into conflict with the more Leninist ideas of correct political lines that could be imposed on the masses by party cadres. He wrote *Dialectical Materialism and Psychoanalysis* (Reich, 1929/1960) to defend psychoanalysis against Communist criticisms, making clear it did not have to be an inappropriate psychologisation of social issues, which error he attributed to some psychoanalysts. This argument reappeared in the political movements of the 1960s and 1970s, when there was a resurgence of interest in Reich's ideas, in using psychoanalysis to understand and oppose the workings of social oppression, and to create alternative and more inclusive forms of therapy.

Reich put many of his ideas into practice in outreach work and in Sex-Pol. He and other analysts and doctors would speak about sexual concerns, about the politics of everyday life, and would give advice about mental health. Later, individual therapy sessions were provided. It was 'a blend of psychoanalytic counselling, Marxist advice, and contraceptives' (Danto, 2005: 118) and very popular. Calling for a politics of everyday life, Reich could show 'how to relinquish preconceived class barriers and allow the individual to emerge from class constraints' (Danto, 2005: 116). Along with this practical work Reich engaged in theoretical debates about how psychoanalysis and Marxism could be synthesised.

All the left analysts of the time saw psychoanalysis as the study of individuals in a given society, with social structure reproduced in psychic structure. Importantly, and especially for consideration of the subsequent ideas of contemporary psychoanalysts (see Chapter 8), Reich saw this process not as one of mirroring nor as direct structural reflection, but of the *anchoring* of the social order in individual character structure, via the vicissitudes of libidinal desire. He used this to explain how and why the exploited sections of the population tolerate or identify with the ideologies of the powerful upper social classes, often at the expense of their own apparent interests – an abiding political question. Reich argued that there was no simple or mechanistic connection between economic structure and character structure, but rather that the forms of sexual repression and inhibition common to different strata of society made some groups, because of their differing relationships to authority within the family, more accessible to nationalistic and fascistic politics. In *The Mass Psychology of Fascism* (Reich, 1933/1970) Reich argued that the right made much more use of ideology – people's emotions, beliefs and attitudes, their needs for identification with a strong figure – than did the left, who at that time thought that only objective conditions and correct political analyses would be effective in creating resistance and revolution.[6] We can see echoes of this in current political debates.

Reich emphasised the contradictoriness of the dynamics of conformity and rebelliousness, as well as the power of identifications with upper-class figures. While the family structures and forms of sexual repression that Reich saw are no longer so common in modern Western societies, his analysis is still relevant (as I have found in teaching) to contemporary patriarchal societies with high degrees of sexual suppression and ignorance, and gender oppression, in which religion, which Reich saw as a mystical solution, plays a dominant role. Reich's ideas, especially the use of psychoanalysis in political activism, have had a huge after-life in subsequent social movements, also inspiring new forms of radical and socially conscious therapy.

Fenichel

The writings of Fenichel are less known, yet there is much of relevance to any modern concern with psychoanalysis and class. Fenichel was close to Reich in the early years of the Ambulatorium and later often supported him against the increasing criticism of Freud and other analysts. Eventually however he broke with him. Fenichel himself illustrates many of the difficulties in achieving what was his consistent project, that of a variously social or Marxist psychoanalysis, neither culturally nor biologistically reductionist, which retains the depth and complexity of classical psychoanalysis, but which also includes and integrates what he called 'the social factor'. Jacoby (1983) records both Fenichel's enduring loyalty to Freud and classical psychoanalysis, and his equally enduring pursuit of the bridge between this and Marxism. 'For Freud, against Freud' appears to sum up his loyal opposition. However, impressive as Fenichel's efforts were in convening discussion groups of left psychoanalysts, in his own political writings and later in the *Rundbriefe* of exile, his extensive clinical articles are mainly devoid of any reference to social factors. He seems to have kept the two strands of his interests largely separate, creating, as Jacoby says, a bifurcation in his work. This was perpetuated by the omission of his political and social concerns in Simmel's obituary of him (Simmel, 1946), written in the context of the psychoanalytic diaspora in America, the developing panic about communism, and the conservatism of American psychoanalysis. In such ways was the amnesia concerning the radical socially committed aspects of psychoanalysis enacted.

In the *Rundbriefe*[7] Fenichel trenchantly criticises both the 'flat culturalism' (Jacoby, 1983: 106) of the neo-Freudians such as Karen Horney, the biologistic reductionism of the more conservative analysts and the sexual reductionism of Reich. In doing so, he leaves himself little space between all these poles of error for a more positive evolution of ideas, or any resolution of the conceptual issues involved. He was 'fighting against two fronts' (Jacoby, 1983: 87), against those analysts who had no appreciation of social reality and against Marxists who denied individual psychic formations and the role of the unconscious – a difficult position familiar to later generations of political radicals concerned with therapy. However, Fenichel argued that psychoanalysis and Marxism could only be conjoined in practice and not solely theoretically, confronting scepticism with solid work. This is an important argument that has not had the attention it deserves. It foregrounds the materiality of individual suffering and the foundations of psychoanalytic knowledge in clinical practices. Fenichel did indeed devote much energy to the running of the clinics and especially to devising appropriate methods of recording their activities and the characteristics of their clientele. Such data was used to establish the public transparency needed for the wider acceptance of psychoanalysis, something of renewed importance now.

However, these two strands of Fenichel's thought did come together in some writings where he argued both for the universal applicability of psychoanalysis and for the importance of differences arising from social circumstances (Fenichel, 1934).[8] He thought that the Oedipus complex had to be understood socially, within the history and function of the family, and that specific experiences gave rise to neuroses, at the same time as asserting the universal validity of psychoanalytic laws within a capitalist society. He argued that 'the neuroses of our culture are amazingly similar in all classes; that some differences which do nevertheless exist lead back to differences in the living conditions of middle-class and proletarian children' (Fenichel, 1967: 310). He continued that, due to the proposition that the ideology of a society is the ideology of its ruling class, the 'moral views of the proletariat are everywhere amazingly like those of the middle-classes, in any case similar enough to allow a man [sic] of broad sympathies to make contact with people belonging to different classes' (Fenichel, 1967: 310).

This latter point of Fenichel's raises but does not explore the intricacies of cross-class relationships, something I address later in contemporary accounts of class within therapy relationships. The notion that 'broad sympathies', now perhaps rendered as empathy, were needed is a necessary starting point. However, in the light of modern considerations of power, knowledge and discourse, and of the psychic structurings of class, such sympathies alone are insufficient, as later chapters illustrate. Nonetheless, the achievements of the free clinics were such that working-class people did find it possible to make use of psychoanalysis, and much of this was due to the conviction of their founders as to the general applicability and value of psychoanalysis, as well as to their political concerns with the inequality of access. The argument, novel at the time, that those in oppressed circumstances may adopt dominant ideologies is now familiar to any conjuncture of psychoanalysis and politics, with concepts such as interpellation, internal oppression, identification with the aggressor and recently normative unconscious processes (see Chapter 8) put forward as explanatory mechanisms.

In an article about money still cited today (see Chapter 9), Fenichel lays out an extended argument about the interaction of historical and economic factors with the instinctual drives and psychic structures of individuals (Fenichel, 1938). Capitalism, he argues, modifies instinctual structures, creating the drive to amass wealth; it makes use of instincts but is not a product of them. He argues strongly against the over-psychologisation of the desire to become wealthy, seen by many contemporaries as reducible to anal eroticism. Rather, such unconscious motives, which he elaborates at some length, are *harnessed* by the social system. The dynamics of capitalist systems, with their relentless pursuit of profit, are the external conditions under which individual desires and motivations exist. Capitalism, understood as an autonomous social force, makes the pursuit of wealth both a rational and a neurotic activity. Fenichel asked how a society avoids rebellion, when the majority cannot ensure their basic needs but wealth abounds, and concluded that as well as force, the 'cunning' trick was to produce a drive to accrue wealth with fantasies of a better future, creating identifications with richer people. He argued that ideologies of thrift (today's austerity) functioned to obscure true class interests, and to create illusions of personal advancement (today's 'strivers').

This chapter has outlined the intense and creative engagement of these left analysts with the aim of a class-inclusive psychoanalysis, and the popularity of this project. This history is a welcome if insufficiently known counterweight to the blanket stereotyping of psychoanalysis as only concerned with the privileged. That it was crushed by fascism and did not re-emerge in the conservative post-war period illustrates the ways that psychoanalysis itself is part of any particular historical moment. Such political contextualisation, which most psychoanalytic education tends to ignore, is part of what is needed in the evolution of any more inclusive project. What we can also learn is how much detailed commitment and struggle is needed to make such projects happen, how fragile they can be to changing political circumstances in a world where resources are so unequally distributed and where opposing vested interests may be at stake. This is a story that repeats over and over in later contexts.

We have further seen how the placing of psychoanalysis in working-class contexts provoked questions concerning its clinical practices and produced many innovations. In this way, the enlargement of the social reach of psychoanalysis can enhance its wider practice, and inform the mainstream (were it willing), a process which is still evident in the many new understandings arising from modern critiques concerning gender, sexuality and 'race'. Like the free clinics, these have led to practical clinical projects as well as theoretical challenges. The free clinics also raised questions of how the social world can be represented within psychoanalytic theory and whether its laws can be assumed to be universal.

The limited clinical data from these clinics, as well as the theorising of psychoanalysis at that point in time, does not allow much insight into how class may have entered into clinical material, including the therapy relationship itself. Rather, this has mostly emanated from modern attention to the dynamics of the therapy relationship, and to greater reflective awareness of the cultural assumptions and subjectivities of the therapist, as I address later. Further, despite their explicit concerns with extending the reach of psychoanalysis, these radical analysts did not question some of the premises on which psychoanalysis was based. I argue next that it is these founding premises which embed the theoretical disarticulation of psychoanalysis from the social world, leading to its disavowal of class.

Notes

1 At least to non-German speakers.
2 See Engstrom (2005). Other reviewers, e.g. Altman (2006), Roazen (2006) and Fisher (2007), are much more positive. I have found Danto's immersive chronological detail very evocative but also difficult to extract themes from. Her positive assessment of Reich's substantial contributions to the clinics may fuel criticism, given how he has been written out of much psychoanalysis.
3 This slightly confusing name derives from how these analysts saw themselves as children of Freud, not that it concerned the analysis of children.
4 Anna Freud, who later founded the Hampstead War Nurseries, also participated in such work, as did many of her subsequent colleagues.
5 This illustrates the narrow space available for a politically committed psychoanalytic practice, something not confined to Reich's case, see e.g. Plotkin (2011) for Bleger's experiences in Argentina.
6 This capturing of the emotional territory of political arguments by the right is seen for example in anti-abortion campaigns, in the current right-wing assault on people on welfare benefits, in Brexit debates and in the popularity of Trump.
7 My references to the *Rundbriefe* are only to the ones translated into English or referred to by Danto (2005). The bulk remains untranslated and, as far as I can ascertain, uncommented on.
8 Although, as Jacoby shows, only in the introduction to this classic work.

References

Altman, N. (2006) 'Freud's free clinics', *International Journal of Psychoanalysis* 87: 1408–12.
Bibring-Lehner, G. (1932) 'Seminar for the discussion of therapeutic technique', *International Journal of Psycho-Analysis* 13: 257–9.
Crick, P. (2016) '90 Years of the London Clinic of Psychoanalysis'. Unpublished paper.
Danto, E. A. (2005) *Freud's Free Clinics: Psychoanalysis & Social Justice, 1918–1938*. New York/Chichester: Columbia University Press.

Deutsch, H. (1932) 'The training institute and the clinic', *International Journal of Psycho-Analysis* 13: 255–7.
Diercks, C. (2002) 'The Vienna psychoanalytic polyclinic ("Ambulatorium"): Wilhelm Reich and the technical seminar', *Psychoanalysis and History* 4: 67–84.
Eitingon, M. (1923) 'Report of the Berlin Psycho-Analytical Policlinic', *Bulletin of the International Psycho-Analytic Association* 4: 254–69.
Engstrom, E. (2005) 'Review of Elizabeth Ann Danto, Freud's Free Clinics', H-German. Available at: www.h-net.org/reviews/showrev.cgi18481148316623. Accessed June 2016.
Fanon, F. (1952) *Black Skin, White Masks*. New York: Grove Press.
Fenichel, O. (1934) *Outline of Clinical Psychoanalysis*. London: Kegan Paul.
Fenichel, O. (1938) 'The drive to amass wealth', *Psychoanalytic Quarterly* 7: 69–95.
Fenichel, O. (1967) 'Psychoanalysis as the Nucleus of a future dialectical – materialistic psychology', *American Imago* 24: 290–311.
Fisher, D. (2007) 'Classical psychoanalysis, politics and social engagement in the era between the wars', *Psychoanalysis and History* 9: 237–50.
Freud, S. (1918) 'Lines of advance in psychoanalytic therapy'. In Strachey, J. (ed) *The Standard Edition of the Complete Psychological Works of Sigmund Freud* 17: 157–68.
Freud, S. (1930) 'Preface to *Ten Years of the Berlin Psycho-Analytic Institute*'. In Strachey, J. (ed) *The Standard Edition of the Complete Psychological Works of Sigmund Freud* 21: 257.
Frosh, S. (2009) *Hate and the Jewish Science*. Basingstoke: Palgrave Macmillan.
Fuechtner, V. (2011) *Berlin Psychoanalytic*. Oakland: University of California Press.
Hitschmann, E. (1932) 'A ten years' report of the Vienna Psycho-Analytic Clinic', *International Journal of Psycho-Analysis* 13: 245–54.
Jacoby, R. (1983) *The Repression of Psychoanalysis: Otto Fenichel and the Political Freudians*. New York: Basic Books.
Meisel, P. and Kendrick, W. M. (1985) *Bloomsbury/Freud: The Letters of James and Alix Strachey, 1924–1925*. New York: Basic Books.
Plotkin, M. (2011) 'José Bleger: Jew, Marxist and Psychoanalyst', *Psychoanalysis and History* 13: 181–205.
Reich, W. (1929/1960) *Dialectical Materialism & Psychoanalysis*. London: Socialist Reproduction.
Reich, W. (1933/1970) *The Mass Psychology of Fascism*. London: Souvenir Press.
Reich, W. (1945) *Character Analysis*. New York: Simon and Schuster.
Roazen, P. (2006) 'Freud's free clinics', *Journal of American Psychoanalytic Association* 54: 1036–40.
Simmel, E. (1929) 'Psycho-analytic treatment in a sanitorium', *International Journal of Psycho-Analysis* 10: 70–89.
Simmel, E. (1946) 'Otto Fenichel', *International Journal of Psycho-Analysis* 27: 67–70.
Steiner, R. (2000) *'It Is a New Kind of Diaspora': Explorations in the Sociopolitical and Cultural Context of Psychoanalysis*. London: Karnac.

3

ELISION AND DISAVOWAL

The extrusion of class from psychoanalytic theory

We have seen in the previous chapter how theoretical questions concerning the integration of social factors with psychoanalytic work were a preoccupation of many of the psychoanalysts involved in the clinics, albeit secondary to the task of running and maintaining these. This debate subsequently took off in many directions, mainly, apart perhaps from Erich Fromm, divorced from clinical work and often, as in the post-war Frankfurt school, increasingly in the form of a psychoanalytic sociology. In all such critical theorisations of Marxism and psychoanalysis, the emphasis is mainly on ways to stitch them together rather than to understand how the grounds for their disarticulation were created in the first place. This chapter addresses points in the development of psychoanalytic theory where such disarticulation from the social world arises. Anne McClintock (1995), in *Imperial Leather*, names this an aporia – a radical disjunction. Here I identify significant points in the construction of theory by Freud that led to the extrusion of class from psychoanalytic discourse, leaving a theoretical vacuum which has also had effects on clinical work.

My approach is to focus on what is absent, foreclosed or rejected from a text, in order to understand its presuppositions and its foundational assumptions. I look at several of Freud's case histories and other writings where class is descriptively present in the accounts he gives of his patients' lives and their significant others, but where it does not figure at all in the interpretations or theorisations offered, or, as in the Wolf Man case, is explicitly rejected. In attempting to understand this disarticulation, I have learned much from the approach taken by Jean Walton (Walton, 2001), in relation to 'race' and racial difference as these appear and then disappear from various psychoanalytic texts. This is just one of many instances where theoretical work on 'race' in relation to psychoanalysis can suggest avenues of thought as regards class. Walton uses an examination of Joan Riviere's classic account of femininity as masquerade (Riviere, 1929), as well as other clinical writings, to demonstrate that while racialised fantasy and difference form an important part of the *content* of the patient's material they are omitted from any of the analyst's *interpretations* or *theorising*, or indeed from the extensive secondary literature on this case. Walton sees the discarding of the racialised identifications, fantasies and desires that are present as serving the purpose of a universalising account of gender and sexuality that takes no account of significant social formations and powerful social imaginaries. This she names as a process of disavowal. In what follows we can see similar processes of elision and disavowal in relation to class in some of the founding texts of psychoanalysis, and also in the ways some identities built on privilege may be structured by these processes.

The abjected nurse

McClintock (1995) uses the notion of disavowal to argue that Freud founded his Oedipal theory on the elision of the working-class female employee, depriving her of any theoretical status and presenting the Oedipal account as free of any economic or class structures, as universal. There is much to support this account, as will be illustrated later on. She argues that the categories of gender, 'race' and class exist and operate in and through each other, often in contradictory and conflictful ways, so that they are not as hermetically distinct and separate as is often assumed. Psychoanalytic accounts of gender may make no reference to 'race' or class, as Walton illustrates, yet these are often the unspoken (abjected) terms at play.

Class was palpably and extensively present in the family lives of many of Freud's patients and of Freud himself. There are numerous references in various of his case histories and also in *The Interpretation of Dreams* (Freud, 1900) to nurses and governesses, working-class or lower middle-class servants and other employees in the households of middle- and upper-class families. The presence of working-class employees within these families introduces a significant class aspect into the care and development of these children, as well as structuring their relationship with their parents. The family is of course only one context in which class operates, but it is a key one for psychoanalysis, as it is the site of the formulation of Freud's theories of sexuality and the Oedipus complex. Furthermore, the care of children is part of the territory of the embodiment of class. Norbert Elias' epic study of class signifiers and socialisation (Elias, 1939/1994) focuses on matters such as hygiene, manners, bodily comportment, clothes, and taste. These have a bodily aspect inscribed early in the care of children, and are often unconsciously carried, albeit instantly recognisable, in body language of various kinds. Nurses, nannies and maidservants frequently had much more bodily and intimate relationships with children than their own parents did. Jane Gallop argues that the most insistent locus of intrusion into the idealised family is the maid/governess/nurse, naming this as the intrusion of the symbolic into the imaginary, or 'the hole in the social cell' of the nuclear family (Gallop, 1982: 144). Here I attempt to trace this 'hole in the social cell' through some of the many references to the significance of such working-class employees in the early Freudian literature.

It is well known that Freud's self-analysis, conducted mainly through letters to Wilhelm Fliess, was entwined with his formulation of the Oedipus complex. Strikingly, for present purposes, this is put forward in the context of various dreams, memories and associations concerning his nurse, in a period of intense self-analysis. Freud does not provide any details about her identity; indeed she is not even given a name, but subsequent references and secondary literature name her as Monica Zajic (Glenn, 1986) and describe her as working class, Czech and Catholic, at a time when Freud's family were living in Moravia (Grigg, 1973; Swan, 1974). Jim Swan suggests that her ethnic, social, cultural and economic status was one of considerable inferiority, a potent mixture to carry into a caring relationship with an infant from a different social milieu and one which might inspire many conflictful feelings, conscious or otherwise (Swan, 1974).

Freud analyses his significant early relationship with her: 'I can only say shortly that *der Alte* [my father] played no active part in my case . . . that the prime originator [of my troubles] was a woman, ugly, elderly but clever . . .' (Freud, 1897: 261, brackets as original). Making reference to his memories of early sibling jealousy, cruelty and his current travel anxiety he says: '[I]f I succeed in resolving my own hysteria, I shall be grateful to the old woman who provided me at such an early age with the means for living and going on living. As you see my old liking for her is breaking through again' (Freud, 1897: 262).

The following day, he says, in response to a dream of the previous night: 'She was my teacher in sexual matters and scolded me for being clumsy and not being able to do anything' (Freud, 1897: 262). And later: 'Besides this, she washed me in reddish water, in which she had previously washed herself. [The interpretation is not difficult; I find nothing like this in the chain of my memories, so I regard it as a genuine ancient discovery.]' (Freud, 1897: 263, brackets as original). He then recounts an apparent memory of 'the old woman' making him steal some money and give it to her, which he invokes as a parallel with himself in the present taking money from his patients for his 'bad' treatment of them. Subsequently his mother corrects this memory to the effect that the nurse had stolen the money herself and on being found out, was dismissed and sent to prison. Freud, reflecting on his mistaken memory, says 'I = she', suggesting that he was identifying with her in his memory and associations (Freud, 1897: 264).

Freud underlines the extent of the emotional disturbance created for him by the nurse's sudden disappearance in a memory of how distraught he was on a later occasion of not being able to find his mother, and fearing that, like his nurse, she could vanish completely. Following this, reflecting on the course of his self-analysis, he then provides one of the earliest statements of what became the Oedipus complex: 'One single thought of general value has been revealed to me. I have found, in my own case too, falling in love with the mother and jealousy of the father, and I now regard it as a universal event of early childhood' (Freud, 1897: 265).

The leap in Freud's text from these vivid memories and associations concerning his nurse to the bald, generalised statement of the Oedipus complex, without even a paragraph break, is indeed an aporia, into which the working-class employee is propelled and thus abjected.

This whole sequence is striking for suggesting how, in these letters of self-analysis, Freud could credit the figure of a nurse as having an often decisive importance in his development: arousing him sexually in disturbing ways, but providing him with an affectionate attachment that he then lost, and also with the basis for a subsequent identification. It also underlines the extent of the physical intimacy involved in the relationship. Swan, in an extended commentary on these passages, argues that the figure of the nurse not only played a crucial role in Freud's own development but also in the formulation of his theories. He remarks on the nurse's role in both arousing and shaming the infant Freud, and compares this with the much more distanced description Freud gives of his more passive later interest in his mother:

> What needs explaining is how the theory of the Oedipus complex accounts for the boy's guilty impulses towards his mother but ignores

the boy's arousal at the hands of his nurse, especially in view of how much more attention the nurse gets from Freud than his mother does.

(Swan, 1974: 19)

Swan maintains that there are in effect two mothers: the one whose name and nakedness Freud can only mention in Latin (Freud, 1897: 262) and the other whom he remembers as the agent of disturbing sexual experiences. This allows Freud to depict the mother of the Oedipus complex as pure in her sexuality, as only the object of attraction from the son, rather than in any way seductive or intrusive, with the 'bad', humiliating aspects of the now banished nurse projected into the oedipal father.

Freud's postulation of the Oedipus complex and the role of children's erotic fantasies was also the site of the abandonment of the seduction theory. In abandoning that, and its implication of intrusive external influences, the figure of the nurse was also abandoned. It is paradoxical if not contradictory, and certainly significant for subsequent theory, that a working-class figure can be attributed such an important role and yet also be banished, both in actuality and from the theory, present but absent. Prophecy Coles in *The Second Mother* shows how extensively these female employees have been afforded no importance in theories of child development and in clinical work, despite the evidence of significant attachment and involvement, and how the traumas associated with their departure have frequently been minimised or denied any recognition (Coles, 2015). She argues that the 'impression' Freud's nurse made on him continued to puzzle him, but that he failed to find 'a significant place for his nurse in his emotional life' (Coles, 2015: 69); nor, we may add, in his theories.

The return of the nurse

Like all expelled figures, traces remain or return. McClintock (1995) argues that the nurse, 'the repudiated working-class other: the expelled abject' (1995: 89), returns to haunt the dreams of Freud himself and also his patients. She argues that servants, seen merely as parental surrogates and temporary intruders into the 'family romance', should rather be recognised as major sources of love, splitting, conflictual identifications and desires. There is now a considerable secondary literature on such passages from Freud, the import of which is often to trace the significance of his nurse in his subsequent dreams (e.g. Grigg, 1973), or to suggest reinterpretations of his case studies where servants are concerned (e.g. Glenn, 1986; Colombo, 2010).

Jean Laplanche, in his reworkings of Freud, makes use of the discarded figure of a nurse to link Freud's abandonment of the seduction theory to the writing out of the primacy of the other (Laplanche, 1999). This unnamed nurse occurs in a chain of associations and memories that Freud recounts in the course of analysing one of his own dreams. Referring to an inn-hostess who was making dumplings in the dream, Freud writes:

> Love and hunger, I reflected, meet at a woman's breast. A young man who was a great admirer of feminine beauty was talking once – so the story went – of the good-looking wet-nurse who had suckled him when he was a baby: "I'm sorry," he remarked, "that I didn't make a better use of my opportunity." I was in the habit of quoting this anecdote to explain the factor of "deferred action" in the mechanism of the psychoneuroses.
> (Freud, 1900: 203–4)

Laplanche argues that, in this recounting of the story of the young man:

> Freud, who has abandoned the theory of seduction, forgets or rather scotomises *the nurse*, in whom he refuses to see a new figure of the 'perverse adult' of the letters to Fliess. Here, she is hardly anything more than the support of an object without enigma. But what object, what consumption is at issue here? Is it the milk which is to be ingested? Is it the breast which is to be . . . sucked . . .? Incorporated . . .? Caressed . . .? Stimulated . . .? As for the nipple, precisely the erogenous part of the object, it is cruelly absent, as is any reference to the pleasure the other seeks there.
> (Laplanche, 1999: 258, italics/gaps as original)

Laplanche thus criticises Freud for reducing the nurse to the barest of simple functions, someone without complexity, her breast purely as an object for the infant, and not as an erotic zone for her. By characterising Freud's depiction of her as 'object without enigma' Laplanche implies that the nurse is not seen as a fully constituted other, not a subject in her own right, not someone formative for the child's unconscious, nor the conveyer of enigmatic perhaps untranslatable messages. We could add the nurse's desires and needs deriving from her class status and history to Laplanche's list of omitted characteristics. Laplanche also argues:

> After all – and one is slightly ashamed to say so – psychoanalysis with and since Freud has omitted to note that repression and the unconscious

exist in the other before being present in the child: in the Wolf Man's parents, in *Grusha*[1] and in the beating father.

(Laplanche, 1999: 158, my italics)

As I argue later, Laplanche's reorientating of Freudian theory towards the primacy of the other allows more scope for the inclusion of the desires of significant working-class employees, and for the transmission of unconscious communications, including those of class.

Daria Colombo, in a contemporary revisiting of this terrain, cites the many references to servants scattered throughout Freud's writings, often occurring with greater frequency than references to mothers (Colombo, 2010). She points out that while Freud abandoned his original seduction theory, he never doubted the reality of the many seductions by nursemaids, governesses and other servants that he heard about. Colombo examines both the Dora case and also that of Lucy R who was herself a governess (Freud, 1893), as well as others more briefly. She argues that relationships with servants 'function not only as vehicles for split-off aspects of the maternal transference, but also as important independent object relationships' (p. 840). These various servants, she says, are both marginal and central: marginal as persons of little power in the families and households where they worked, and also marginal in psychoanalytic theory; central however to the early lives of many children and in the many references to them, especially in their sexual engagements with their charges. They were thus given some historical and psychic truth at the same time as constituting a theoretical blind spot. Colombo interestingly argues that much of the scotomising of these women servants was because they represented an active, unruly female sexuality which ran counter both to bourgeois morals of the time and also to Freud's own theories of female sexuality as essentially passive. They were, in Freud's words, seen as persons of 'low morals', only remembered as 'worthless female material' (Masson, 1985: 241). Thus were working-class women depicted, and abjected, given neither reality nor fantasy status.

In this secondary literature, two things are going on simultaneously. First, there are the biographical arguments about the importance of Freud's own nursemaid to his subsequent dreams, identifications, recollections and references to nursemaids, as reported by him or interpreted by others post-hoc. Second, there are the theoretical critiques of the lacunae and contradictions in the manifest presence of the servants in the text with their writing-out from theory and with the privileging of the oedipal theory as involving only the parents, and, as we see next, with the theory of the primal scene. Most commentators run the two aspects together, which may have some legitimacy given that Freud's own theorising developed from his self-analysis. However, it is not necessary to speculate about the putative biographical aspects of Freud's motivations and possible countertransferences to insist on the theoretical elisions at play in the various texts, elisions and disavowals that have had such determining influences on the framework of subsequent psychoanalytic theorising.

Class and the Wolf Man

The Wolf Man text (Freud, 1918) provides one of the clearest examples of the writing-out of class from theory, and its return in another form. This case is the site of Freud's main theorisation of the primal scene, and is also the site of a striking erasure from the theory of the social relations so vividly portrayed in the descriptive case material. Here I trace some of the ways that class permeates the text and the significance of this. The racial and class disavowals of this text have been critiqued by Luz Calvo, using post-colonial theory. He argues for a reading such that 'the subject is constituted through fantasy scenarios in which difference is conceived as a tangled web of sexual, racial and class positions' (Calvo, 2008: 57).

The Wolf Man came from an aristocratic Russian family and one of his symptoms was a compulsive attraction to working-class women. Freud describes this as: 'all the girls with whom he subsequently fell in love – often with the clearest indications of compulsion – were also servants, whose education and intelligence were necessarily far inferior to his own' (Freud, 1918: 22). Freud suggests at this point that if all these servant girls were substitutes for the figure of his intellectually superior sister whom he had to forgo, then an *intention to debase* was contributing to his object choice.[2]

Freud's account contains many references to various nurses and female servants who played key roles in the child's life and also, it seems, in the construction of his sexual fantasies and later practices. At the outset, Freud describes how little the mother had to do with the children of the family, and that there were several substantial and crucial periods when both parents were absent. There are multiple references throughout the text to the various caring and educational roles that his nurse performed, and also to the roles that various governesses and tutors carried out. There are strikingly fewer references to the mother. The boy was mainly looked after by a nurse, an old peasant woman '[W]ith an untiring affection for him. He served her as a substitute for a son of her own who had died young' (Freud, 1918: 14). Freud makes some reference here to the nature of the nurse's possible desire for the boy, which may well have been crucial to their relationship, framed as it was for her by her loss, but he gives her no further status as a desiring or grieving subject, rather as only an employee. Thus are the subjectivity of the other and the enigmatic messages she may have conveyed dispensed with.

In Freud's account the nurse, 'his beloved Nanya' (a phrase Freud often repeats), with whom he shared a bedroom, becomes an important object of the boy's libidinal strivings, frustrations and conflicts. There is ample evidence of the intensity and loyalty of the boy's feelings towards her, in the face of criticism, and contempt expressed by the governess (another employee) and also by his sister. Indeed it seems that the marked change in his behaviour as a child occurred during the period of conflict between these two adult employees. This was also associated by Freud to the earlier seduction by his sister, carried out while she told him sexualised stories about his Nanya. Freud sees the boy's masturbation in front of his Nanya as attempts to seduce her, only to be met with refusal, disapproval and threats from her. He then, Freud says, begins a secret search for another sexual object. Freud describes the boy's regression to a sadistic-anal pregenital organisation in which 'his principal object was his beloved Nanya', whom he tormented. The earlier seduction by his sister had, Freud says, forced him into a passive sexual role, and he 'pursued a path from his sister via his Nanya to his father' (Freud, 1918: 27). Later Freud describes how the child only recovered from the anxiety with which the wolves' dream (a crucial part of the text) ended by having his Nanya with him at night. Freud renders this as a flight back from father to nurse, as objects of his desires. In all these many important ways, the nurse rather than the mother appears as the cardinal female object of the boy's early and turbulent emotional life, yet she is never described as anything more than a substitute for the mother.

As the case narrative proceeds with its constructions and reconstructions, another servant, Grusha, enters the account as formative in the Wolf Man's subsequent sexual compulsions. This scene was produced by a chain of associations from a screen memory involving another peasant girl. Freud describes the scene with Grusha as the first experience the Wolf Man 'could really remember', arrived at 'without any conjectures or intervention' by Freud. This certainty contrasts with the many conjectures in the text surrounding the alleged witnessing of the putative primal scene between the parents. Freud links the boy's sexual excitement at the sight of Grusha, on her knees scrubbing the floor 'with her buttocks projecting', to the posture his mother allegedly assumed in the earlier hypothesised scene of copulation from behind with the father, such that Grusha 'became his mother to him' and 'like his father . . . he behaved in a masculine way towards her', by urinating on the floor. He earlier remarks, as suggested by a linguistic confusion, on how Grusha 'had become fused with his mother' in the Wolf Man's memory. Freud continues: 'The compulsion which proceeded from the primal scene was transferred on to this scene with Grusha' (Freud, 1918: 93). Freud then goes on to describe the subsequent compulsiveness with which the Wolf Man fell in love with several peasant girls in similar occupations and postures to Grusha, and how this compulsion dominated his love choices. Notably Freud remarks that it was not just the posture but also the *occupation* of the young woman that was to have such a decisive influence on his subsequent conditions of being able to fall in love. In this respect we can see that something associated with class (occupation) had made its mark in the text.

Despite these abundant references to many different employees and to the significant roles of the Nanya and Grusha in the Wolf Man's early childhood, they are only rendered as substitutes or surrogates for the mother, a unidirectional displacement without any theorised significance. Freud preserves the primacy of the constructed primal scene by interpreting the significance of the physical debasement of Grusha's kneeling only in terms of his association to the posture of the mother in the parental coupling, not as something in itself full of emotive social meaning and difference. In conducting this argument, he wants to disprove any greater significance of what he calls the Wolf Man's 'intention to debase' (Freud, 1918: 95), which he sees as a rival to the primal scene explanation, an argument he keeps going throughout the text. Freud contends that the Wolf Man did not respond in any fruitful way to this alternative interpretation and concludes that this militates against any overestimation of such an 'intention to debase', rather than the primal scene hypothesis. It is notable that Freud poses this as an either/or choice, not as both being contributing factors. By invoking an 'intention to debase' Freud is assuming this as a defining feature of class relations on the part of those of the upper classes towards those of the working classes, which, while plausible, is not elaborated. He returns later to the question of the status of the 'intention to debase' in a discussion of the importance of the dumb water carrier who Freud says served the patient as a father-surrogate.

Although these servants are described as having far-reaching impacts in the childhood and adult life of the Wolf Man, class is not given any significance. Rather Freud argues: 'A child pays no regard to social distinctions, which have little meaning for him yet; and he classes people of inferior rank with his parents if such people love him as his parents do' (Freud, 1918: 98).

This is a strong assertion in one of the founding papers of psychoanalysis that class differences as such cannot be expected to impinge on or affect a child, and that the alleged 'inferior rank' of working-class employees will not register. It undoubtedly has had far-reaching effects over the subsequent course of psychoanalysis. The child's supposed lack of ability to perceive social difference is contradicted by Freud's argument a few pages later, in relation to the primal scene hypothesis, that 'we have rated the powers of children too low and that there is no knowing what they cannot be given credit for' (Freud, 1918: 103). Yet the early and formative relationships that the upper-class Wolf Man had with working-class employees are dismissed in favour of the (often absent) parental couple, at the same time as being extensively described. The question of how a child internalises social differences between significant figures and, in the wider world, of how class becomes part of the psyche, is rendered a non-question within the canon. This is a form of disavowal, of knowing and not knowing, and is a prime site within psychoanalysis for the elision and extrusion of class.

Calvo (2008) rereads the Wolf Man case in the light of the racial transference that occurs at the beginning of the analysis. Freud says in a letter to Ferenczi, the patient 'confessed to me, after the first session: Jewish swindler, he would like to use me from behind and shit on my head' (Brabant and Giampieri-Deutsch, 1992: 138). Calvo argues that this racial dynamic is disavowed by Freud in an ironic joke about money[3] and that this leads to the eliding of the structuring role of racial difference. Calvo's analysis is valuable for the ways in which he then reads Fanon alongside Freud to emphasise the ways in which subjects are constituted through powerful social imaginaries and the circulation of fantasies of miscegenation. He also links his extensive rereading as regards 'race' to the elision of class. He considers that Freud overlooked the primal importance of the boy's relations with Grusha and other servants, and the structuring rather than secondary role of social difference: 'These distinctions of high/low recur as organising tenets of the Wolf Man's desire, demonstrating that social difference and oedipal scenarios are intertwining fantasies and sites of dense condensation' (Calvo, 2008: 62). Social forces and imaginaries are thus given a dynamic equivalence with the intra-psychic processes; in such ways social position can structure sexual desire. This approach locates the workings of social formations as part of the earliest structuring of subjectivity, rather than as an externally imposed effect on an already existent psyche.

The challenge is to identify such 'intertwining fantasies and sites of dense condensation' in the case of class, something that some contemporary work considered later is beginning to illuminate. An upper-class/middle-class example of this, namely class-related sexual debasement, is also described in 'The Universal Tendency to the Debasement in the Sphere of Love' (Freud, 1912). Here Freud observes how the frequent choice of a woman of a lower class by men of a higher class is a means to complete sexual satisfaction, a consequence of their need for a debased sexual object, inhibited with respected and respectable women. Thus such splitting between love and sex has a class dimension, again described but not theorised as to how class comes to signify debasement. Instead the debasement that is attached to sex, as something degrading, is seen as coming only from internal sources and the childhood repression of sexuality, rather than, or as well as, from the social configuration. Here, as in the Wolf Man case, we can see how for upper-class white heterosexual males the class and sexual dynamics are intertwined. McClintock (1995) provides many similar examples from the era in which psychoanalysis was first formulated. Such eroticisation of class difference can also be found in many historical accounts of gay male sexuality.

I suggest that Freud's notion of the 'intention to debase' depicts one aspect of class relations, and the ways people are constituted by them, that has a powerful significance, both in its materiality and in being one of the many circulating fantasies about class. Because the 'intention to debase' is used as a foil for Freud to disprove as a putative alternative to the primal scene hypothesis, the significance of it is easily overlooked. This is that the up/down, inferior/superior aspects of class are central to many aspects of class experience and class relations, as later considerations show, however much we may for other reasons wish to resist or dispute this. The Wolf Man case itself suggests the early age at which bodily distinctions between high and low, and the accompanying fantasies, are transformed and intermingled with social distinctions. It was at such a juncture that psychoanalysis turned away from any further exploration of the implantation of class relations in the psyche of the developing child.

Cross-class love and loss

We can see from the foregoing how working-class employees are present in the founding texts of psychoanalysis at key moments in the evolution of theory, yet discarded as of any importance in their own right. The work these employees did, the services and relationships they provided, in caring for the children (and indirectly in the creation of the theory), are rendered invisible, as servants so often were and are required to be (Lethbridge, 2013). Thus, the ways in which middle-class and upper middle-class identity and defence structures can be significantly built on excluded working-class others are not investigated psychoanalytically. These servants remained the 'worthless female material' of Freud's letter to Fliess, excluded from the theory of the 'family romance' of the Oedipus complex, yet in many cases crucial to the child's development. These various relationships also exemplify the vicissitudes of and barriers to 'crossing the boundaries of inequality', a central notion in Sennett's (2003) discussion of class and respect.

The ways these working-class employees come to figure or be forgotten, in the minds of others, illustrates powerfully Judith Butler's notion of ungrievable lives, those which are not valued enough to be recognised as worthy of grief. However, a few psychoanalytic writers, including Coles (2015), have questioned the contemporary lack of psychoanalytic interest in surrogate or second mothering. Sara Scheftel (2012), like Laplanche earlier, describes this as a 'scotoma' in the literature, and Harry Hardin (1985) remarks on the contrast between the absence from theory and the frequency in his clinical practice of various forms of substitute primary caretaking. He contests the commonly accepted argument that the mother, even if largely absent, trumps the nurse/nanny, an echo of Freud's eclipsing of his nurse by the image of his mother. In this and subsequently (Hardin and Hardin, 2000), he and his co-author trace the vicissitudes of care by servants/employees through detailed clinical examples. They highlight the intense, often very physical, attachments involved and the trauma for the child when employees leave or are sacked. They argue that the importance of such loss for the child and subsequent adult is significantly unrecognised, often forgotten or repressed, ungrievable but sometimes surfacing in fragments of sensory memory or symptoms of detachment in relationships. They criticise the lack of recognition of surrogate–mother transference in clinical work (Hardin and Hardin, 2004). Coles (2015) suggests that the neglect of the nanny or nurse lies in their unacknowledged emotional importance, the traumatic nature of the losses sustained, the conflicts inherent in substitute care, covered over by an idealisation of the mother, all of which may contribute to later melancholia. To which I would add their lack of any social power.

The difficulties of the nannying job, another 'impossible profession', are taken up more fully by Scheftel (2012). She describes the very rapid repression by the child of caregivers who leave as part of their devaluation. She sees the nanny as falling into a divide between mother and baby, likely to disappoint the child or else elicit resentment towards the mother, a kind of negative 'problematic and potentially split psychic space'

(Scheftel, 2012: 253). The nanny may be the repository of all kinds of projections from the mother, whose own conflicts may lead her to deny, hate or make invisible the very person on whose help she is dependent. The nanny is required to remain in the background, her necessary presence overlooked. Scheftel considers this normal for many cross-class relationships, where underpayment and disdainful or abusive behaviour can reflect the entitled dynamics of domestic employers. Skeggs, in her research on class and gender, quotes one nanny:

> They treat you like shit. What I've noticed is that they never look at you . . . they just tell you what to do. . . . Some of them want you to know you're shit in comparison to them. . . . Even the kids. They learn really early on that you're not worth the ground they walk on.
> *(Skeggs, 1997: 92)*

What is remarkable is that in the face of huge disparities of power and recognition, very often (albeit with exceptions, see Sonntag, 2006) these working-class women do forge significant loving relationships with their more privileged charges.

Such denial of the subjectivities of domestic employees, or of their significance, has meant there are few clinical accounts where the patient herself is a domestic employee. One exception is Freud's case of Miss Lucy R, a governess and putatively lower middle class (Freud, 1893). Her duties meant that she could only come for short sessions – a material constraint often echoed in the exigencies of providing psychoanalytic therapy in poor communities (see Chapter 4). She felt conflicted between her loyalty to the children who needed her (their mother was dead), and her desire to leave an uncomfortable situation and return to her own mother. Freud analyses her symptoms (recurrent smells of burnt pudding) as deriving from the repression of the conflict of her love for her employer that she wanted to forget. On Freud interpreting this she said very eloquently that she was not ashamed of this love, but that it was distressing to her because she was only a poor girl in his service as an employee and thus did not have the same 'independence' towards him she would to anyone else. She felt people would laugh at her if they knew. She traced the arousal of her love for the employer to his unusual declaration of how much he depended on her to bring up his children. Freud considers the 'operative trauma' to be an occasion when the employer, angry with her for an incident, threatens to dismiss her. This display of power crushed her hopes that he loved her in any way, but her symptoms disappeared with these interpretations. Two aspects of being a servant stand out: the powerlessness she felt as an employee, which Freud does not take up, and also the vulnerability and confusion of being needed and depended on, but not loved as an equal.

Furthermore Freud gives little space to her fantasies of love. Colombo (2010) highlights Freud's apparent insistence that Lucy R should stay in service, rather than follow her own desires, that is, reconcile herself to her role as an exploited servant; replace the dead mother as caretaker of the children but not as someone more equal, as wife or lover of the father. Colombo comments how unusually the death of her fantasy is accepted with remarkable complacency by both Freud and Lucy R; her love 'makes no difference'.

Elsewhere Freud emphatically denied that servants were interesting or adequate as psychoanalytic subjects, as Vicky Lebeau (1995) argues. In a letter to Jung he said: 'What with their habits and mode of life, reality is too close to these women to allow them to believe in fantasies. If I had based my theories on the statements of servant girls, they would all be negative' (Freud, 1907: 64). He continues: 'we can tell these persons their story without having to wait for their contribution. They are willing to confirm what we tell them, but *one can learn nothing from them*' (Freud, 1907: 64, my italics).

Freud in this passage gives up on servants, re-inscribing them with his version of their story, not open to hearing theirs. Whether Freud means the servants do not have the kind of fantasies that psychoanalysis can make use of, or whether they do but do not believe in them is left ambiguous. However, the distinction between reality and fantasy, the borderline with which much psychoanalysis works, now becomes inflected by class. Thus was a limit placed on who was suitable for or interesting to psychoanalysis: this was justified in terms of 'too close' to reality, an often repeated theme, closing down any psychoanalytic exploration. The class dimensions of this have reverberated through the subsequent history of psychoanalysis, disenfranchising many working-class subjects, and taking for granted what 'reality' might mean.

Identities built on privilege

I suggest that the vagueness and blankness with which many of these working-class caregivers come to be portrayed by both writer and patient is a function of their generally devalued status as poor and working class, scarcely remembered by the adult and unrecognised in psychoanalytic discourse or as psychoanalytic subjects – an aporia indeed. Thus the powerful social framing at play, replicated in the theory, leaves unaddressed not just the subjectivities of employees themselves, but also the ways in which middle- and upper-class identities can be structured by this abjection. Certain kinds of middle- or upper-class identity and defence structure can be partly built on the unrecognised love and loss of the working-class caretaker. Donald Winnicott, for example, described a patient whose 'actual nanny gave much colour to the False Self organisation' (Winnicott, 1960: 142).

Relational psychoanalysis, with its emphasis on intersubjectivity, has opened up this ground further. Melanie Suchet addresses the intersection of socially structured relationships, privilege and the melancholia of profound attachment to, and loss of, family employees in a retrospective portrayal of her black South African nanny, Dora Moketzie (Suchet, 2007). While recognising the ambiguities of such a search from a position of her own white privilege, she attempts to retrieve Dora from the annihilations of racial and social class privilege, and the necessarily narcissistic perceptions of the child she was. Asking the question 'who was she?', Suchet speaks of a time before she was aware that the hands that so gently held her and bathed her were black, or that she was white. She evokes the sensuous nature of Dora's loving care, while remarking that she came to know *without it being spoken*, that she herself was part of the ruling class, and that to be white was to have power, even as a child. She expresses the confusion she felt as to who they were for each other: Dora as someone she 'loved effortlessly', her 'nanny-mommy', but who was not recognised as a person worthy of love and loss, part of the family yet a servant from another world about which Suchet knew nothing. She tracks the vicissitudes of this deep, loving relationship that was socially devalued and ambiguous within the family. Suchet asks when it was she realised her 'idyllic childhood' and happiness were at Dora's expense – that Dora seldom saw her own child who occasionally came to visit, that she and her family lived a life of poverty and oppression of the most stark kind.

Suchet's article is important for the ways she analyses and deconstructs a form of white identity built on privilege and the unrecognised emotional labour of a working-class woman. She coins the term 'the melancholia of the beneficiary' encapsulating the experience of loss and the diminishment of the sense of self for those who have benefited from the privileges of whiteness and class. Melancholia is a place of loss in which the socially disparaged other can persist unconsciously, not grieved or grievable. Suchet sees her re-membering of Dora, as a loving parental figure whose strength and endurance she feels marks her, as part of the re-evaluation of the self through an integration of what has been disavowed or foreclosed. She sees the confrontation with shame and the relinquishing of the previously idealised self as a first step in 'unravelling' privilege. Suchet acknowledges there is no way of escaping or transcending the profound racialisation and privilege of her relationship with Dora. She argues that the process she describes is part of living fully in the awareness of 'race', of surrendering 'the brittle defensiveness of whiteness' to be able to see the socially disparaged other as 'a like subject', rather, I would add, than perpetuating distance and disavowal. In this way the social framing that 'tears asunder the ability to love fully, to admit that love and to value both the black and the white mother' can be held up for questioning and deconstruction (Suchet 2007: 882). Sarah Hill (2007), in a commentary on Suchet's paper, argues that in any such process the real and material social context has to be foregrounded, a reminder that 'a narcissistic injury or lack is of a different order from a racist injury' (2007: 897), or indeed from one originating in class inequality and discrimination. Otherwise, the crucial dialectic between the psychic and the social collapses, and the social is inadvertently reduced to the psychic – a danger inherent in all such explorations.

Adrienne Harris (2007) takes this analysis further in her commentary. She observes that in the context of working mothers in Western societies and the globalisation of childcare, many children are now raised in multiple class and 'race' contexts, with the employment of childcare workers from diverse backgrounds. She, like previous authors, observes how often in clinical work:

> [O]ne comes upon some odd *elision* in a patient's narrative. Lost nannies, caretakers, or housekeepers without names or apparent meaning, any number of different missing pieces of a developmental attachment puzzle are often erased in family memories and certainly in our institutional, professional memories and narratives.
>
> *(Harris, 2007: 890, my italics)*

She depicts the complexity of trying to disentangle the 'use of another' in the Winnicottian sense from its other usages that relate to class, economic necessity and exploitation. She sums this up as 'the mix of gift and unwilling extraction and necessity' involved in childcare arrangements.

Harris argues that the construction of self in acts of domination and the continuation of privilege is a deep infrastructure in any white person's life, something that can constitute what she calls a *'psychose blanche'* – a psychic absence that can only be papered over. This she sees as a 'spot' of dissociation, despair and failed symbolisation (again an aporia), in contrast to Suchet, whose article assumes that this can, via the kind of process she depicts, be symbolised and altered. I suggest that class position also can be deeply constitutive of a privileged person's identity and personality in ways that may well resist symbolisation, and therefore lack articulation and reflection. In Harris (2012) she further argues that this means that even authentic expressions of social concern will be inevitably compromised, a way of expressing the pernicious divisions between people that social inequality creates, and an important corrective to any self-idealising.

Disavowal

This chapter has pinpointed the elision and disavowal of salient cross-class relationships in the lives of some of Freud's patients, as well as of Freud himself. This disavowal has allowed the creation of a universalised account of the Oedipus complex, and the assumption of the primacy of the constructed primal scene. These working-class figures do, however, continue to persist and haunt the subsequent adults as scotomised but often crucial figures. It is argued that the elision of these working-class employees allows psychoanalysis to continue with the construction of the primacy of the nuclear family, where questions of 'race', class and power are extruded. This is one important way in which the disarticulation of psychoanalysis from significant aspects of the social world arose. To bring significant cross-class relationships within the context of domestic employment more into the clinical and theoretical picture is to conceive of the working-class employees as persons in their own right, as 'like subjects', to use Jessica Benjamin's important term, with their own histories and subjectivities. This requires a form of theory that would embrace the ways in which class enters into and structures intimate emotional relationships, and also where the primacy of the other is more fully considered, as Laplanchian theory suggests. This would also throw light on the foreclosures and defensive structures of upper- and middle-class privilege, as some psychosocial and clinical work, addressed in later chapters, does.

The importance of naming the extrusion of class as disavowal is, I suggest, that disavowal is a process more widely involved in the way we deal with painful or unwelcome social realities. Disavowal is a mode of defence in which, as Hinshelwood (2008) describes, conscious awareness of painful realities is rejected. Freud originally evolved the concept in relation to male fetishism but it has a wider applicability to any unwelcome knowledge that is known but not known, denied or pushed aside. Two incompatible positions are held at the same time, so a compromise position results between two conflicting forces or ideas which exist side by side but do not influence each other. This Freud characterises as splitting of the ego, which occurs to enable 'normal reality awareness to survive while in another part of the ego it is strenuously denied' (Hinshelwood, 2008: 507). It results in the weakening of the ego, and we can see a parallel to this at a social and a disciplinary level. The way this operates may differ depending on the social positioning at any one point in time of the subject – as more or less privileged, and in relation to more or less privileged others. The disavowals concern knowledge of these others and their social realities, of how social realities impinge on and construct the self. Disavowal is an accommodation to realities we know about but feel powerless to affect or unwilling to engage with. The disavowal of the social world as of relevance to psychoanalysis means that the extensive knowledge, for example, of class as it is lived and felt about from other disciplines is ignored. My contention is that this weakens and isolates psychoanalysis in any attempt to reach out beyond what seems like its hermetically sealed province. It has also created a theoretical vacuum in which the languages and concepts to talk about class are not readily available within psychoanalytic frameworks.

Hinshelwood raises the question of the different ways and degrees to which the ego can be split, from conscious, maybe neurotic, conflict in which the ego can recognise both sides, through various forms of repression, disavowal and fragmentation to foreclosure in psychosis. Such differentiation is the stuff of detailed clinical work. Many writers have described the internal dividedness produced by class, and I suggest this can operate through all kinds of disavowal and splitting. Several writers on the affective aspects of class have also used notions of disavowal to describe the vicissitudes of living class in a divided society (see Chapter 5). Sennett and Cobb (1972) are at pains to distinguish the kind of divided self that they see as part of working-class consciousness from those described in cases of schizophrenia. However, Gary Walls (2006) makes a link with clinical work in how the often necessary double consciousness engendered by racism can be seen in symptoms of various kinds.

Notes

1 Grusha was the servant girl the memories of whom played an important part in Freud's analysis of the Wolf Man.
2 Here Freud is pursuing an argument with Alfred Adler and his postulation of the primacy of motives of power and prerogative. These, Freud avers, would have explained the case if he had not pursued the analysis further. Adler, who worked contemporaneously with a mainly working-class population of patients, described a symptomatic picture of inferiority complex, resulting from their socially underprivileged positions.

3 'On the whole I am only a machine for making money. . . .' Brabant and Gampieiri-Deutsch 1992: 138). Calvo argues that while making no explicit mention of the anti-Semitism that drives the transference, Freud's remark seems to make fun of racist discourses that associate Jews with money.

References

Brabant, E. F. and Giampieri-Deutsch, P. (1992) *The Correspondence of Sigmund Freud and Sandor Ferenczi, Vol. 1, 1908–1914*. Cambridge, MA: Harvard University Press.

Calvo, L. (2008) 'Racial fantasies and the primal scene of miscegenation', *International Journal of Psycho-Analysis* 89: 55–70.

Coles, P. (2015) *The Second Mother: Nurse and Nannies in the Theory of Infant Development*. London: Routledge.

Colombo, D. (2010) '"Worthless female material": Nursemaids and governesses in Freud's cases', *Journal of the American Psychoanalytic Association* 58: 835–59.

Elias, N. (1939/1994) *The Civilizing Process: Sociogenetic and Psychogenetic Investigations*. Oxford: Blackwell.

Freud, S. (1893) 'Miss Lucy R'. In Strachey, J. (ed) *The Standard Edition of the Complete Psychological Works of Sigmund Freud*, vol. 2: 106–24. London: Hogarth.

Freud, S. (1897) 'Letters to Fliess'. In Strachey, J. (ed) *The Standard Edition of the Complete Psychological Works of Sigmund Freud*, vol. 1: 261–5. London: Hogarth.

Freud, S. (1900) 'The interpretation of dreams'. In Strachey, J. (ed) *Standard Edition of the Complete Psychological Works of Sigmund Freud*, vols 4 and 5. London: Hogarth.

Freud, S. (1907) In McGuire, W. (ed) (1964) *Freud/Jung: The Freud/Jung Letters*, 32F, 64–5. London: Penguin.

Freud, S. (1912) 'On the universal tendency to debasement in the sphere of love'. In Strachey, J. (ed) *Standard Edition of the Complete Psychological Works of Sigmund Freud*, vol. 11: 177–90. London: Hogarth.

Freud, S. (1918) 'From the history of an infantile neurosis'. In Strachey, J. (ed) *Standard Edition of the Complete Psychological Works of Sigmund Freud*, vol. 17: 3–124. London: Hogarth.

Gallop, J. (1982) *The Daughter's Seduction*. New York: Cornell University Press.

Glenn, J. (1986) 'Freud, Dora and the maid', *Journal of the American Psychoanalytic Association* 34: 591–606.

Grigg, K. A. (1973) '"All roads lead to Rome": The role of the nursemaid in Freud's dreams', *Journal of the American Psychoanalytic Association* 21: 108–26.

Hardin, H. T. (1985) 'On the vicissitudes of early primary surrogate mothering', *Journal of the American Psychoanalytic Association* 33: 609–29.

Hardin, H. T. and Hardin, D. H. (2000) 'On the vicissitudes of early primary surrogate mothering II', *Journal of the American Psychoanalytic Association* 48: 1229–58.

Hardin, H. T. and Hardin, D. H. (2004) 'On: Miss A', *International Journal of Psycho-Analysis* 85: 1509–11.

Harris, A. (2007) 'Discussion on "unravelling whiteness"', *Psychoanalytic Dialogues* 17: 887–94.

Harris, A. (2012) 'The house of difference, or white silence', *Studies in Gender and Sexuality* 13: 197–216.

Hill, S. (2007) 'Homage to Dora: Commentary on paper by Melanie Suchet', *Psychoanalytic Dialogues* 17: 895–902.

Hinshelwood, R. (2008) 'Repression and splitting: Towards a method of conceptual comparison', *International Journal of Psycho-Analysis* 8: 503–29.
Laplanche, J. (1999) *Essays on Otherness*. London: Routledge.
Lebeau, V. (1995) *Lost Angels: Psychoanalysis and Cinema*. London: Routledge.
Lethbridge, L. (2013) *Servants: A Downstairs View of Twentieth-Century Britain*. London: Bloomsbury.
Masson, J. M. (1985) *The Complete Letters of Sigmund Freud to Wilhelm Fliess: 1887–1904*. Cambridge: Harvard University Press.
McClintock, A. (1995) *Imperial Leather: Race, Gender and Sexuality in the Colonial Contest*. New York: Routledge.
Riviere, J. (1929) 'Femininity as masquerade', *International Journal of Psycho-Analysis* 10: 303–13.
Scheftel, S. (2012) 'Why aren't we curious about nannies?', *The Psychoanalytic Study of the Child* 66: 251–78.
Sennett, R. (2003) *Respect*. London: Allen Lane.
Sennett, R. and Cobb, J. (1972) *The Hidden Injuries of Class*. New York: Norton.
Skeggs, B. (1997) *Formations of Class and Gender*. London: Routledge.
Sonntag, M. (2006) 'I have a lower class body', *Psychoanalytic Dialogues* 16: 317–31.
Suchet, M. (2007) 'Unravelling whiteness', *Psychoanalytic Dialogues* 17: 867–86.
Swan, J. (1974) '*Mater* and Nannie: Freud's two mothers and the discovery of the Oedipus complex', *American Imago* 31: 1–64.
Walls, G. (2006) 'Racism, classism, psychosis and self image in the analysis of a woman'. In Layton, L., Hollander, N. and Gutwill, S. (eds) *Psychoanalysis, Class and Politics: Encounters in the Clinical Setting*. New York: Routledge.
Walton, J. (2001) *Fair Sex, Savage Dreams: Race, Psychoanalysis, Sexual Difference*. Durham, NC: Duke University Press.
Winnicott, D. (1960) 'Ego distortion in terms of true and false self'. In Winnicott, D. (ed) (1965) *The Maturational Process and the Facilitating Environment*. London: Hogarth.

4

PSYCHOTHERAPY FOR THE PEOPLE?

Psychoanalysis in some public sectors

This chapter considers some of the ways in which psychoanalytic therapies have existed or do now exist within various public sectors, especially the third or 'voluntary' sector of community clinics. I address some of the cultural, economic and clinical issues arising when psychoanalysis engages with working-class clientele, and the challenges this creates for established practices. Some of the themes arising in the historic free clinics emerge in these different historical contexts. Issues of technique, cultural context and the structuring influence of social forces persist, added to by greater attention to the role of the therapists' own attitudes and cultural awareness. I consider what we can learn from these different kinds of free and low-cost clinics and bodies of work.

The influence of Freud's widely cited visionary speech about free clinics (Freud, 1918) lives on, in the inclusive spirit of many of the projects considered here. Strikingly, this speech is also quoted below the masthead of the UK Association for Psychoanalytic Psychotherapy (APP) in the NHS, whose psychotherapists have provided what they describe as 'psychoanalytically informed care' for more than a half century. However, the ambivalence (explored further later) also contained in Freud's speech about the status of psychotherapy continues to negatively affect the recognition of the value of free and low-cost work. Thus the journal of the APP refers to work in the NHS as 'applied' psychoanalysis, with its implications of not 'pure'. Here I argue that this contrast between the supposedly 'pure' forms of intensive private practice and the lesser frequency and shorter duration of those deemed 'applied' has dogged much of subsequent discussion and also the politics of the field. The exigencies of the present time demand a radical re-evaluation of these hierarchies and binaries, which are predominantly matters of class and inequality, and which negatively affect the wider standing of psychoanalysis.

The idea of free or low-cost psychoanalytic clinics, available to working-class people, went into abeyance after the demise of the Vienna and Berlin clinics and in the wake of World War II. A much more conservative era in psychoanalysis ensued, especially in the USA, but also in Europe, oblivious to its previous history, a kind of Laplanchian 'going astray' that Stephen Frosh (2009) regards as a loss of moral valence. Harvey Taylor, in his assessment of where psychoanalysis now stands, describes this as the 'truncation of the original broad vision of the pioneers' (Taylor, 2013: 3). The post-war era was marked by an amnesiac blotting out of the politically radical aspects of the past, the adoption of socially conformist standards of mental health and gender roles and the extreme pathologisation of homosexuality (Lewes, 1989; O'Connor and Ryan, 1993/2003). The notion that working-class people were not 'analysable' gained widespread acceptance, confining them to physical and pharmacological treatments. There appears to have been almost no contemporaneous challenge to this distorted perception. Moskowitz (1996b) shows how the ghosts of 'analyzability' still linger, especially affecting 'minority' patients. Several contributors to a contemporary book about psychoanalysis in disadvantaged urban communities still saw the need to argue against this canard (Foster et al., 1996). More recently, analysts working with Latino populations in the USA have also argued against this still expressed prejudice (Gaztambide, 2014; Gherovici, 2016).

In the social ferment of the 1960s and 1970s, many reworkings of psychoanalysis took place, challenging its conformist aspects and harnessing its socially radical potential. These challenges critiqued the prevailing ideologies of psychoanalysis, especially in relation to women, gender and 'race'. Some left and feminist groupings, alert to the importance of everyday life in political struggles, took on board the usefulness of psychoanalysis as a tool for understanding how the dominance of state power was underpinned by processes of individual repression, reproduced within the family. This has some continuity with the engagements of the earlier left psychoanalysts who saw psychoanalysis as an emancipatory tool at both the personal and social level. 'The personal is political' became a widespread motif. The notions of 'internalised oppression' and of 'interpellation' led to many advances in locating individual subjectivities within a wider social framework of political subordination. There was a resurgence of interest in some of Reich's writings. The anti-psychiatry movement inspired by Laing and others developed forms of psychoanalytic practice for those deemed psychotic, who had otherwise been subjected to pharmacological treatments and hospitalisation.

Psychoanalytic therapy in the UK, following the 1929 settlement with the medical profession, was never fully integrated into state provision. However, within the NHS it grew considerably in the post-war period, concomitant with the development of the welfare state. It included adult and child psychoanalytic psychotherapy, group analysis, family therapy and therapeutic communities within hospitals. Although always limited in extent, and often contested, nonetheless, as Andrew Cooper and Julian Lousada (2010) describe, psychoanalysis did have a solid presence in the wider mental health world and also within mid-twentieth-century social work. Much of this is now attenuated, replaced by CBT and other therapies, or abolished.[1] Sally Sales (2011), describing the political and theoretical contexts in which CBT has become so dominant, argues that working-class people especially are increasingly being consigned to brief manualised forms of treatment, an increasing concern also with campaigning organisations.[2]

However, in the UK, many psychoanalytically trained clinicians and trainees do still work in primary and secondary care in the NHS and in child psychotherapy departments. Recent evidence submitted by the umbrella bodies to the UK Parliament estimates that 25 per cent of registered psychoanalytic therapists work in the NHS, in some way.[3] Such work also continues in the public hospitals and clinics of the USA, as well as in various community settings. This means that many psychoanalytic therapists do encounter patients from a diversity of class and ethnic backgrounds. Although the detailed clinical work of NHS psychoanalytic psychotherapists has a predominant place in the APP's journal, *Psychoanalytic Psychotherapy*, a cursory survey suggests that discussions of class and ethnicity are infrequent, and cited, if at all, as 'background' factors. It is surely timely for the public sector work described in this journal and others to be given a higher profile as to its social and clinical importance. As Paul Wachtel (2002) argues, there is a need for a conceptual framework and reflection on what public sector and community work may throw up for psychoanalysis, some of which I put forward later on. In what follows I mainly consider psychoanalysis within community and third-sector clinics of various kinds.

Free and low-cost clinics

The reworkings of psychoanalysis did not remain at the level of ideology alone but also led to a plethora of innovative practical community projects, providing socially conscious forms of psychoanalytic psychotherapy, accessible to those previously excluded financially or put off by mainstream elitism, bias and prejudice. The extent of this field was and is huge, and deserves more extended research. Broadly speaking, there are three overlapping categories of such projects: those with an explicitly emancipatory agenda, that seek to combine therapeutic and political forms of struggle; those whose aim is to contest and remedy mainstream psychoanalytic bias and ideologies that exclude or wrongly pathologise groups identified by, for example, gender, ethnicity or sexual orientation; and those whose main aim is to extend access to psychoanalytic psychotherapy to those excluded from it by financial or other factors – a social justice agenda. Many projects occupy more than one of these categories but by far the largest number are those with a social justice agenda. All such projects tend to be precariously funded by a mixture of state (local authority, central government) and charitable sources, and often have sliding scales of charges.

Here I consider the issues that are raised by the transposition of psychoanalysis in its explicit engagements with class and poverty. Within a very broad definition of psychoanalytically informed therapy, the diversity of such projects, both past and present-day, is extraordinary[4] and is testimony to the continuing concern and desire of many psychoanalytic practitioners to remedy the exclusive nature of psychoanalysis. However, the available literature is scant and scattered; in-depth accounts of most projects, let alone an encompassing survey, have as yet to be written. Much useful information is probably hidden within the funding applications and annual reports that organisations produce. The kind of documentation on which Danto (2005) was able to draw was due to the priority that the early left psychoanalysts gave to outreach work, to popular writings and to the publication of their detailed records. The issue of the accessibility of psychoanalysis to working-class people is no longer part of mainstream psychoanalytic consciousness in the way it was then. Thus the knowledge that such engagements can bring is neglected, and the work of such diverse clinics does not gain the understanding or recognition it merits. Here I attempt to identify the main issues, using some of the available literature and my own experiences.

Political motivations and understandings

There are many different motivations for working in public or voluntary-sector clinics. In the case of politically radical clinics, the motivations may be explicit. I have devoted considerable space to these, as they, unlike most other projects, are often written about. Many of the issues identified apply to work in other more numerous but less documented settings.

Marie Langer, who trained in pre-World War II Vienna and subsequently in Buenos Aires, embodies many of the ideas of the historic free clinics, albeit in a different environment and historical period. She is a transitional figure, making reference in her writings to Reich's Sex-Pol, which she regarded as before its time, and also incorporating aspects of the Kleinian theory of her training. Much of Langer's work, from the 1950s onwards, took place in the context of conflicts within and splits from the Argentinian Psychoanalytic Association. Increasing state repression and terror led to her eventual exile and psychotherapeutic work in Mexico and Nicaragua. Langer's accounts of work in disadvantaged communities foreshadow many of the themes in later projects.

Langer, in her various journeys through psychoanalysis, Marxism and feminism, impressively maintained a necessary dialectical tension between clinical work and political activity, and between theory and practice. She challenged the demands of classical psychoanalysis as untenable in practice: '[T]he placing of social reality "in parentheses" during treatment and the supposed "objectivity" of the psychoanalyst. Both are unsustainable.' (Langer, 1989: 156). She further argued that an object-relations approach, as opposed to one based solely on drives/instincts, allowed more possibility for embracing the social, an argument also made by a later radical pioneer, Sue Holland.

Langer addressed issues of clinical practice that have since become familiar. She argued that it is important to distinguish between aspects of the analytic frame that are necessary for clinical reasons and those that are ideological or useful for the analyst. She and her colleagues adapted the psychoanalysis of their training to provide less frequent sessions, face-to-face rather than on the couch and dialogue with the patient rather than analytic silence. They also addressed the importance of countertransference as a 'working tool' rather than an obstacle. This is now common within most theoretical orientations but was then being pioneered, partly through the work of another Argentinian psychoanalyst, Heinrich Racker. All contemporary discussions of practising psychoanalysis in poor communities emphasise the importance of these factors.

Langer also critiqued the notion of neutrality, the idea that analysts can be completely ideologically neutral and not influenced in their work by their own political and moral commitments. Like Langer, the pioneers of contemporary feminist approaches to psychotherapy argued that supposedly neutral stances unquestioningly reflect the status quo (Eichenbaum and Orbach, 1982). Langer also queried the then common view that the fee was an important part of the treatment, regarding this as more to do with the economic needs of the analyst, and maintaining that any resistance or idealisation connected to free treatment could be addressed within the therapy. Furthermore, she strongly disputed that working-class patients could not verbalise sufficiently well to undertake psychoanalysis. Rather, they understood the interpretations offered and had as good or as bad capacity for insight as 'bourgeois' patients in private practice. Many working-class patients:

> who were very deprived, really needed that hour in which they had the right to listen and to be listened to. That someone was interested in their fate and was witness to it, was much more unusual and therefore more appreciated and therapeutic than it is for our private patients.
>
> (Langer, 1989: 176)

This is a powerful observation also made by some of the therapists I interviewed (see Chapter 7).

Reflecting subsequently, Langer said:

> In our therapeutic work we remained faithful to our psychoanalytic technique of interpreting unconscious conflict. While we refrained from offering advice, suggestions or didactic interventions, our interpretations of our working-class patients' discourse included a critical perspective of the class and gender determinants of their unconscious pain and rage.
>
> (Hollander, 1997: 76)

She also described how the economic and social circumstances of the patients were taken into account: time constraints, cost of transport, domestic demands, childcare, all might mean that deep regression was to be avoided.

Langer noted how commonly unconscious guilt feelings and self-blame would derive from a conviction that individuals were the only ones responsible for their 'failures', an ideology that has been intensified in the current era. The aim was to help such patients to discriminate between their responsibility for aspects of their personal history, and that of their family and of society. Class-consciousness was part of Langer's aims, achieved through work in groups that built on insights into individual problems, to place these in a wider social context, and also to forge bonds of solidarity, and a sense of belonging, something also embodied in Holland's model, described later.

Strategies for combining therapeutic and political forms of struggle are also put forward by Paul Hoggett and Julian Lousada, describing a project, Battersea Action and Counselling Centre (BACC), where I also worked (Hoggett and Lousada, 1984). They argue that to offer a therapeutic service for working-class people it was necessary to understand both the fragmentation of everyday life within capitalism and also how the therapeutic/helping professions were experienced by the community at large. This latter included people's experiences of psychiatry and social work as an aspect of social control, of the widespread prescription of psychotropic drugs, of the perceived stigma of mental illness, and the fear of being seen to be receiving therapeutic help. Whereas, for the practitioners involved, psychoanalytic therapy might seem an undisputed good, this was not necessarily so for the intended clients, an issue that surfaces in many other accounts. Rather, the cultural resonances and the social codes implicit in its practices can seem alien, unwanted and sometimes coercive. Beverley Skeggs argues that the reflexive, knowing, inner self is a specific historical production, enabled through different practices: '[F]orced telling for welfare for the working-class, and authorial exhibitionism for the middle-class' (Skeggs, 2004: 119).

Such factors can lead to justified suspicion towards an invitation to take up counselling or therapy. Daniel Holman (2013), in an appraisal of the role of class in taking up talking therapy for depression and anxiety, identifies several factors. He uses Bourdieu's theoretical schemas (see Chapter 5) to argue that the underuse of such services by working-class people can be understood in terms of cultural dispositions structured by social conditions. Clinical encounters, where 'institutionally sanctioned ways of talking, thinking and feeling are especially apparent' (Holman, 2013: 12), can constitute 'a form of symbolic violence over working-class lives'. Simon Charlesworth, in *A Phenomenology of Working Class Experience*, emphasises the ways in which the interview situation itself constitutes a form of cultural domination, leading to inhibition, self-negation and apparent inarticulacy, in which the ordinary expressiveness of everyday speech is lost, felt as worthless (Charlesworth, 2000).

Other notable features of BACC were a full-time nursery and crèche, a small advice service, and a vegetable co-op, as well as psychotherapy. In this way the centre embedded itself in the local community and tried to address some of its material needs, lessening suspicion, as well as distinguishing itself from state interventions. This came from an understanding that whereas it might be very difficult to approach a mental health service openly, it was perhaps easier to talk about practical difficulties. This might then lead on to talk about issues for which therapy could be offered.

Freud himself in his 1918 speech suggested that psychoanalysis with working-class people might necessitate some attention to their material needs. Some of the contributors to Foster et al. (1996) describe how addressing practical or advocacy needs can enable a better comprehension of the patient's experiential and material world, which may be very unfamiliar to the therapist. The question of how this impacts on the therapeutic work and its frame is one many practitioners in such settings tussle with. An argument can be made that such provision facilitates confidence in the therapist's understandings and commitment, and thus sustains the therapeutic work, despite the departure from usual practice. Ruth Fallenbaum (2003, see Chapter 8) provides an example in which after much reflection she agreed to an advocacy role.[5] Economic insecurity and deprivation can thus be felt to invade the clinical frame, and disturb the usual setting; but none of this is beyond analytic reflection within the work. Taking psychoanalysis out of its private practice location, where the social world does not impinge so intrusively, demands that the space for and of psychoanalytic therapy is protected but without resort to rigidity or lack of realism.

The attempt at BACC to address some material needs within a therapeutic centre reflected the understanding of how interconnected these needs are with emotional ones, rather than bracketing off the latter into a completely separate sphere. However, there was also a clear recognition that the spheres of private and public life should not be conflated or reduced to one another, but that the dynamic tensions between them should be sustained. Reductionism could take the form of psychologising political involvements, interpreting rebellion as Oedipal protest, for example, a then common psychoanalytic trope, or of seeing emotional issues as unimportant and self-indulgent compared to material ones, to be overcome by political activity, at the time an attitude typical of many left groups.[6] These considerations all illustrate the complex position that such projects inhabit in attempting to encompass both politics and therapy. Some of the earlier left psychoanalysts did see psychoanalysis as having a socially liberating role. However at BACC we were clear that any emancipatory change through therapy was not itself to be seen as a form of political action, although it might lead to that through a reorientation to aspects of reality and a different self-evaluation.

Hoggett and Lousada also emphasise the central role of language in articulating mental distress: the frequent unavailability of a vocabulary other than a medicalised one, and the lack of people who are able to listen without overly entangled responses. The desire to share some therapeutic knowledge, including enabling a language of the emotions, led BACC and the subsequent Lambeth Mental Health group (Banton et al., 1985) to offer counselling skills courses and workshops to people in the community. These empowering efforts proved very popular, and are an echo of Freud's and Ferenczi's recommendations for psychoeducation in working with disadvantaged groups (Gaztambide, 2012).

When a Tory council gained power, BACC was immediately closed down, illustrating the precarious position that radical mental health projects occupy in the wider political arena. BACC reflected an era in which the welfare state was seen by the left as an aspect of social control, and not, as now, as an essential service, free at the point of use, embodying an ethic of collective support while being under virulent attack from neo-liberalism. However, the 'therapeutic' interventions of the current welfare system may still embody aspects of social control – witness the ways economically disadvantaged families are now being renamed 'troubled' ones.[7]

One of the main initiators of BACC was Sue Holland, who set up a much more enduring project on a large working-class estate in White City, London. Holland's psychoanalytic approach was based on Ronald Fairbairn's form of object relations, which she saw as providing a potentially more social view of the individual than classical Freudian theory. This she combined with Paolo Freiere's notions of conscientisation. Holland and Holland (1984) outline how they saw global forces transformed into intra- and inter-psychic relations:

> [A] comprehensive therapy must include not only a recalling of repressed "rejected" part-objects and part-self representations, but *also* "conscientisation". . . concerning a people's own historical roots through which, for example, a mother's failing and rejection can be understood in its political and economic context.
>
> *(Holland and Holland, 1984: 100)*

Interestingly, some US community activists are now using Freiere's ideas in combination with psychoanalysis (LeRoy, 2016).

In White City this meant providing initial one-to-one psychotherapy to address the familial and intra-psychic aspects of depression and to lessen the need for medication, and then a transition to groups which allowed hidden and shared histories to be unravelled. This enabled not only a recognition of commonalities of suffering and loss, but also of collective strengths, with possibilities for action to bring about desired changes. Holland described this dialogical and intersubjective process as moving 'through psychic space into social space and so into political space', with participants having the choice to exit at any point (Holland, 1995). One of the notable features of the long-lived White City project is how the integrity of the project's political values were sustained alongside its dependence on state funding and also through significant shifts in wider political rhetoric.

The necessity for understanding history as it impinges on an individual, as well as intra-psychic dynamics, is a theme that runs through these politically inspired projects. Strong arguments for this are also made by those working clinically with people exposed to social traumas of various kinds, for example, Barbara Fletchman-Smith (2003) in the case of the legacies of slavery, and Francoise Davoine and Jean-Max Gaudillière (2004) with reference to wars and genocide. Valerie Walkerdine (2015), building on her psychoanalytically informed work in a working-class community subjected to the devastations of deindustrialisation, argues that such an approach is essential in understanding how class is transmitted through generations. Recognition of historical and social frameworks gives depth and meaning to experiences otherwise felt to be entirely individual, or else not explicable; 'small' histories carry echoes of 'large' ones. This constitutes the restoration of the 'social link', the foreclosure of which, Davoine and Gaudillière argue, can lead to psychosis. Such attention to history is part of the framework needed when psychoanalysis is practised outside its usual contexts, and indeed within them.

Psychotherapeutic culture and class

Many projects and clinics situate themselves in economically deprived areas with the inclusive aim of increasing access to therapy. They are informed by an assumption of psychoanalytic therapy as an undisputed good, unfairly distributed, even if, as sometimes, in need of revision.

Such conscious sociogeographic placement means that many factors arise concerning the cultural interface between the profession of psychoanalytic therapy, its staff and the intended clientele. Some of this has been recorded in several American books, which provide the greatest detail about contemporary psychoanalysis in such localities (e.g. Altman, 1995/2010; Foster et al., 1996). As Altman and also Rendon (1996) record, the US community health movement made important contributions to challenging and changing the prejudice against working-class people being offered psychoanalytic therapy. The growth of a socially conscious relational psychoanalysis has also provided many practitioners with the frameworks to work in these settings. We thus have a considerable body of literature which does not repeat the prejudices of the past but looks more openly, critically and dynamically at what may be involved.

Many of these writers are emphatic that working in disadvantaged working-class communities presents a challenge to the cultural embeddedness of psychoanalysis, and to some of its values and practices. In their view, the problems derive not from the fundamental nature of psychoanalytic theory but with its implementation. They pay particular attention to the pre-existing perceptions, attitudes and professional identities that therapists may bring to such engagements, as well as to how the stimulation of particular subjective reactions may impede useful work. They eschew what Foster refers to as 'condescending' alterations in technique, but argue strongly for a more pluralistic, socially well-informed approach in which both analyst and patient are regarded as mutual participants in the therapeutic relationship. Many authors advocate a less rigidly interpretive approach, in favour of an exploratory dialogic one, in which the analyst is more open to how a patient may convey his or her realities, and less inclined to impose theory on a patient. In part, the authors are taking issue with the dominance of classical and ego psychology forms of psychoanalysis, and advocating a turn to a more relational approach, although not, as Altman does, dispensing altogether with classical psychoanalysis. Moskowitz (1996a) indeed argues that the recognition of the primacy of love and aggression gives psychoanalysis the potential to transcend cultures, and advocates for the integration of both schools.

From Fanon (1952/1967) onwards, it has been a basic argument of culturally aware approaches to psychoanalysis that the familial structures and relationships to power implicit in Freudian theory may not obtain in other cultures. This is especially so in those cultures which are subjected to historical forces of domination, exploitation and racism. Individual autonomy, separation and independence may be valued very differently in poor urban and immigrant communities, where the family plays a different role in relation to the state, compared to that of the indigenous bourgeois nuclear family. Foster (1996) gives several clinical illustrations of how a less theoretically driven interpretive mode seeks to understand the specific social formations of families, and the importance of family solidarity in the face of oppressive conditions.

Gaztambide (2014), in a commentary on a conference held to discuss psychoanalytic work in poor Latino communities in the USA, amplifies this further. In one particularly salutary passage, citing another participant's contribution, he illustrates the importance of:

> [B]eing exquisitely attuned to the patient's metaphors, cultural symbols, and ways of thinking. Padron's presentation implicitly raised the question of what is "concreteness" but a metaphor we have yet to connect to, a symbol we have not yet deciphered, a language we have not learned to speak? A very moving aspect of Padron's work was the way in which his interpretations of Antonio's [the patient's] conflicts contained a "both/and" rather than an "either/or" quality in relation to sociopolitical themes in the patient's life. . . . He holds both psyche and culture as sources of meaning, while at the same time searching for psychological depth, adding another dimension of psychological meaning to sociopolitical realities.
>
> (Gaztambide, 2014: 34)

This argument, that 'concreteness' is a mode of expression that needs more deciphering, rather than always being a block to psychoanalytic understanding, is important. It is a challenge to any facile writing-off of some people as unsuitable for psychoanalysis, as well as to creative analytic skill. The question of 'analysability', the allegation that working-class Latinos are 'too concrete', not psychologically minded enough, and have too weak ego strength to engage with psychoanalysis, thus becomes a question of analysts' perceptions and desires, their capacity to understand and communicate. This is a very important reordering of perspective, putting the emphasis more on the abilities and interests of the analyst, rather than on the alleged deficits of the analysand.

Likewise, Foster emphasises that where there are large cultural or class differences between analyst and patient, work is needed on both parts for some joint understanding. Disparate social worlds may give rise to 'mutual subjective arousal' (Foster et al., 1996: 15), inhibitions and anxieties, and these can limit therapeutic work unless they are addressed. Part of what is needed is for the therapist to be able to recognise and process her own subjective reactions to what she learns or perceives of the circumstances of a patient's life. One common reaction I have noticed in my supervision experience is the despair and hopelessness that can be generated in the practitioner when faced with the weight of accumulated deprivation and adversity borne by many working-class and otherwise disadvantaged patients. Lee Whitman-Raymond (2009) also comments on how trainees, who often work with the most economically deprived patients, may feel overwhelmed by their circumstances, compounded by feelings of shame at feeling this, and by the difficulty of acknowledging or addressing the huge social differences involved. This puts particular demands on the capacity to find and enable the space for psychoanalytic work.

Diane Reay (2000) argues that the 'complex self-hoods' of working-class children have not adequately influenced psychoanalytic theorising, and that a more sophisticated understanding is needed of social jealousy, fear, denial, longing and envy, an understanding which she provides in much of her work. Javier and Herron (2002) also argue that 'the poor person' has not been well understood by psychoanalysis: 'Thus for most analysts who find themselves working with a patient who is economically deprived, there is a sense of confusion' (Javier and Herron, 2002: 151). Substantial inequalities of wealth and circumstance are not differences that most analysts will have been trained to think about, unlike gender differences, for example. These authors see the consequences of poverty as liable to create a distancing between the economically disadvantaged patient and the better-off analyst, with the potential to lead to unsatisfactory outcomes if these intersubjective dynamics are not available for reflection. Javier and Herron suggest:

> Possible attitudes by analysts are to feel sorry for the patient and in turn emphasize the social reality of poverty to the exclusion of personal responsibility, or to reverse the process and blame the patient. . . . (T)he analyst is also faced with a fear of revealing an offending attitude.
> *(Javier and Herron, 2002: 160–1)*

They also see the challenges in such work as arising from the virulence and schisms of class divisions and differences, which all participants in the encounter are subjected to and which make the development of a working alliance especially complex. They illustrate the complexities for the therapist of maintaining the tension between realistically seeing the patient as subjected to adverse social circumstances and seeing him or her as having agency in their predicaments, while not colluding with any tendency to excessive self-blame, an echo of Langer's injunction, and also something which some of the therapists I interviewed (see Chapter 7) wrestled with.

In psychotherapeutic work with women in a deprived urban environment, Pamela Trevithick (1995) describes how low confidence about articulating thoughts and feelings, stemming from a lifetime of negative experiences, may make the beginning of any therapeutic process extremely difficult. She notes how the inhibition of curiosity, resulting from chronic low self-esteem and adversity, can block helpful experiences and learning. She argues that explanations of personal intersubjective and wider cultural processes, as well as positive affirming input, are all needed to facilitate the take-up and taking-in of therapy. This chimes with the arguments that recognition and understanding of historical and current cultural contexts are necessary as part of any therapeutic enterprise with oppressed and poor populations, as is some relevant psychoeducation. In a further article, drawing on Winnicott, she argues that recognition of present-day failures of the environment, and the provision of adequate holding and sometimes of material help, are all necessary (Trevithick, 1998).

Similar conclusions, framed in different theoretical terms, are found in Miriam Rosa and Ilana Mountain's (2013) account of what they term 'clinical listening' with socially excluded young people in Brazil. Their work derives from a Lacanian perspective combined with Bourdieu's notion of symbolic violence. It is a relatively unusual attempt to engage with extremely marginalised 'street kids'. Whereas the previous writers make an appeal for the 'subjectivity' of working-class patients to be more adequately recognised, these authors argue that their intended clientele should be recognised as desiring subjects, rather than subjected to discourses that disenfranchise them, for example, those which see them as unanalysable or which reproduce existing power relations.

Rosa and Mountain see social marginalisation as a form of symbolic violence, where there is domination through communications in which the domination is disguised. This collective reification can result in 'blind submission, autistic closure, or irruptions of violence' (2013: 13) on the part of the young person. It creates 'discursive helplessness' (i.e. having no recognised voice) and thus no 'appeal to the Other'. Such desubjectivisation is traumatic. The authors emphasise how their analytic work takes place in precarious conditions, where there is often huge need, lack and urgency. Clinical listening requires ethical and political positioning, whereby the webs of domination and exclusion are made more apparent without any attributions to the supposed characteristics of the subject. In this way their approach has much in common with the overtly political approaches described previously.

Just as Foster et al. (1996) and Altman (1995/2010) emphasise the importance of understanding the countertransferential responses of analysts in work with disadvantaged clients, so too these authors delineate the kinds of resistances that may occur when clinical listening becomes unbearable. These include too hasty onward referrals; too much focus on the social situation, something Whitson (1996) also mentions; and only seeing subjects as victims. Conversely, analysts can assume unrealistic possibilities of choice, similar to the bifurcated thinking that Javier and Herron (earlier) describe. Analytic resistances also include too much adherence to theory and mistaken diagnoses; too much emphasis on differences, which can entrench stereotypes and distance. Listening can become unbearable for the analyst, because of the extremity of pain and deprivation involved and also because of the potential for feeling complicit in the social order that produces these circumstances, by reason of being more privileged. This I suggest is an insufficiently acknowledged source of therapist confusion and dysfunction.

Clinical listening, according to Rosa and Mountain, involves not the repetitive recounting of trauma, but rather, by supposing the 'desiring Other', a witnessing, a rescuing of memory and a recognition of desire in the transference, by which they mean the desire to be heard and understood, and have meaning attributed to experiences. Such listening can undo the suppression of subjectivity. It is 'transgressing in relation to the bedrock of the way society is organised, and it implies rupturing the tie that institutionalises a refusal to listen to the subject' (Rosa and Mountain, 2013: 14), a way of describing one main function a therapist may be able to perform in socially oppressive conditions.

Compared to the elaboration of their theoretical positions, Rosa and Mountain's description of their clinical work with particular clients is somewhat brief, albeit very moving. They note how the children initially regarded psychoanalytic listening with distrust, one more strategy of domination over them, even though their participation was voluntary, something which may well have felt compromised by their compulsory institutionalisation. The therapist gained their confidence by 'giving room to the symptom', recognising the subject's defences that, necessary for psychic survival, are engendered by being in the position of a 'leftover' in the social structure. This counters any tendency to over-hastily interpret or even attack defences in socially marginalised people, something which can occur. By meeting the ways in which the subjects present themselves, even the most traumatic circumstances can be given meaning and context. This restores 'desire in the transference'.

The advantage of this theoretical position is that it does not deal in any supposed psychological characteristics of socially excluded people, and therefore does not run the risk of inadvertent pathologisation or othering, which a more psychologised approach, however well intentioned, can do. By seeking to understand the position of socially excluded subjects discursively it attempts to create an egalitarian, they would say, ethical, approach. This egalitarianism is reflected in how they see the process being one of clinical listening rather than therapy, with all that the latter might imply about the goals and professional knowledge of the therapist setting the agenda. Although the benefit of their approach for their intended clientele remains to be shown more definitively, I would argue that for an analyst struggling with work in a poor inner city and assailed by the many emotions this can stir up, their approach could well be helpful. It can help the analyst think not so much in terms of the personality characteristics that extreme social exclusion might create (and that might be thought to render participation in analysis problematic) but of the ways in which the social order can exclude and disenfranchise certain subjects from access to any inclusive process of recognition and understanding, rendering their often traumatic experiences devoid of meaning or context. This puts the emphasis much more on the value of the process of listening and the establishment of an other who wants to hear. Furthermore, the authors are, to my mind, appropriately realistic about how, on the one hand, clinical listening can have modest mutative effects for the subject but, on the other, they recognise that radical social change is needed. This can help counteract any omnipotent tendency or its sequel, despair, by the analyst confronted with extreme poverty.

Patricia Gherovici, an analyst in inner-city Philadelphia, also concurs with this Lacanian emphasis, enjoining therapists to understand how 'concreteness', passive relation to authority and a focus only on the present are all symptoms of structural violence rather than supposedly inherent cultural attributes (in Gaztambide, 2014). Latinos, she avers, are certainly capable of psychoanalytic work and rather than consigning them to non-analytic or directive therapies, a 'strict and untendentious' (à la Freud) analytic approach would entail listening to clients as desiring subjects, thus facilitating ownership of their own subjectivity. Gherovici (2016) argues strongly that 'real' problems do not mean people are unanalysable: 'It is like saying poor people do not have an unconscious.'

It can be argued that all these recommendations are simply aims that any good psychoanalytic therapy would pursue: openness and less rigidity in using theoretical ideas, cultural and other self-reflections on the part of the analyst, some degree of social understanding and exploration of how the patient might perceive both the analyst and the therapeutic enterprise. This, although true in some ways, neglects the question of why this has been and still is hard to achieve with working-class and ethnic-minority patients in poor urban communities. It denies the specificity of the issues at hand, the historical injustices and sources of pain involved, and concomitantly the need for analysts to undertake serious reflection on their own attitudes, emotional responses, social understandings and theories, any of which may hinder therapeutic work in poor communities.

Pure gold or copper alloy?

The divisions within the psychoanalytic field, especially those between psychoanalysis, psychoanalytic psychotherapy and psychodynamic counselling, are transparently class divisions. The inequality of access is barely mitigated, and certainly not rectified, by the limited availability of lower-cost or 'affordable' longer-term private psychoanalytic therapy with trainees, or with those analysts and therapists who donate their time to low-cost clinics or who have sliding scales.[8] How widespread these often-cited practices are, or how far these scales slide, is currently unknown, since the role of money in the discipline is seldom debated, as Chapter 9 discusses further.

This situation has led to an insidious and perverse dynamic, whereby psychoanalytic work under the most difficult and challenging circumstances receives the least recognition and esteem and tends not to be carried out by those with most experience. This has structured the psychoanalytic field from the beginning, despite the best efforts of the early pioneers. The ambivalence at the heart of Freud's (1918) statement on the need for 'a psychotherapy for the people' runs through most discussions on providing psychoanalytic therapy outside private practice settings. Freud wrote that any 'large-scale' application of 'our therapy will compel us to alloy the pure gold of analysis freely with the copper of direct suggestion; and hypnotic influence, too. . . .' He continued: 'But, whatever form this psychotherapy for the people may take, whatever the elements out of which it is compounded, . . . its most effective and most important ingredients will assuredly remain those borrowed from *strict and untendentious* psycho-analysis' (Freud, 1918: 167–8, my italics).

These passages serve a double function of both exclusion and inclusion. They drove a wedge between psychoanalysis and the assumedly lesser form, psychotherapy, suitable for those who cannot pay. Gaztambide (2012) argues that this laid the ground for the restrictive development of the notion of analysability, which led to many working-class and minority clients being excluded from the 'pure gold' of psychoanalysis. This reflects a historic process whereby those excluded on economic, educational and cultural grounds are then perceived to possess the very characteristics that would seemingly justify their exclusion – a way in which the fundamental inequity of the situation is elided and disowned, and the idealisation of 'pure' psychoanalysis is not challenged for what it contains and conceals – namely, a defence of privilege.

Aron and Starr (2013), in their arguments for a progressive and less divided psychoanalysis, also suggest that the way Freud drew his distinction between psychoanalysis and psychotherapy has had far-reaching and adverse effects in how this difference has continued to be seen, with the concomitant idealisations, denigrations and misunderstandings. As is well documented, Freud was always concerned to radically differentiate psychoanalysis from any association with hypnosis or suggestion. Because Freud linked the difference between psychotherapy and psychoanalysis to the assumed role of suggestion (which he was at pains to repudiate as any part of psychoanalysis), psychoanalytic psychotherapy has been wrongly seen as necessarily involving something akin to this, as being more directive and supportive, not 'properly' analytic. This is far from the reality of most psychoanalytic psychotherapy, something not sufficiently recognised by those who make this disparaging judgement. There is a largely inconclusive literature on where and how to draw the distinction (e.g. Frisch et al., 2001), a symptom of the disavowal of the underlying status and economic forces at play. The second part of Freud's assertion, that 'psychotherapy for the people' will, to be effective, use the approach of 'strict and untendentious' psychoanalysis, has been frequently ignored. And yet this is exactly what those working at lesser frequencies aspire to and do often provide, in both private and public settings.

Aron and Starr argue that ideology, economics and professional insecurity all affect where and how the boundaries between psychoanalysis and psychoanalytic psychotherapy are drawn. This creates a binary emptied of the social and economic factors that structure it. In the heyday of American psychoanalysis, post-World War II, the distinction and distance between the two was at its greatest, at a time when psychoanalysis was most in demand, most lucrative and most conservative. It was also the period when the idea that working-class clients were not analysable was at its height, cementing the economic, cultural and symbolic capital of psychoanalysis. There was thus a marking out of territory by the psychoanalysts, an assertion of identity related to social hierarchy and a disdain for any other use of psychoanalysis. In the UK, despite the influence of the social justice ideology of the welfare state, and the presence of psychoanalysis within this, the hierarchy between 'pure' psychoanalysis and allegedly 'applied' psychoanalytic psychotherapy prevailed, as it still does today. Such hierarchical territoriality contributed in the 1990s to the splitting of the newly established umbrella body for psychoanalysis and psychoanalytic psychotherapy into separate organisations, eliding their common usage of psychoanalytic theories and practices.[9]

Cooper and Lousada (2010), in their critique of the resistance of psychoanalytic institutes to adapt to social changes and to the diminished market for psychoanalysis, comment on the attitudes of 'hubris and arrogance' with which psychoanalytic institutes view other therapeutic practices. Their explanation of this lies in several factors: the ways in which psychoanalysts may see themselves as part of a cultural establishment, the clinging to tradition and the uncritical belief many have of their uniqueness. They also see the dynamic features and anxiety inherent in the psychoanalytic situation as rendering analysts vulnerable to the imputed judgement of the 'analytic super-ego'. Cooper and Lousada argue that psychoanalysts:

> depend for their continuing self-esteem and hierarchical dominance upon being able to successfully project inferiority or weakness into psychoanalytic psychotherapists, who in turn do the same for 'counsellors'. But the projections also operate both ways, since the supposedly persecuted groups may fiercely criticise the 'analytic arrogance' of the supposedly dominant.
>
> *(Cooper and Lousada, 2010: 36)*

Their description of 'excess hierarchy' in the psychoanalytic field captures well the often difficult relationships between those trained at certain organisations and other psychoanalytic practitioners, and also in the restrictive practices as to eligibility for particular roles, such as those of training analysts. It surfaces in the battles fought about who can legitimate whom, and who has the entitlement to various labels or trade descriptions – who can call themselves or be recognised as a psychoanalyst, for example.[10] These are all struggles over symbolic capital, underpinned by economic capital, although seldom recognised as such. Cooper and Lousada go on to argue that the task facing psychoanalytic institutions now, in the face of the many external changes taking place, is to hold on to the unique skills and capacities that a psychoanalytic education can confer in understanding unconscious processes and unconscious communication, without the assertion of the moral superiority or cultural arrogance – gold versus copper – that they critique.

These arguments do not deny that there are often important differences, rather it is a question of how these are valued, and what they are taken to mean. Psychoanalytic therapies inherently take time – that is part of their value and importance – and within capitalism time is money. Frequency and duration are the main poles of distinction commonly drawn between psychoanalytic psychotherapy and psychoanalysis,[11] and also between what is possible in private practice settings and in community or public sector ones. It is inherently a class issue, because of the economic factors involved and also because of how less frequent, for example, once weekly, work is often seen as of lesser value and given much less recognition. Quantity, as Teresa Mulvena (2004) in her review of the issues surrounding frequency points out, becomes quality. This is a process that Marxists have long ascribed to the workings of capitalism.

Most practitioners who work with the limits imposed by funding or other constraints will have experienced the frustration of not being able to work for longer or more intensively with many particular clients. Often, although importantly not always, more is felt to be better, by both patient and therapist. Time limits may sharpen therapeutic efforts, and a theoretical understanding of the timelessness of the unconscious does allow for the possibility of rigorous and intensive psychoanalytic work under more limited circumstances. However, this does not address those aspects of therapeutic efficacy that depend upon the open-endedness, duration and consistency possible under better-resourced conditions and sustained relationships.

The available literature on outcome research in relation to frequency (for example, Frosch, 2011) suggests that more frequent work is often better, in terms of outcome, although not invariably. It is also widely acknowledged that other factors, such as the emotional quality of the analytic relationship, the experience of the analyst, and the degree to which he or she is internalised by the analysand, can all be crucial whatever the frequency. And it is also true that unduly long-term psychoanalysis can sometimes be harmful, in perpetuating a stultifying dependency, as opposed to a useful one. Further, conflicts of interest can be created in the open-ended nature of private practice with well-off patients, whereby the analyst stands to gain from prolonging the treatment, as several writers on money and psychoanalysis have argued (see Chapter 9).

The situation is also structured by how most psychoanalytic trainings require a particular frequency of sessions, both for the therapist's own analysis, and for working with patients. They mostly do not train people to work at a lesser frequency or for fixed short-term durations, despite the availability of accumulated knowledge and experience, a shortcoming that Taylor (2013) and many others see as having had serious consequences in limiting the contribution psychoanalysis makes within the public sector. Yet this is often the situation in which psychoanalytic practitioners find themselves, in private practice as well as in public sector work. Aron and Starr cite studies that show that in the USA most graduates of psychoanalytic institutes, despite their training in high-frequency work, see most of their patients once weekly, and only a few more frequently, who are often themselves trainees. It is widely recognised that this is true in the UK too. Inevitably, without relevant training or support, this is felt as inferior, and practitioners, haunted by the ideal of intensive open-ended work, can feel deskilled and despairing. Cherry et al. (2012), based on surveys of analytic practice, suggest that trainings need to change to recognise the lower-frequency work that most analysts commonly do, and also their use of additional techniques. Some trainings now do recommend (although do not require) that their trainees gain experience of less frequent work.

Alloys of course can be superior to pure metals, in their greater strength or fitness for particular purposes, even if, unlike gold, not of such great market value. Cooper and Lousada ask what the psychodynamic counsellor has to teach the psychoanalyst about the practice of therapy and the nature of unconscious processes, a politically astute question.[12] They suggest that this question is neither surprising nor contradictory, just because such counsellors are more likely to work in 'the complex messy world of front-line mental health services' (2010: 44). There is much that can be learned by practice at this interface, especially in respect of 'race', ethnicity and class. It is important for the future of psychoanalysis, as well as for the benefit of patients, that such work is better recognised, understood and valued, without denying its limitations. Some of the writings cited in this chapter, as well as the arguments of this book, could contribute to that, were there the political will.

Freud also suggested that the 'new conditions' of free clinics would require psychoanalysts to adapt their techniques. The considerations of this chapter, and also of Chapter 2, have shown that the innovations made in these settings are far from being 'suggestion' or 'dilution', but rather additions to and enhancements of psychoanalytic practice more generally. As with the historic free clinics, and as with Ferenczi's technical recommendations, engagement with a wider clientele in diverse settings has driven new creative approaches (see e.g. Lemma and Patrick, 2010). Notably, the most recent innovations in psychoanalytic therapy have come from public sector work. Much of this is researched, evidence-based and responding to the needs and challenges of mental health institutions, although also felt by some to be unwarranted adulterations of the 'pure gold' of psychoanalysis. These innovations, which are beyond the scope of this book, include Mentalisation-based Therapy, Dynamic Interpersonal Therapy (DIT), Parent–Infant Psychotherapy (PIP) and psychoanalytic consultations and supervision for mental health staff. Psychoanalytic interventions and consultation can take many forms (see e.g. Campbell, 2006; Carrington et al., 2012; Evans, 2016) and are a particularly effective way of extending psychoanalytic thinking to a variety of situations, as are Balint groups, which have a continuing life. My own experience, as a supervisor/consultant to an NHS inpatient unit, is that many staff, not least nurses, are very receptive to psychoanalytic input, if it is presented in succinct ways that are of immediate relevance to their work (e.g. Land, 2004; Evans, 2016).

All such innovations and adaptations are based on core psychoanalytic concepts but extend psychoanalytic technique and sometimes integrate other approaches. Such readiness to engage with the social world is essential to the survival of psychoanalysis, and to any considerations of social justice and fairness. Taylor (2013) makes a strong plea for the broadening out of what is comprised by 'psychoanalysis' to include diverse uses of psychoanalytic theory, with equivalent value accorded to each, in the interests of a 'new settlement'. If all the many scattered and committed individual efforts and projects within the various public sectors could gain greater collective existence and recognition, it would create a more effective political pressure for the value of psychoanalytic work within our mental health institutions.

This chapter has illustrated the diversity of thought and practice that psychoanalytic practice in many different free or low-cost contexts has given rise to. It has emphasised the importance of sociopolitical histories in the lives of both analysands and analysts. What stands out, apart from the overriding issue of funding, is the absence of much mainstream interest, recognition or teaching of such work. This reflects the divisiveness inherent in the internal politics of psychoanalysis, its lack of reflection on its own social status and also its separation from the wider world of modern mental health provision. If psychoanalysis as a profession could become more socially aware and inclusive in its trainings and social locations, and encompass the many diverse uses to which it is put, it would not only do justice to these many efforts, but also garner itself more public acceptability – an enduring argument since the earliest days.

Notes

1 The extent of these changes is hard to assess, as no survey exists. The therapeutic communities of the Henderson and Cassel Hospitals no longer exist.
2 Such as the Alliance for Counselling and Psychotherapy: https://allianceblogs.wordpress.com

3 Evidence from UKCP and BPC to the Public Accounts Committee Inquiry into IAPT services. Available on BPC website, June 2016.
4 Within a small part of London alone I know of or have known of the following: Red Therapy, Battersea Action and Counselling Centre (BACC), The Barefoot Psychoanalyst, Open Door Young Person's Consultation Centre (Haringey), The Women's Therapy Centre, The Maya Centre, City Road Youth Counselling, The Brandon Centre, Off Centre (Hackney), Nafsiyat Intercultural Therapy Centre, The Fanon project, PACE – therapy for LGBT people, The Blues project (CAPP), the Lambeth Mental Health Group, The Lorrimore Centre, White City Mental Health project, The Inner City Centre, various Mind centres. There are many more in other areas, and countries, and also ones I will not have heard of. Some of these listed projects are now defunct.
5 A common contemporary example is therapists being asked by patients to provide detailed evidence of mental health difficulties for entitlements to benefits.
6 The slogan 'Don't break down, break out!' was typical of this attitude.
7 The recent suggestion that obligatory counselling should be enforced as a condition of unemployment benefits is another worrying example.
8 This practice is similar to the much-vaunted UK practice of private schools offering subsidised fees or free places to poor 'bright' children, which props up rather than changes the inequitable system.
9 It is only recently that the three main regulatory bodies have opened formal talks about how they may cooperate in facing issues that they all have in common – a belated recognition of their similarities and the necessity to find joint ways of engaging with the changing political landscape.
10 Some practitioners who work psychoanalytically and have trained outside the main IPA organisations do call themselves psychoanalysts – a development that challenges the hegemony of the 'elite' organisations.
11 Even though there is little consensus about whether there is a fundamental distinction and what it might be based on (e.g. Frisch et al., 2001).
12 It is interesting to note that the British Psychoanalytic Council, which Lousada has been chair of, now accredits psychodynamic counselling courses – a recognition of core similarities, even if the symbolic hierarchy is preserved.

References

Altman, N. (1995/2010) *The Analyst in the Inner City: Race, Class, and Culture through a Psychoanalytic Lens*. New York: Routledge.
Aron, L. and Starr, K. (2013) *A Psychotherapy for the People: Towards a Progressive Psychoanalysis*. New York: Routledge.
Banton, R., Clifford, P., Frosh, S., Lousada, J. and Rosenthall, J. (1985) *The Politics of Mental Health*. London: Macmillan.
Campbell, J. (2006) 'Homelessness and containment – a psychotherapy project with homeless people and workers in the homeless field', *Psychoanalytic Psychotherapy* 20: 157–75.
Carrington, A., Rock, B. and Stern, J. (2012) 'Psychoanalytic thinking in primary care: The Tavistock psychotherapy consultation model', *Psychoanalytic Psychotherapy* 26: 102–20.
Charlesworth, S. (2000) *A Phenomenology of Working Class Experience*. Cambridge: Cambridge University Press.
Cherry, S., Meyer, J., Hadge, L., Terry, M. and Roose, S. P. (2012) 'A prospective study of psychoanalytic practice and professional development: Early career interviews', *Journal of the American Psychoanalytic Association* 60: 969–94.

Cooper, A. and Lousada, J. (2010) 'The shock of the real: Psychoanalysis, modernity, survival'. In Lemma, A. and Patrick, M. (eds) *Off the Couch: Contemporary Psychoanalytic Applications*. London: Routledge.

Danto, E. (2005) *Freud's Free Clinics: Psychoanalysis and Social Justice 1918–1938*. New York: Colombia University Press.

Davoine, F. and Gaudillière, J.-M. (2004) *History beyond Trauma*. New York: Other Press.

Eichenbaum, L. and Orbach, S. (1982) *Outside In . . . Inside Out*. Harmondsworth: Penguin.

Evans, M. (2016) *Making Room for Madness in Mental Health*. London: Karnac.

Fallenbaum, R. (2003) 'The injured worker', *Studies in Gender and Sexuality* 4: 72–92.

Fanon, F. (1952/1967) *Black Skin, White Masks*. New York: Grove Press.

Fletchman-Smith, B. (2003) *Mental Slavery: Psychoanalytic Studies of Caribbean People*. London: Karnac.

Foster, R. (1996) 'What is a multicultural perspective for psychoanalysis?' In Foster, R., Moskowitz, M. and Javier, R. (eds) *Reaching across Boundaries of Culture and Class: Widening the Scope of Psychotherapy*. Lanham: Jason Aronson.

Foster, R., Moskowitz, M. and Javier, R. (eds) (1996) *Reaching across Boundaries of Culture and Class: Widening the Scope of Psychotherapy*. Lanham: Jason Aronson.

Freud, S. (1918) 'Lines of advance in psychoanalytic therapy'. In Strachey, J. (ed) (1955) *The Standard Edition of the Complete Psychological Works of Sigmund Freud*, vol. 17: 157–68. London: Hogarth.

Frisch, S., Hinshelwood, R. and Gauthier, J. (2001) *Psychoanalysis and Psychotherapy*. London: Karnac.

Frosch, A. (2011) 'The effect of frequency and duration on psychoanalytic outcome: A moment in time', *Psychoanalytic Review* 98: 11–38.

Frosh, S. (2009) 'Where did class go? Psychoanalysis and social identities', *Sitegeist* 3: 99–116.

Gaztambide, D. (2012) '"A psychotherapy for the people": Freud, Ferenczi and psychoanalytic work with the underprivileged', *Contemporary Psychoanalysis* 48(2): 141–65.

Gaztambide, D. (2014) '*Melancolia bajo un palo de mango*: A review and critique of "Psychoanalysis in El Barrio"', *Division Review* 11: 33–6.

Gherovici, P. (2016) 'A poor brain is as worthy as a rich brain: Psychotherapy faces a privilege problem'. Available at: http://gu.com/CMP=Share_iOSApp_Other. Accessed 9 June 2016.

Hoggett, P. and Lousada, J. (1984) 'Therapeutic intervention in working class communities', *Free Associations* 1: 125–52.

Holland, S. (1995) 'Interaction in women's mental health and neighbourhood development'. In Fernando, S. (ed) *Mental Health in a Multi-Ethnic Society: A Multidisciplinary Handbook*. London: Routledge.

Holland, S. and Holland, R. (1984) 'Depressed women: Outposts of empire and castles of skin'. In Richards, B. (ed) *Capitalism and Infancy*. London: Free Association Books.

Hollander, N. (1997) *Love in a Time of Hate*. New Brunswick: Rutgers University Press.

Holman, D. (2013) 'What help can you get talking to somebody? Explaining class differences in the use of talking treatments', *Sociology of Health and Illness* 35: 1–18.

Javier, R. and Herron, W. (2002) 'Psychoanalysis and the disenfranchised: Countertransference issues', *Psychoanalytic Psychology* 19: 149–66.

Land, P. (2004) 'Thinking about feelings: Working with the staff of an eating disorders unit', *Psychoanalytic Psychotherapy* 18: 390–403.

Langer, M. (1989) *From Vienna to Managua: Journey of a Psychoanalyst*. London: Free Association Books.

Lemma, A. and Patrick, M. (eds) (2010) *Off the Couch: Contemporary Psychoanalytic Applications*. London: Routledge.

LeRoy, M. (2016) Urban liberation and psychoanalysis: Free associations at the grassroots', *The Psychoanalytic Activist*, online newsletter, 30 March. Available at: https://psychoanalyticactivist.com/2016/03/30/urbanliberationandpsychoanalysis/. Accessed August 2016.

Lewes, K. (1989) *The Psychoanalysis of Male Homosexuality*. New York: Quartet.

Moskowitz, M. (1996a) 'The social conscience of psychoanalysis'. In Foster, R., Moskowitz, M. and Javier, R. (eds) *Reaching across Boundaries of Culture and Class: Widening the Scope of Psychotherapy*. Lanham: Jason Aronson.

Moskowitz, M. (1996b) 'The end of analyzability'. In Foster, R., Moskowitz, M. and Javier, R. (eds) *Reaching across Boundaries of Culture and Class: Widening the Scope of Psychotherapy*. Lanham: Jason Aronson.

Mulvena, T. (2004) 'Once-weekly work: Less of the same or something different'. Unpublished Paper.

O'Connor, N. and Ryan, J. (1993/2003) *Wild Desires and Mistaken Identities: Lesbianism and Psychoanalysis*. London: Karnac.

Reay, D. (2000) 'Children's urban landscapes'. In Brewer, S. (ed) *Cultural Studies and the Working Class*. London: Cassell.

Rendon, M. (1996) 'Psychoanalysis in an historic-economic perspective'. In Foster, R., Moskowitz, M. and Javier, R. (eds) *Reaching across Boundaries of Culture and Class: Widening the Scope of Psychotherapy*. Lanham: Jason Aronson.

Rosa, M. and Mountain, I. (2013) 'Psychoanalytic listening to socially excluded young people', *Psychoanalysis, Culture and Society* 18: 1–16.

Sales, S. (2011) 'The making of docile working class subjects: CBT, class and the failures of psychoanalysis', *Journal of Psycho-Social Studies* 4: 126–38.

Skeggs, B. (2004) *Class, Self, Culture*. London: Routledge.

Taylor, H. (2013) *UK Psychoanalysis: Mistaking the Part for the Whole*, British Psychoanalytic Council Discussion Paper. London: BPC.

Trevithick, P. (1995) 'Cycling over Everest', *Groupwork* 8: 5–33.

Trevithick, P. (1998) 'Psychotherapy and working class women'. In Seu, B. and Heenan, C. (eds) *Feminism and Psychotherapy: Reflections on Contemporary Theories and Practices*. London: Sage.

Wachtel, P. (2002) 'Psychoanalysis and the disenfranchised: From therapy to justice', *Psychoanalytic Psychology* 19: 199–215.

Walkerdine, V. (2015) 'Transmitting class across generations', *Theory and Psychology* 25: 167–83.

Whitman-Raymond, L. (2009) 'The influence of class in the therapeutic dyad', *Contemporary Psychoanalysis* 45: 429–43.

Whitson, G. (1996) 'Working-class issues'. In Foster, R., Moskowitz, M and Javier, R. (eds) *Reaching across Boundaries of Culture and Class: Widening the Scope of Psychotherapy*. Lanham: Jason Aronson.

5

LIVED EXPERIENCES OF CLASS

Psychosocial and sociological perspectives

The last chapter showed how psychoanalytic work in low-cost and free clinics and disadvantaged communities could benefit by some reflective understanding of the social circumstances of the clientele and of the class formations affecting both them and the therapists themselves. Here I attempt to glean something of what psychoanalysis can learn from how sociologists and psychosocial researchers have investigated class as it is lived, experienced and felt about. Several years ago I set out to explore this growing body of contemporary research, through immersion in some of the literature and through an attachment to one of the UK's leading sociology departments.[1] This enterprise came from realising that for any psychoanalytic concern with class, if it was not to be simply reductive, I had to go outside of psychoanalysis, to a wider knowledge and theorisation of class, and attempt some interdisciplinarity of thought, as regards the social and the psychoanalytic. I found much of relevance to the subjective, psychological and emotional aspects of class, and to the many ways in which class forms and inhabits our psyches, all within a framework of structural social forces. This, I contend, provides a necessary basis for any psychoanalytic exploration of the conscious and unconscious ways in which class may form us and also enter into clinical relationships, in private as well as public sector work.

In the course of this project I learned much about *processes*: the manifold historic processes of distinction that proliferate in the terrain of class, the everyday practices that constitute class as something to be continuously done, the often hidden feelings that accompany this, and the unceasing processes of judgement and moral evaluation that divide people externally and internally. I also learned about the pain, ambivalence, anxiety, defensiveness and sometimes pride involved in the 'emotions of class', and how it is possible to study these in a way that brings to life the complexities of feeling, self-conception and perception.

Much of this research has emanated from the recent 'affective' turn in sociology, although pre-dated by older interests. This represents a turn away from the preoccupation with stratification and class-consciousness, towards a much greater interest in cultural aspects of class and the personally experienced subjective and emotional dimensions, the ways in which 'class is in everything about a person' (Walkerdine et al., 2001: 39). Some of this research uses psychoanalytic methodologies to enhance its methods; other theorists use psychoanalytic concepts to enlarge their theorising or to further explain their findings. Yet other work does not make explicit reference to psychoanalysis but, in dealing with emotions, provides much of potential psychoanalytic interest.

Such work, of which I can present only snapshots, could add greatly to any clinical attempt to recognise and understand class-inflected experiences, relationships and emotions, within and outside the therapy relationship.

Starting points

Here I outline some of the points of orientation within sociology, which I have found helpful in addressing class psychoanalytically. I ask what kinds of language, themes and concepts are used in talking about personally experienced and affective aspects of class, and how do these connect with psychoanalytic concepts? How can reading such work with psychoanalytic ears illuminate some of the processes identified?

Elias

Norbert Elias' epic study, *The Civilising Process* (Elias, 1939/1994), is an historical survey, in great depth and detail, of the class distinctions prevailing at different periods in Western Europe. What this reveals is that while the precise criteria differentiating one class from another change historically and according to locality, class distinction per se does not. There is always an upper and a lower class, and often others. Elias is emphatic that class should be seen as a total *figuration*, comprising all classes as interrelated parts of a totality. This supports the relevance of addressing middle- or upper-class positionings within any field, in addition to the much more studied working-class ones. Elias emphasises the immense psychic work of socialisation and the enforcements that are needed to sustain distinctions between classes. This focus on the *processes* by which class distinction is produced, maintained and reproduced is relevant to contemporary concerns with the intergenerational transmission of class, and the multitudinous practices through which individuals become classed subjects.

Elias notes how within the modern period class boundaries have become less fixed and more permeable, and also more subject to internalised rather than external control, in judgements of the self. He makes use of Freudian concepts of id, ego and super-ego to argue that such structural differentiations within individuals are connected to the structures of relationships within society at large, and the particular forms of drive and affect control at play. He attributes a decisive role to changes in feelings of shame and delicacy in generational processes of class differentiation. This, and his focus on matters of manners, hygiene, etiquette and taste, allows us to see the deeply embodied and personally experienced markers of class, which are often instantly and subliminally apprehended. Elias' massive work leads him to emphasise 'how deeply the stratification, the pressure and tensions of our own time, penetrate the structure of the individual personality' such that the child 'feel(s) the entire tension of a society, even before he or she knows anything about them' (Elias, 1939/1994: 445). This suggests how class and class difference become part of a person from the earliest age, long before any consciousness of social distinctions; absorbed and felt before they can be thought.

Elias' work is distinctively psychosocial, antedating the modern identification of this as an independent discipline. He sees an 'indissoluble interrelationship' between how individual personality and social structures evolve, and he argues against the dichotomisation implied by the concepts of 'individual' and 'society', seeing them instead as inseparable albeit different aspects of the same human beings.

Bourdieu

Pierre Bourdieu's theorisations of class allow us to see the many subjective, qualitative and quantitative micro-distinctions through which class is lived and perceived. His analysis of different forms of capital – economic, cultural, social and symbolic – underlines the complexities of class and inequality (Bourdieu, 1984).[2] In positing cultural capital as on a different axis from economic capital, Bourdieu opened up an enormously fertile field for investigating the force and operation of distinctions and differentiations, often the bases for instant and subliminal apprehensions of class.

Classes exist for Bourdieu 'not as something given but as *something to be done*' (Bourdieu, 1994/1998: 12, original italics). Thus any kind of static psychology of class is eschewed, with the emphasis instead on the constitutive nature and processes of practices and dispositions, the makings of class. This has been central to much subsequent psychosocial work on class. Class is produced and lived within the positions occupied in social space and the structures of the distribution of different kinds of capital. The critique of any psychology of class with inherent attributes, and the emphasis instead on its processes and practices, is a dynamic model of how people become and live as classed subjects. This has a synergy with psychoanalytic dynamic processes and mechanisms, as Bourdieu suggested in his later work. Relationality is also central to Bourdieu's work: the sense of one's place in social space always involves a sense of the place of others.

Bourdieu's analyses of the multitudinous processes of distinction that are part of daily social being, his ideas of relationality, dispositions and habitus have psychoanalytic resonances, as will be seen further on. His work has illuminated a huge body of empirical research on the lived experiences of class, what Skeggs (1997) calls the 'mundane, reiterative everyday experiences' that are formative of and also a product of structural inequalities.

Inequality and stratification

Despite the generally acknowledged decline in self-identification as belonging to a class (itself a topic of research and theorising), many sociologists argue that class differentiations based on multiple criteria rather than clear-cut boundaries are still a vital aspect of how people live, intensified by changing inequalities. Savage expresses this as class being construed more as difference than as belonging (Savage, 2000). Tyler (2015) describes a process of 'class decomposition' in the transition to present-day forms of finance capitalism, in which fewer people recognise themselves as part of a class, aided by the increasing individualisation of poverty, the fragmentation and casualisation of work and neo-liberal ideologies and practices that blame the poor for their circumstances and celebrate the rich. Inequality, however, as Tyler argues, remains a matter of class. Issues of life chances, opportunity and achievement, wealth and poverty, cultural positionings and taste, social networks and marginality and media representations all remain of intense concern, often sites of struggle, resentments and antagonisms.

For Skeggs also, class is an identifier of inequality. She is emphatic about its ubiquity, its fundamental marker being exclusion, such that inequalities proliferate and pervade all aspects of life. This leads to the emotional politics of class, 'fuelled by insecurity, doubt, indignation and resentment (but also lived with pleasure and irreverence)' (Skeggs, 1997: 162). Charlesworth's phenomenological study of working-class life in the wake of deindustrialisation underlines the persistence and damage of social exclusion, poverty and cultural constraints: 'From conditions of scarcity . . . their position of exclusion comes to dominate their experience because it is the fundamental condition in relation to which their experience is constituted' (Charlesworth, 2000: 172).

Recently Skeggs and Tyler have advanced critiques of the whole enterprise of class stratification and classification, which are very relevant to understanding the deep, ambivalent and often unspoken emotions that class can arouse. Classifications necessarily contain presuppositions and evaluations, however much they purport to be describing an objective reality, and in doing so enact forms of power. 'Class is a historic representation of a categorisation of a person's value and this was always a moral classification' (Skeggs, 2015: 214). The kinds of attributes used to assign people to classes are always symbolically valued in some way; hence the terms 'upper' and 'lower' or the hierarchical numbers of official classifications. In this sense classification is a performative act, creating what it purports to describe. Class names reveal 'structural conditions of inequality' (Tyler, 2015: 496).

These considerations about classification underline the powerful moral and emotional impacts of these acts of categorisation and naming, however much, especially within any discipline such as psychoanalysis that prioritises the uniqueness of the individual, these may be resisted. They fuel the widely reported ambivalence and ambiguities in any talk about class, as will be seen later.

Class emotions

Language is key in psychoanalysis, and one starting point is with research on how people talk about class. Andrew Sayer (2005), in his study of everyday speech and feeling about class, draws on empirical sociological work and on moral philosophy. He argues that most sociology has sidelined the normative and moral significance of class, focusing only on people as the occupiers of social positions, or as the bearers and performers of class practices, rather than on their values, dispositions, emotions and beliefs. Rather, it is moral values such as social justice and respect for persons which render class such a contested and troubling subject. As I found in my research (see Chapter 6), questions about what class people belong to often evoke unease and evasion, hesitant and complex responses. Sayer claims this is because 'class', far from being merely a descriptive term, is understood as one of injustice and moral evaluation, a highly charged issue. Any psychoanalytic approach has to take this moral aspect into account, which it often does not easily do.

Sayer seeks, with many examples, to capture the complexity of ways in which people talk, feel and respond to class. 'Ordinary' class concerns always involve evaluations of some kind, infused with feeling, whether acknowledged or not, and this should not be separated from the more cognitive aspects of class experience and knowledge:

> Feelings about class are suffused with tensions: between ethical evaluation and economic evaluation; between status and worth; between judgements of moral luck in terms of deserved and undeserved advantages and disadvantages; between acknowledgement of injustice and defensive rationalisation and evasion; and between recognising class as ethically problematic yet being able to do little or nothing about it.
>
> *(Sayer, 2005: 225)*

Sayer's emphasis on the 'intractability' of the tensions surrounding class suggests how deeply class permeates us intra-psychically and interpersonally. Other work illustrates further this fraught terrain, something which it might be thought psychoanalysis is well equipped to explore.

Ambivalence, anxiety and ambiguity

The conflicting emotions, the ambivalences and ambiguities aroused by and about class are evident in many studies. As a contemporary survey suggests: 'What people say about class on the one hand, and how they actually enact and perform class in their everyday lives on the other, are very different' (Savage et al., 2015: 388).

Skeggs' (1997) detailed ethnographic work with a large sample of working-class women is invaluable in portraying the complexity of their emotions linked to class. She provides detailed economic, occupational and educational data pertaining to the women but also remarks how it is easier to define them by what they were not, that is, not middle class. Class was experienced as exclusion: from access to most forms of economic, cultural and social capital, and with very few legitimating forms of recognition. They were, Skeggs says, never in a position to construct distance from necessity, something which is central to Bourdieu's understanding of class distinctions, and also suggested by Layton in her psychoanalytic work on class (see Chapter 8).

Skeggs found that many of these women did not wish to identify themselves as working class, and refused this categorisation by dissimulating and disidentifying. She argues that this dissimulation is itself part of class, a form of resistance or refusal, something akin to disavowal. For many of the women, 'working class' was a pejorative category, one implying poverty, lack of respectability, something dangerous, dirty and valueless. Skeggs attributes this to the historic and contemporary representations of class, and also to experiences of being negatively positioned by others. She portrays the huge efforts many women made to distance themselves from this label, in their concerns with respectability, appearance, domestic styles and self-improvement. Pride in being working class was relatively unusual, and many wished to pass as middle class, although with uncertainty and anxiety as to whether that was possible:

> They know that there are certain ways of being and doing to which they do not have access. This generates resentment. There was not a clear split between those who wanted to pass and those who resented. The two affects were held together.
>
> *(Skeggs, 1997: 92)*

Holding together such different affects is part of the ambivalence and dividedness in the emotions surrounding class, and something that psychoanalysis can recognise with its understanding of divided and conflicted subjects. It underlines how economic class position and class identity are not necessarily the same, and makes the latter more complex and ambivalent than often assumed.

Other sociologists have observed how questions about class provoke considerable unease. In a study of spontaneous talk about class, Devine (2004) found that those from middle-class or lower middle-class backgrounds rarely used the category, whereas those from working-class backgrounds often did. With the latter, the discussion included issues of status, of inferiority and superiority, and judgements of worth. Considerable feeling was expressed with an acute awareness of the moral judgements that might be made of working-class people. Resentment and anger about the adverse effect of class on their lives, and the apparent ease of achievements for those from middle-class backgrounds were also voiced:

'Arguably, an undercurrent of class conflict, of struggles over moral worth, became apparent. This underlying tension might explain why the British middle class do not articulate, and indeed go to some length to distance themselves from the class label' (Devine, 2004: 208). Such middle-class distancing, with its unspoken feelings, can be recognised as operating within the psychoanalytic field.

Sayer suggests that the widely reported unease, embarrassment, evasion and ambivalence associated with talking about class is not a denial of class but rather an implicit acknowledgement of unjustified structural inequalities. This complexity, and the corresponding potential for anxiety of many kinds, is the kind of ground in which psychoanalysis has something to offer. It also suggests that speaking about class within a clinical context may be fraught with these kinds of emotions, anxieties and disavowals, for all concerned.

I have had many opportunities to speak with groups of psychotherapists, counsellors and trainees about class. The discussions often have a sense of pervasive anxiety, which can be hard to identify. They become both charged and inhibited. Some participants express fears of giving offence, others of exposing what they consider shameful aspects of their backgrounds or of being looked down upon. Those who see themselves as more privileged sometimes retreat into a kind of defensive guilt, or assert that class is not important, it is just individuals that matter. This defensive use of liberal individualism can, as Cooper describes in the painful processes of addressing institutional racism in therapy organisations, flatten or deaden the particularity of any articulation of such experiences (Cooper, 2010). In one workshop,[3] with trainees on a course where understanding difference and diversity was a prominent feature, nonetheless some said talking about class felt like a taboo, suggesting the unspoken fears of what might be unleashed. Others felt there was not a language with which therapists could think about class. This conceptual vacuum suggests the untheorised psychosocial conjuncture that class within the psychoanalytic field occupies, the gap or aporia that opens up and that stymies people's thoughts. It is this gap that Chapter 3 identified as part of how class got left out of psychoanalytic discourse.

Judgements, dividedness and interiority

Many authors from within different theoretical traditions have underlined the salience of evaluative judgements, made or imputed, as a part of everyday consciousness of living with class. Not only are these damaging and wounding in many cases, but also insidiously internalised.

In their pioneering, now classic, work, *The Hidden Injuries of Class*, Sennett and Cobb (1972) view class as a matter of daily existence rather than as an abstraction. They explore with in-depth interviews the 'complexity of working-class consciousness'. Many of their interviewees felt they were judged and not respected as equals by middle-class people. They attributed a kind of superiority to the latter, as being more 'internally developed', with the power to judge but also as having more chance to escape from the force of circumstances, and to develop the 'defences' of personal control that education can bring. The authors emphasise how personally their interviewees took their class position, comparing and judging themselves as inadequate, but also resenting these emotions. This is 'the burden of class', an existential wound, in which class denies 'any feeling of secure dignity in the eyes of others, and of themselves' (Sennett and Cobb, 1972: 170). They describe how 'social differences . . . appear as questions of character, of moral resolve, will and competence' (Sennett and Cobb, 1972: 256). They attribute this to the flaw in a putatively egalitarian meritocracy, in which social success or failure can only be seen as the result of individual differences in ability and effort, thereby becoming one of the insidious ways in which class is internalised as personal failure.

Sennett and Cobb show how class creates a dividedness within the person; a split between the conscious understanding of the injustice of unequal opportunities and an 'inner conviction' of personal responsibility, self-blame and shame. Dividedness, disavowal and split or double consciousness are related themes that surface frequently in psychosocial understandings of how people live with and within social divisions. Disavowal, through the splitting it involves, can lead to a diminution in effectiveness and resilience. It can also render people especially vulnerable to the actual or perceived judgements of 'superior' others, to the middle-class gaze. Skeggs also emphasises the prevalence of judgements that the working-class women in her study felt exposed to. Class 'is still a hidden injury' (Skeggs, 1997: 95). It 'becomes internalized as an intimate form of subjectivity, experienced as knowledge of always not being "right"' (p. 90). Her interviewees continually doubt their own judgements.

Skeggs sees this confluence of emotion as presupposing a real and/or imagined superior other. She illustrates with extensive quotations the many ways and areas of life in which her participants felt judged, and/or judged themselves, under surveillance, constantly uneasy and convinced they could be found wanting or undesirable; and sometimes resisting this negative evaluation of themselves. 'The working-class are constantly aware of *the dialogic other* who have the power to make judgements about them' (Skeggs, 1997: 167, my italics). The middle-class gaze, she says, takes on a life of its own, not needing to be enacted to be felt. This echoes Bourdieu's description of symbolic violence: '(D)ominated lifestyles are almost always perceived, even by those who live them, from the destructive and reductive point of view of the dominant aesthetic' (Bourdieu, 1994/1998: 9). Psychoanalytic notions of identification with the aggressor underline how such a position can be held unconsciously. Skeggs points out how contemporary pathologising representations, especially in the media, exacerbate these processes, intensified in the current era of impoverishing and demonising a section of the working class, as Tyler (2008) shows.

It is significant that Skeggs uses concepts of internal dividedness – the dialogic other, disidentification – to capture part of how class is lived. This is despite her Foucauldian sociological framework, with its emphasis on how subjectivity is produced, which eschews notions of interiority or depth. To my ears, her depiction of such dividedness demands the use of psychoanalytic concepts.

Diane Reay, in her extensive psychosocial research on class and education, does make use of the notions of interiority, internalisation and depth. She aims to establish the psychic economy of class as a legitimate concern for social science. She argues, in 'Beyond consciousness? The psychic landscape of social class', that despite contemporary ideologies of classlessness,[4] class is 'still deeply etched into our psyches' (Reay, 2005: 911). Elsewhere she emphasises how 'living class in a deeply unequal society like the UK is a powerfully defended and defensive experience' (Reay, 2015: 21). Throughout her research she studies both working-class and middle-class subjects, something relatively unusual and especially important for present purposes. She describes the 'psychic landscape of class' as lived both consciously and unconsciously: 'My contention is that *beneath* socio-economic categorisation, *underneath* class practices, lies a psychic economy of class that has been largely invisible in academic accounts and commonsense understandings' (Reay, 2005: 912, my italics).

Arguing that sociology has falsely seen 'psychic responses' to class as only a matter of individual psychology, she comments on how much of the recent interest in the lived processes and relationships of class was pioneered by feminists, many themselves from working-class backgrounds. Feminism is intrinsically psychosocial, and thus in a good position to challenge traditional disciplinary boundaries and binarisms, and forge new ways of thinking. Reay argues, as do other authors, that emotional and psychic responses to class and to inequalities are part of the makings of class, intrinsic to its formation and operation, not just add-ons to structural features. She understands the complex psychosocial dynamics of class to be essentially relational: these involve comparisons, affiliations, differentiations and judgements, and strike at the heart of how people may feel about themselves.

Reay shows, with many telling examples, how the working-class pupils in her study had by the age of ten already internalised negative judgements of themselves: 'These girls, in the context of schooling, inhabit a psychic economy of class defined by fear, anxiety and unease where failure looms large and success is elusive; a place where they are seen and see themselves as literally "nothing"' (Reay, 2005: 917). She describes how her extensive research was 'permeated by the petty mundane humiliations and slights of social class. . . . Class recognitions, visceral aversions and feelings of inferiority and superiority are routine' (Reay, 2005: 917). She summarises her powerful data as: '[C]lass is produced in a complex dynamic between classes with each class being the others' "Other"' (Reay, 2005: 923). Such a formulation lays the ground for the powerful projections and emotions that surround class difference, and emphasises the relationality of all class experience.

Judgements and comparisons depend upon perceptions of difference and the making of distinctions. Bourdieu's emphasis on the ceaseless work of distinction is amplified further in his massive *The Weight of the World* (Bourdieu, 1999), in which many of the interviews read like clinical engagements, in bearing witness to the intensity, pain, and conflicted identifications that stem from lack of recognition and low social standing. Distinctions constantly proliferate, something Skeggs also remarked upon; the women in her study 'were continually making comparisons between themselves and others, creating distances and establishing distinctions and tastes in the process' (Skeggs, 1997: 82).

It is perhaps hard for anyone not subjected to such invasive forces to really acknowledge and want to know about how being working class can expose a person to harms and wounds of many kinds, to being the recipient of pejorative perceptions, disdainful judgements and discriminatory actions, let alone the economic inequalities and structural disadvantages. Just as it can take a huge effort of will and imagination for a white person to take on board the impact of being subject to racism, the daily experiences of micro-aggressions and denials as well as the larger ones, so too with class. An example of this is that I, in my middle-class bubble, had not expected and indeed was shocked by how some of the therapists in my study from working-class backgrounds had experienced being the target of class contempt (see Chapter 7). The academic research that I cite in this chapter, as well as other experiences, can open our eyes, as it did mine, to the far-reaching impacts of class that we might be ignorant of or rather not know about, but which have the potential to profoundly hurt and constrain people, and in which we are structurally complicit.

Studying the middle classes

Reay's work on the middle classes also illustrates the often judgemental aspects of such identities. Empirical sociological interest in the middle classes is relatively recent and, compared to the volumes of work on the working classes, uncommon. However, for any understanding of how class works in and through persons, as a whole figuration of a social field, and how dominant values operate alongside economic inequalities, it is essential to address the more privileged classes and their subjectivities. As inequality widens and intensifies, studies of elites are becoming more common (e.g. Savage et al., 2015). For any discourse such as psychoanalysis that has largely been the province of the middle and upper classes, the unspoken, hidden and taken-for-granted nature of its class mores and practices means it is especially important to address the psychic embodiments and effects of such hegemony.

Elias suggests that foresight, rationality and affect control are part of the upper and middle classes' means of sustaining distinction, status and domination in the modern period. This has required a vigilance and cultivation of super-egoic functions. Reay et al. (2013) render this as middle-class privilege working in and through individual qualities under individual control. Foucauldian thought also emphasises the increasing historical use of psychological processes as a means or technology of domination. In *Class, Self, Culture* Skeggs (2004) provides an historicised account of how different notions of the self and of the individual inflect differently with class. She describes how excess, vulgarity and stasis are projected onto the working classes, with the middle classes 'owning' responsibility, respectability and reflexivity. Through such processes and discourses, differently classed selves and classed judgements are produced and sustained. She depicts how 'property and propriety have long been central to the middle-class self, how ownership, exchange and morality are always intimately connected' (Skeggs, 2004: 175). Interestingly for any psychoanalytic approach, she argues that it is methods of telling and knowing that make the self, and also make class difference. 'The concept of the self (in particular the reflexive, knowing, inner self) is a specific historical production, enabled through particular methodologies' (Skeggs, 2004: 119). As argued in Chapter 4, this can lead to different class-related attitudes to psychotherapy and psychoanalysis, including working-class wariness.

Much of the empirical work involving the middle classes has taken place in relation to education, a crucial site of class division and confrontation, a key to middle-class cultural and economic reproduction, as well as a source of upward mobility. In *Growing Up Girl,* Walkerdine et al. (2001) put forward a framework that combines both Foucauldian and psychoanalytic approaches for understanding the different educational trajectories and outcomes of working-class and middle-class girls. Their study was in-depth and longitudinal, and notably draws on psychoanalytic methodologies and concepts in the analysis of their data.

The educational trajectories of the two groups were hugely divergent, with even the most successful working-class girls doing much less well than the least successful middle-class ones. The authors argue that the production of educational success is intimately tied up with emotional processes, with the ability to turn emotionality into rational discourse as one of the factors in middle-class achievement. They see child-rearing practices that encourage 'rational autonomy and nice feelings [as] central to the bourgeois order' (Walkerdine et al. 2001: 119), an echo of Elias' emphasis on upper- and middle-class self-restraint. Hanley (2016) emphasises how disconcerted she initially was by the seeming niceness and rationality with which the middle-class people she met presented themselves: 'Darkness is managed or hidden' (Hanley, 2016: 115).

Such emotional constraints are central also to the middle-class imperative to maintain and reproduce their status. Walkerdine et al. note especially the powerful fear of failure in middle-class families, with endemic and intense feelings among the girls of not being good enough, despite very high performance. Any 'failure' was felt to be an individualised one, rather than leading to any reflection on the values and demands of their cultural locations, and simply required harder and harder work: 'It is difficult to overstate the way in which very high academic performance is routinely understood as ordinary and simply the level that is expected' (Walkerdine et al., 2001: 179).

The authors describe the role of their own working-class backgrounds in 'making strange' the apparent 'impenetrable normality' of such success, and observe their sense of contradiction and confusion in interviews with middle-class girls. They 'were presented with apparently seamless success but at the same time deep anxieties surfaced, anxieties that increasingly seemed to underpin that very performance, supporting our view of success as part of a defensive organisation' (Walkerdine et al., 2001: 167). Whereas the working-class girls who did well seemed able to take pride in their performance, the middle-class ones found it harder to do so, or to consolidate a sense of achievement. The authors suggest that this pursuit of excellence covers over a terror of its opposite – of falling off the edge of rationality and middle-class status, into an abyss of unreason, uncertainty and their own suppressed desires, often projected into and typified by feared working-class others. As clinicians we often see the most extreme manifestations of this in some of the symptoms of anorexia, a condition infused with a relentless drive for perfection and one which has an unusually large proportion of middle-class, high-achieving young women, compared to other psychiatric conditions, although it is by no means exclusive to them.

Reay et al. (2013) argue that middle-class responses to inequality have not been much researched, and that it is important to unpick the 'unacknowledged normality' of middle-classness and whiteness. They use the complexities thrown up by parental choice of urban comprehensive schooling as a tool to do so. Their focus is the section of the white middle class they characterise as having egalitarian values, who attempt to engage with difference and inequality in choosing to send their children to urban comprehensives. These are contrasted to those with more exclusivist orientations and a 'fortress mentality'.

The authors describe the combinations of guilt, defensiveness, empathy and conciliation in these 'egalitarian' parents' attitudes. Despite their 'desirous openness', anxieties of all kinds proliferated, with a 'complex mixture of pity, sympathy, disgust and fear towards the working-class "other"' (Reay et al. 2013: 105). They often objectified the latter in pejorative ways, manifesting the wish to maintain distance, despite being committed to the value of engaging with difference. Fears of contamination also abounded. The authors saw their subjects as struggling to manage the tension between this 'desirous openness' to proximate different others and their 'subliminal elitism', that led them to assert and defend their 'distinction' through the claiming of some kind of superiority, usually 'brightness'. They were 'attempting to do class, distinction work under conditions of anxious proximity' (Reay et al. 2013: 116), thus illustrating the middle-class use of class as a defence.

Reay et al. describe these middle-class subjects as also divided: looking defensively inwards and protecting 'their investments of capital and their children's futures, but also looking outwards, towards otherness, tentatively recognising a value in difference that is more than just tokenistic' (Reay et al. 2013: 165). The authors invoke psychoanalytic concepts in naming this as disavowal: 'What is seen to be shameful, in this case any responsibilities for very visible inequalities, is split off and projected into subordinate groups' (p. 117).

Their study lays out, in many evocative examples, the internal conflict that the social order creates, illustrating how class can divide (some) more privileged people internally, albeit differently so from those less well off. It is a depiction that some readers may identify with – certainly I did – and which is also relevant to any engagement with working-class circumstances from a middle-class position, as in the inclusive projects of Chapter 4, or work in the public sector. What it brings out is that alongside the values of democracy, fairness and openness that Reay et al. attribute to their subjects, there is often an undercurrent of something more fearful and hostile. This, as the authors point out, is something that psychoanalysis is well placed to understand. From within psychoanalysis Layton (2011) also described how the 'tolerant middle' can conceal a hierarchy of values, privileging self-control and devaluing strong displays of emotion, in the mental health field as elsewhere, such that therapists may 'unconsciously perform' such cultural values. Just as racist feelings or homophobia may exist alongside a conscious commitment to equality or non-discrimination, so too class contempt, conscious or otherwise, may and does coexist with other attitudes and beliefs.

Reay, Crozier and James were surprised how often their subjects saw working-class circumstances as a cultural rather than an economic and structural issue, an effect perhaps of the insidiousness with which structural disadvantage readily comes to be seen primarily as a matter of personal responsibility and choice, something which current ideologies reinforce. It is in this way, Steph Lawler (2005) argues that taste – the 'other' to disgust – can come to displace inequality as an explanatory schema, an aspect of how the middle classes can appropriate being 'cultured' for themselves. The denial or sidelining of economic factors in favour of cultural distinctions is something that the psychoanalytic field is likely to be prone to, especially given the legacy of the exclusion of working-class people from psychoanalysis on grounds of their supposed lack of verbal ability and educational credentials – that is, their cultural capital.

The more hostile and fearful aspects of class distinction, such as mockery and disgust, have, as Tyler argues, become increasingly acceptable through various media representations, whereas other forms of overt hatred have become less legitimate or even illegal (Tyler, 2008). Owen Jones's book *Chavs: The Demonization of the Working Class* is replete with such examples (Jones, 2011). Lawler argues that such far-reaching negative and stigmatising representations *produce* working-class people as other and abhorrent to middle-class existences. By doing so they constitute middle-classed identities as not being the 'repellent and disgusting "other"' (Lawler, 2005: 431). Lawler sees class-related disgust as a powerful indicator of the interface between the social and the personal, a sign that some norm has been violated, and often felt immediately in the body: 'It indicates how the drawing of distinctions is laden with negative affect' (Lawler, 2005: 438). To this I would add that identities based on disavowal and repudiation of denigrated others are especially likely to be insecure, readily threatened and thus in need of over-assertion. Lawler argues that the forms of distinction and contempt that she describes are not just contingently related to class but rather are 'at the very heart of an identity and a subjectivity that is classed' and are 'unconsciously incorporated . . . an effect of unequal social and cultural processes' (Lawler, 2005: 440). Her work suggests the need for further psychoanalytic exploration of such class dynamics, in understanding how those excluded by structural forces can come to be so denigrated.

Although many people may consciously and genuinely eschew such attitudes, we cannot be complacent as to their possible existence within us in ways we might not wish to know about. The concepts of institutional racism and everyday sexism have taught us much about the manifold ways, unconscious as well as conscious, in which prejudice, hostility and hatred may be embodied socially and personally. There are many subtle, covert and unconscious ways of enacting class distinction, and as psychoanalytic therapists we have the tools to acknowledge and address these, if we so wished. The denial or disavowal of structural and economic factors, and the separation of the psychological and cultural from these, exemplify the 'unlinking' that Layton suggests runs through much contemporary discourse.

Bourdieu and psychoanalysis

Reay (2015) argues that Bourdieu often fails to engage fully enough with the affective aspects of class, despite in many ways laying the ground for doing so. However he increasingly if ambivalently incorporated psychoanalytic concepts into his writings, recognising them as intrinsic to his theories, as Steinmetz (2006) depicts.

In *Distinction* Bourdieu invokes the notion of a 'social psychoanalysis', arguing that taste, 'one of the most vital stakes in the struggles fought in the field of the dominant class and the field of cultural production', is where sociology is especially akin to a social psychoanalysis (Bourdieu, 1984: 11). He argues that: '[T]he social relations objectified in familiar objects, their luxury or poverty . . . impress themselves through bodily experiences which may be as profoundly unconscious as the quiet caress of beige carpets or the thin clamminess of tattered garish linoleum' (Bourdieu, 1984: 77). Bourdieu continues: 'Experiences of this sort would be the material of a social psychoanalysis which set out to grasp the logic whereby the social relations objectified in things and also, of course, in people are *insensibly internalised*, taking their place in a lasting relation to the world and to others' (Bourdieu, 1984: 77, my italics). What is of particular note here is Bourdieu's positing of the embodied, non-conscious internalisation of social relations (here class relations) as these manifest themselves in cultural practices and in relation to others. These particular passages have been made much use of in Layton's incorporation of Bourdieu's work into her clinical understandings of class (see Chapter 8). His notion of internalisation fits well with the schemas of relational and object-relations psychoanalysis.

Bourdieu criticises the more essentialist and ahistorical aspects of psychoanalysis in his critique of 'substantialism' but makes extensive use of psychoanalytic terminology at other points. Steinmetz (2006) cites many examples of Bourdieu's use of concepts such as repression, denegation, identification, libido and defence, and yet also his ambivalence towards them. He argues that psychoanalysis could fill in some of the holes in Bourdieuian theory, especially as regards how disparate life experiences either become integrated or fail to be, in the formation of a biography or habitus; and also in how the 'dominated' often need the approval and recognition of the 'dominant'. These are aspects that I also suggested earlier are of psychoanalytic relevance.

In later writings Bourdieu recommends that sociology and psychoanalysis, rather than being seen as alternatives, should unite their strengths, but he acknowledges that they would have to overcome their mutual suspicion, a highly recognisable description. The psychosocial work cited here does illustrate the creativity unleashed by attempting to do so. Bourdieu summarises the task of this disciplinary collaboration as understanding how:

> [T]he social order *collects, channels, reinforces or counteracts* psychological processes depending on whether there is a homology, redundancy and reinforcement between the two systems, or to the contrary, contradiction and tension. *It goes without saying that mental structures do not simply reflect social structures.*
>
> (Bourdieu, 1999: 512, my italics)

This passage is especially important in view of the tendency (see Chapter 8) of some contemporary psychoanalytic writers to read off mental structures from what they perceive of as social structures, as a direct reflection in all instances. Rather Bourdieu allows for a more differentiated relationship, one in which psychological processes have some degree of autonomy and complexity but interact with and are ultimately shaped by the conditions of the social world. Bourdieu thus leaves space for the autonomous operation of unconscious mental processes as well as asserting the primacy of social forces.

Reay suggests that it is through the conceptual lens of the habitus that psychoanalytic understandings of affect can be fused with sociological theorisations, allowing us to analyse what Bourdieu calls the genesis of 'investments' in a field of social relations. She argues that dynamic emotional processes may become 'sedimented in certain habitus', such that the learning 'that comes through inhabiting pathologised spaces within the field often results in a predilection for shame, fear, anxiety or even righteous indignation, while the internalisation of social inequalities in the privileged can result in dispositions of superiority, entitlement, disdain but also a predilection for guilt, ambivalence and discomfort' (Reay, 2015: 12).

Such a psychosocial extension of the concept of habitus gives, Reay argues, 'a sense of how blurred the lines are between psychic processes and social processes' (Reay, 2015: 13), an argument of particular relevance for the project of this book. Reay illustrates this with examples drawn from multiple interviews in the educational field over years, in which she draws on psychoanalytic concepts. In one example, she describes a working-class boy as caught between two different but compelling fields, that of white, working-class masculinities and that of educational achievement and neo-liberal imperatives of self-improvement. This is 'an untenable space' requiring an exhausting amount of psychic and interactive work, struggle and conflict, to 'maintain his contradictory ways of being, his dual conception of self' (Reay, 2015: 13). She regards this as an example of Bourdieu's notion of divided habitus, something also eloquently described in other writings on social mobility (see Chapter 6). Reay describes the toll on this boy of trying to resolve these tensions, 'the complex, at times contradictory interweavings of ambivalence, defensiveness and pride that make up his divided habitus' (Reay, 2015: 14), which she links to the dilemmas facing many of the men in Sennett and Cobb's study (described earlier). The French sociologist Didier Eribon vividly describes his sense of living in two 'irreconcilable worlds' which 'co-exist in everything you are' (Eribon, 2013: 18), producing a 'level of tension that was hard to bear, and above all, highly destabilizing' (Eribon, 2013: 167).

Reay also elaborates the divided habitus of the middle-class parents she studied: 'Dealing with the discomforts of privilege in disadvantaged contexts all too often results in varying degrees of repression, sublimation, dis-identification, splitting and projection' (Reay, 2015: 19). Here again we can see how psychoanalytic concepts can illuminate the ways in which class becomes the site of internal dividedness and conflict, albeit very differently so for those positioned differently in social space. Reay invokes the notion of a psychic economy of social class: 'feelings of ambivalence, inferiority and superiority, visceral aversions, recognition and abjection . . . internalised and played out in practices' (Reay, 2015: 21). Reay's concept of a psychic economy of class, drawing on psychoanalytic processes, places the complexity of living and experiencing of class firmly within the purview of psychoanalytic theory, as does the other work reviewed here, in different ways.

The considerations of this chapter suggest how fertile, as well as how necessary for any interest in class, the collaboration of sociology and psychoanalysis can be. I have described some of the ways in which a psychoanalysis interested in class could draw on relevant sociological and psychosocial work. This provides useful language, frameworks and concepts with which to understand how people inhabit their particular class locations, including unconsciously, as well as how they are impinged upon by social forces. This goes some way to filling the conceptual gap I have shown psychoanalysis has in relation to class. It brings out how class is always relational, involving distinction and difference as well as identification. It also shows how class is more than that: in the moralism and evaluations of its classifications, that have such powerful emotional impacts; and in its far-reaching structural, material, social and cultural inequalities. Some of the research also shows how sociological and psychosocial work can be enhanced and illuminated by drawing on psychoanalytic concepts. The dense emotionality of class; the many forms of pain, anxiety and conflict involved in living class; the resulting projections and disavowals; these all speak to the kind of divided subject that is the province of psychoanalysis. The following chapters exemplify much of this through the experiences of therapists within the psychoanalytic field and contemporary clinical writings.

Notes

1 At Goldsmiths, University of London, from 2004 to 2008, where Victor Seidler and I ran interdisciplinary seminars on psychosocial topics.
2 To give approximate definitions: economic capital includes income, wealth, financial assets and inheritances. Cultural capital includes dispositions of mind and body, as in taste, style, etiquette, etc.; cultural goods; and educational and professional qualifications. Social capital includes resources built on networks of connection and affiliation. Symbolic capital is the form these different types of capital take when recognised and legitimated in the operations of power. All are context-specific.
3 Laurence Spurling and I conducted this in May 2016.
4 Now perhaps less prevalent, with the politics of austerity imposed on working-class lives and incomes.

References

Bourdieu, P. (1984) *Distinction: A Social Critique of the Judgement of Taste*. London: Routledge.
Bourdieu, P. (1994/1998) *Practical Reason*. Cambridge: Polity Press.
Bourdieu, P. (1999) *The Weight of the World*. Cambridge: Polity Press.
Charlesworth, S. (2000) *A Phenomenology of Working Class Experience*. Cambridge: Cambridge University Press.
Cooper, A. (2010) 'Institutional racism: Can psychotherapy change?', *British Journal of Psychotherapy* 26: 486–501.
Devine, F. (2004) 'Talking about class in Britain'. In Devine, F. and Waters, M. (eds) *Social Inequalities in Comparative Perspective*. Oxford: Blackwell.
Elias, N. (1939/1994) *The Civilizing Process: Sociogenetic and Psychogenetic Investigations*. Oxford: Blackwell.
Eribon, D. (2013) *Returning to Reims*. Los Angeles: Semiotext(e).
Hanley, L. (2016) *Respectable*. London: Allen Lane.
Jones, O. (2011) *Chavs: The Demonization of the Working Class*. London: Verso.
Lawler, S. (2005) 'Disgusted subjects: The making of middle-class identities', *The Sociological Review* 53: 431–46.
Layton, L. (2011) 'The Psychology and Politics of Privilege', *The Psychoanalytic Activist*, March Newsletter, section IX, Division 39 of the American Psychological Association.
Reay, D. (2005) 'Beyond consciousness? The psychic landscape of social class', *Sociology, Special Issue on Class Culture and Identity* 39: 911–28.
Reay, D. (2015) 'Habitus and the psychosocial: Bourdieu with feelings', *Cambridge Journal of Education* 45: 9–23.
Reay, D., Crozier, G. and James, D. (2013) *White Middle-Class Identities and Urban Schooling*. London: Palgrave Macmillan.
Savage, M. (2000) *Class Analysis and Social Transformation*. Buckingham: Open University Press.
Savage, M., Cunningham, N., Devine, F., Friedman, S., Laurison, D., McKenzie, L., Miles, A., Snee, H. and Wakeling, P. (2015) *Social Class in the 21st Century*. London: Penguin Random House.
Sayer, A. (2005) *The Moral Significance of Class*. Cambridge: Cambridge University Press.
Sennett, R. and Cobb, J. (1972) *The Hidden Injuries of Class*. New York: Norton.
Skeggs, B. (1997) *Formations of Class and Gender*. London: Routledge.
Skeggs, B. (2004) *Class, Self, Culture*. London: Routledge.
Skeggs, B. (2015) 'Stratification or exploitation, domination, dispossession and devaluation?', *The Sociological Review* 63: 205–22.
Steinmetz, G. (2006) 'Bourdieu's disavowal of Lacan', *Constellations* 13: 445–64.
Tyler, I. (2008) 'Chav Mum, Chav Scum', *Feminist Media Studies* 8: 17–34.
Tyler, I. (2015) 'Classificatory struggles: Class, culture and inequality in neoliberal times', *The Sociological Review* 63: 493–511.
Walkerdine, V., Lucey, H. and Melody, J. (2001) *Growing Up Girl: Psychosocial Explorations of Gender and Class*. London: Palgrave.

6
CLASS AND SOCIAL MOBILITY WITHIN THE PSYCHOANALYTIC FIELD

Here I consider the class-related experiences and concerns of therapists from diverse backgrounds, as subjects within the profession, drawing on my own research and other writings. These often painful and conflicted experiences suggest much about the implicit structure and hierarchies of the field, in the various enactments and denials of class that abound. Several recent surveys confirm what is informally known, that the psychoanalytic profession lacks diversity as regards ethnicity and class (Cooper, 2010; Axelrod, 2012; Ciclitira and Foster, 2012). This chapter fleshes out in first-person accounts the various understandings of class that therapists have in their backgrounds and in their adult circumstances. The vicissitudes of social mobility are evident in the complex trajectories of those from working-class backgrounds, which I link to other writings on the psychic demands and costs of class transition. Social mobility presents a particular conjuncture of the social and the psychic and illustrates how the divisions of the social world are lived out personally, how class becomes embodied and has its enduring effects.

In a small research project (Ryan, 2006/2013) I interviewed thirteen experienced psychoanalytic psychotherapists. These were psychoanalytically informed interviews in the questions I asked and in the abilities of the subjects to articulate their thoughts and experiences within such a framework. The main focus of these interviews was their clinical work with differently classed patients (the topic of Chapter 7), but I prefaced this with biographical questions about the therapists' own class backgrounds, current class status and also their experiences of class within their trainings, their own analysis and current professional discourses. They worked in a variety of public sector, voluntary and private locations. According to their own definitions, there were six from working-class, two from lower middle-class and five from middle-class or upper middle-class backgrounds. Other details can be found in Ryan (2006/2013). Here the subjects are referred to by alphabetised initials.

Many of the interviews generated intense, complex and painful feelings, for both the interviewees and myself. A few were more distanced. I was left with a sense of how much there is to articulate that is more often left undiscussed and unprocessed, and what a charged yet elusive subject this is. Many expressed great relief and interest in being able to talk about class within a psychoanalytic framework, compared to their previous experiences of lack of discussion.[1]

This sense of a loaded absence is corroborated by other psychoanalysts attempting to address class. Thus Stephen Botticelli suggests: 'At the mention of class, all progressive heads reverently bow – yet within psychoanalysis, few can think of anything to say about it' (Botticelli, 2007: 121). Lee Whitman-Raymond suggests that one factor is 'the unbearability of facing the pain that inheres in many discussions of class' (Whitman-Raymond, 2009: 428). Elisabeth Corpt, in an extended discussion of her journey through the psychoanalytic field, 'Peasant in the Analyst's Chair', asks why, despite her complex feelings about her class origins, she never felt able to raise the subject in her training and first analysis (Corpt, 2013). She suggests that the psychoanalytic institutional context in which she and her analyst were embedded relegated class concerns to the superficial and the extra-analytic. These observations are amplified by what follows, in which I present illustrative selections from Ryan (2006/2013), as well as previously unpublished material.

Biography and ambivalence

The hybridity and heterogeneity of class ascriptions were evident in the replies of therapists from working-class and lower middle-class backgrounds, as regards class of origin. One, A, said: '*Culturally and educationally working-class, occupationally lower middle-class.*' I I defined her family as: '*Lower middle-class . . . well, neither of my parents had an education so from that point of view they were working class.*' Some also referred to housing and location. F said: '*You knew where you were in the pecking order . . . there was them up there and us down here*', reflecting how the divisions of social space 'really and symbolically' are translated into physical space (Bourdieu, 2000: 134). The therapists from middle-class backgrounds mostly expressed less complexity and hybridity.

Questions about present-day class status produced complex, hesitant and ambivalent responses from those from working-class or lower middle-class backgrounds. Most saw themselves as middle class to some extent but qualified or resisted this in different ways. A said: '*It can't be escaped, I'm reluctant, resist this, feels like being invisible, it's a shame to lose where you come from.*' C replied: '*That's a difficult one, isn't it? . . . I feel kind of split . . . divided more than split. . . . I have very middle-class interests, not entirely, and I have working-class interests, certain attitudes.*' E said: '*I suppose I would still say I was working class. . . . I mean that it's in me, but I recognise that I'm obviously middle class in my aspirations and that I'm educated and in my socioeconomic status I'm middle class. I'm influenced by my roots and allegiances that are working class, or identifications and triggers that I'm working class.*' D thought the definition of class in her Mediterranean country was more specifically related to occupation and wealth only, whereas class in the UK '*implies a set of beliefs and values*' which she saw as amounting to an internalised identity.

Such excerpts illustrate the understanding, born of personal experiences, that class as it is lived is not only an economically or occupationally defined entity, but also is a matter of interpersonal perceptions, identifications, lifestyles, values and feelings, that it constructs a person at the deepest level, whatever life changes in social status may be made. One challenge for psychoanalysis is to understand how such constructions relate to psychoanalytic models of the mind, for example how and when aspects of class have their impact developmentally, and how it becomes part of psychic structure.

The therapists from middle-class backgrounds gave briefer and less ambivalent descriptions of their present status, with one exception. P, originally from an ex-colonial country, defined himself as middle class on grounds of education and occupation, but added: '*I suppose sort of middle, I don't know what it means.*' He felt his particular background and ethnic status '*adds to the complexity of not knowing where to place oneself*'. The mainly untroubled self-ascriptions by those from white, middle-class backgrounds reflects the taken-for-granted and dominant nature of such status within professional cultures, and the greater degree of continuity of this with their family origins.

The sense that class constructs something enduring 'in' a person, as E said, despite huge changes is important from a psychoanalytic point of view, as to the persistence and formative nature of early experience. Studies of upward social mobility amply corroborate the ways in which early class formations may persist. This has been expressed in many ways, as, for example, 'the marks of earlier class may still remain' (Raymond, 1999: 128), or as 'class is in everything about the person' (Walkerdine et al. 2001: 39). This suggests that social divisions and inequalities are so great and so fraught, and construct the self and its allegiances so fundamentally, that earlier class experiences will remain as significant parts of a person, whatever the change in circumstance. As well, upward mobility is unlikely to bring with it the inheritance of wealth that better-off classes may have.

Early awareness of class difference

In response to questions about early awareness of class difference, much emotionally significant material emerged, often of a stark nature. E said: '*I had a real sense of the haves and have-nots, I definitely belonged to the have-nots. . . . So I could compare myself . . . I could see the differences about having. . . . Some people lived in big houses. . . . We lived in a perfectly fine house, but it was very cold, and only some parts of the house were furnished, because there was not enough money. . . . I don't know where I had seen stair carpets but I had a sense the right and proper thing was a stair carpet . . . the right and proper thing we didn't have, we had lino.*' Her comparisons of the furnishings in her house with other houses, and the coldness in her house, recalls Bourdieu's use (quoted in Chapter 5, p. 97) of the contrast between lino and stair carpet as an illustration of the way class becomes objectified in material objects and impresses itself unconsciously through bodily experiences. E described her parents as being good providers, yet their lesser economic status was a powerful factor in her relationship with them, influencing '*her entire life*'.

F also described the hierarchical layout of her village: '*The demarcation was very very marked . . . we were just different . . . and it felt like, you knew you were inferior . . . there was a lot of deference by our parents to people at the top of the village.*' C described an early sense of shame at the poverty of his home and his anger at seeing his mother's meekness and humility in the face of the arrogance of the landowner.

Awareness of class difference in educational establishments was frequently mentioned. H said she became aware of class '*without knowing the word*' when she went to grammar school. Visiting friends' houses: '*I would see and feel a difference . . . lots of books, we didn't have anything like that in our house . . . it affected me quite deeply, I think, some sense of inferiority . . . why don't we have these things?*' This left her with a sense '*of something missing*'. Class permeated her relationships with others. She started to feel uncomfortable going to school, and inadequate visiting friends' '*very posh*' families. These friendships '*tended not to go anywhere . . . either I or they didn't pursue it . . . quite unconsciously at the time I sought out people who were from more ordinary backgrounds*'. This is eloquent testimony to the difficulty of forging close personal relationships in the face of social inequalities. Corpt (2013) also recounts the failure of an early cross-class friendship, in the face of huge differences in domestic milieu.[2]

The middle-class therapists mainly described early awareness of class in terms of comparisons with others. K said: '*Very early . . . it was clear to me that my father's work and our home were very different from other people's whose homes I went into, who lived in terraced cottages and came back dirty from work. . . . I knew that sort of thing without it ever being said.*' Asked what she felt about this, K commented: '*I don't think it made any difference to me. . . . I used to play with working-class children and I used to go to their houses all the time.*' Another described a big difference between his grandparents' houses – one a terraced council house and the other a big detached house – but did not recall any talk, sense of conflict or difficulty about these differences.

Other middle-class and upper middle-class therapists were more troubled by their experiences. N said: '*From very very early on I was aware of class difference. . . . My parents were major landowners. I quickly developed a sense of class privilege. In relation to other children . . . I felt both guilty and deeply envious. I wanted more than anything else to escape my own privilege and eat fish and chips out of newspaper.*' Asked what she felt this would relieve her of, she said: '*Guilt and isolation and fear of hatred and dislike from others. . . . I was definitely teased for being rich, not exactly teased, I was marginalised. . . . I became very aware of scrutinising my language for evidence of class privilege.*' J, from a background where snobbery was always blatant and accepted, describes her early anxious concern for those less well off as '*in me from the start, and a big problem to me*'. She didn't want them to '*think about me in a more privileged position . . . there was a sort of reversal process that went on*'. She had subsequently always wanted '*to make things better for people who weren't as fortunate as myself*'. Others had called her '*an inverted snob*'.

These more anxious upper middle-class accounts also illustrate the enduring nature of early class experiences in creating a conflicted sense of self. Rather than a denial or repudiation of the working-class other (which might be found with different subjects), concerns for that other and/or anxieties aroused by them persist uncomfortably in the psyche, as the research described in Chapter 5 suggested. This resonates with Frances Maher's (1999) attempts to understand what her upper-class background had bequeathed to her, both consciously and unconsciously. She describes persistent feelings of marginality and isolation from the issues of others, frequent embarrassment or silence about her class origins, and her attempt to solve this by becoming involved in feminism. J's self-questioning echoes Maher's description of how at school, while being told that because of their privilege they had to make a difference in the world, nonetheless this was within the framework of maintaining class superiority and exclusivity. Maher suggests her own political involvements covered over a 'subconscious sense of cultural superiority', a dynamic that Reay et al. (2013) also identified with their conflicted middle-class interviewees. It is not hard to imagine the degree of unease, hurt or anger that anyone subject to such enacted or unconscious superiority might feel.

From subsequent parts of the interviews it became apparent that guilt about privilege and fear of attack were still powerful emotions that could be aroused countertransferentially, limiting the clinical work of some of these therapists (see Chapter 7).

The psychic demands of class mobility

Class transitions illustrate some of what is involved in the psychic life of class and its enduring effects. The huge struggle and persistence needed against various barriers cannot be overestimated, nor the lifelong effects of lesser economic capital or inherited wealth.

The sense of dislocation attending social mobility, and the feelings of complexity, dividedness, isolation and multiple identities, has been richly described in other literature about class and culture (e.g. Hoggart, 1957/2009), in autobiography (e.g. Steedman, 1986; Kuhn, 1995; Eribon, 2013), in the accounts of women academics from working-class backgrounds (Mahony and Zmroczek, 1997) and in recent sociology. Bourdieu described himself as 'torn by contradiction and internal division' as a result of his huge upward mobility (Bourdieu, 2000: 16). Reay, in an incisive article on social mobility, describes how she has 'spent the last 50 years trying to reconcile the working-class girl I was with the middle-class woman I have become' (Reay, 2013: 673). Bourdieu describes this as a 'habitus divided against itself . . . doomed to a double perception of the self, to successive allegiances and multiple identities' (Bourdieu, 1999: 511). A recent empirical study suggests many, although not all, subjects found their upward mobility problematic, with some unable to fully adapt or acculturate and all having to reconstruct their sense of place within social space (Friedman, 2015).

Bourdieu (1999: 510) depicts many of his upwardly mobile interviewees as experiencing 'success as failure', and a betrayal of those who have nurtured them. He saw his own success as 'a transgression and treachery' (cited in Friedman, 2015: 2). Reay describes how, despite being appreciative of her 'privilege', it was difficult to avoid 'a sense of treachery and overwhelming guilt' (Reay, 2013: 673). She suggests that enduring ambivalence characterises many upwardly mobile people. Combined with the often-reported lack of self-confidence, this makes, I suggest, the achievement of professional success even harder and can heighten vulnerability to (often unconscious) self-sabotage. By contrast, Eribon, who radically cut himself off from his background in order to 'create' himself, felt no guilt, but rather such intense shame that he would hide his family origins.

From within the psychoanalytic field, Dick Blackwell also foregrounds a sense of betrayal accompanying his class mobility. He criticises how upward mobility is seen only positively so that its difficulties and losses are not sufficiently recognised (Blackwell, 1998, 2002). This leaves no adequate space for mourning, and instead creates a confused longing for what had been lost, alongside the experiences of being uprooted and replanted, 'with no original soil', which I would render as a kind of melancholia. He comments on how there is no meaningful transitional space for these psychosocial issues to be addressed – something which it might be hoped therapy or training would provide. Depicting the discontinuity experienced in moving from a working-class coal mining community to being a New York psychoanalyst, Susan Bodnar remarks how she is haunted by her grandmother's injunction to 'remember where you come from' (Bodnar, 2004).

The comments of my interviewees amplify much of this, and suggest how class of origin remains embodied as part of the psyche. Several evoked the experience they had of *'living in two cultures at once'*, and the complexities of identity that this involved. D remarked how upwardly mobile people often feel they do not belong, are *'in between'*, do not feel accepted or don't deserve what they have: *'(class) is something that is internalised and stays with people throughout their lives'*.

F emphasised the isolation that can result: *'I can move in and out of either class in different situations I suppose. . . . It's always remained something I'm painfully aware of now that I'm seen as middle class, but I don't have that middle-class background that would give me a sort of confidence with my peer group.'* The lasting impact of her early class experience had created feelings of shame that had been very hard to tackle, despite: *'politically, emotionally and rationally I think everybody's equal but there's a sort of residue that goes right back to childhood, so it's quite hard to get rid of . . . I can see when it's operating, because I am aware of it, so I can challenge myself, but it's still there.'* Reay also describes the vulnerability to a 'resurgence of the humiliations and shames that populated a working-class past' (Reay, 2013: 673). These comments bring out the enormous amount of psychic work that has to be continuously done, to counter the personal reverberations of the construction of some classes as superior and others as inferior, by those who have been positioned in the latter category. This is a fundamental aspect of how people are formed by class, as others have described (see Chapter 4). F expressed adherence to a principle of universal equality, while showing how very hard it is to make this a psychically operative notion, when emotionally and socially so much appears to contradict this.

Several other therapists also commented on a lasting lack of confidence that made negotiating the middle-class world of professional trainings especially hard. H said: '*I resented my parents for not giving me more confidence because I felt that I was going off into this new world somehow at a disadvantage.*' Her lack of confidence was focused on differences in accent, and a recurrent feeling that she wouldn't be accepted because she was not good enough, an aspect stimulated strongly countertransferentially in her clinical work (see Chapter 7, p. 120). She had had to battle with her resentment towards those who hadn't had to fight so much to get to where they were – a recurrent theme.

B also emphasised what a personal transformation training required, and his concern as to whether he could '*make that jump*'. B's articulation of this resonates with Bourdieu's (1984: 251) description of upward mobility: 'a "social promotion" experienced as an ontological promotion . . . a leap'. A, on going to university, felt in a minority '*in another country . . . I felt shame, inadequacy, then anger*'. The scale and extent of such differences are too often minimised or discounted.

These issues of confidence, intertwined with negotiating social relationships, and also speech and language, were mentioned by others. A referred to the sense that how someone speaks '*absolutely defines you*', and said that part of his class mobility had involved '*getting used to having a voice*'. E said that she had felt '*traumatised by class, my sense of low self-esteem, sense of embarrassment, feeling not as good as, not feeling that I had something to say . . . now I don't feel so raw.*' She described a greater sense in the present of entitlement to speech, to place and status. She, like others, saw middle-class people as having confidence, of having a voice, a view, a sense of their place in the world, an inheritance, not having to make such efforts either financially or culturally.

What might the widely reported lack of confidence speak to psychoanalytically? It is as if the impressive educational and professional achievements, gained without the support and resources that middle-class individuals often have, cannot sufficiently counteract the earlier invasive impact of a class positioning felt as inferior. Such positioning is deeply internalised and constructs fundamental aspects of the sense of self. As Corpt says: 'Early social class identifications persist' (2013: 59). Psychoanalysis, if it is to extend its reach, needs to recognise the power and persistence of these early social identifications. Social mobility can also mean the ordinary separations of growing up are entwined with class issues. These social separations, infused with anger, dividedness, shame and guilt, may well complicate and make harder the necessary internal separations, as N later described for a working-class patient (see p. 125).

Class mobility exposed these interviewees to very great challenges as to their sense of self-worth, in contexts that can appear to invalidate good internalised aspects of the parents. It was as if they could not take their backgrounds – their old habitus – into these new environments in a sufficiently helpful way. Reay (2000: 159) describes the 'concoction of working-class past and middle-class present' as a confusing contradiction, emphasising how deeply social divisions are etched into our psyches. Psychoanalytically this could be seen as creating splits in the ego which may well weaken a person's ability to deal with their present-day circumstances.

The force of class is such that the good, nurturing aspects of the interviewees' parents, while undoubtedly important, often could not sufficiently withstand or protect the then child from the destructive impact of adverse social experiences and of the powerful constructions of themselves as inferior, constructions that the writings of the previous chapter addressed. Here there are probably very important differences between families, with class consciousness and ideology a significant factor. Reay identified her parents' strongly politicised working-class consciousness as an important contribution to her persistence against many odds. In my research D's very political father and her family's oppositional values appeared to have given her some strength in not internalising class oppression, despite very hard financial circumstances. F described her family, low in the social hierarchy of her village, as not having the solidarity and strength of a working-class community that she saw her grandparents as having, and commented painfully on the deferential attitudes of her parents, as did C.

Institutional frameworks

Some features of the institutional framework emerged very strongly, especially the absence of any discussion of class in professional trainings, and subsequently. All the working-class and lower middle-class interviewees and some of the middle-class ones felt that this absence was problematic. H said: *'There was a sort of assumption that we were all the same.'* This assumption of universal class-blind similarity among individuals was a recurrent theme, progressive in many ways, but problematic in its non-recognition of material differences.³ P said that no aspects of 'social reality', including the socio-geographical locations and accoutrements of many consulting rooms, were addressed on his course, even in clinical presentations. The hermetic nature of the therapy milieu that this absence created was emphasised by N, having previously immersed herself in radical politics where she had been attacked for her class privilege: '*It was an enormous relief going into the world of psychotherapy precisely because class wasn't an issue . . . almost total denial of class factors. It was a relief but at the same time I felt inauthentic, concealing the fact that I had grown up with an acute awareness of class and its manifestations. It wasn't directly pathologised, simply not addressed.*'

Many added that even post-qualification there were few arenas in which class issues formed part of any professional discussion. The exceptions were those therapists who had worked at a feminist therapy centre, where class was a recurrent issue in their clinical discussions, as Orbach (2011) makes clear. The critical approach to established theory and practice that feminism engenders enables and requires it to embrace issues of 'race', culture and class, not as an add-on to the formation of the psyche but as an integral part of it.

This widespread silence about class constructs a very powerful institutional framework. It echoes, and is built on, the extrusion of class from the psychoanalytic canon, as Chapter 3 described. It is likely to have far-reaching effects on therapists' abilities to think about and work productively with class-related issues with their patients, as well as on how they find themselves in relation to their own professional identities.

The financial demands of psychoanalytic trainings and the sacrifices entailed in completing them were frequently mentioned by those from working-class backgrounds. The strains of doing so alongside others who were much better off put considerable demands on their capacities to process rather than enact resentment and envy. Chapter 9 considers further aspects of money and political economy.

Many from working-class and lower middle-class backgrounds emphasised the often difficult personal impact of the social milieux they encountered, and anxieties about being accepted. B said he had had to learn the codes of this milieu, and '*was fearful of overstepping certain boundaries, your sense of humour, being out of place, would I fit in . . . it demands a personal transformation*'. This echoes Skeggs' argument, that excess, vulgarity and stasis are projected historically onto the working classes (Skeggs, 2004), leaving the (psychoanalytic) middle classes to occupy the grounds of discretion and politeness.

Several therapists commented on the class markers they felt they encountered in various analytic consulting rooms. G described an analyst: '*[W]hose consulting room was almost as big as a football pitch, she was so far away, and she was very traditional/classical, and I thought how would a working-class patient feel in that kind of room . . . if they are on social security and they go into this huge room that's just used for consulting, not doubling up. . . . I had to process my envy.*' Apart from wealth or the lack of it, the consulting room and its adornments can convey other cultural values. It signals the need for privacy, for quiet, for boundedness, and often for discreetness. As such, it can seem typical of a middle-class study, which is not to question the usefulness of these features, but to indicate their cultural loadings, and how, for some, they may be a source of unease.

Own therapy or analysis

Therapists' own experiences as patients provide some voices from the couch, to put alongside their thoughts about their work as therapists. For some from working-class backgrounds, the difficulty of talking about class and feeling adequately heard continued. F, while very positive overall as to her analyst's ability to understand her, identified her feelings about her working-class background as the sole area where she didn't feel heard. Her analyst she identified as middle class: '*So it was right in the room for me. . . . He'd got that public schoolboy, sort of charming, polite blah de blah. . . . I actually raised how I felt about being working class and those feelings of inferiority and shame, and I felt it was one of those areas he didn't quite understand because he'd hooked into the "you're all equal sort of thing, and I really need to value myself", he couldn't identify with the place where it was painful, or the shame. So I told him that. . . . He was a little bit defensive about it that made me feel . . . there's something about this you can't hear.*' Whitman-Raymond (2009) records a similar experience with her well-off analyst, whom she greatly valued overall: 'His "forgetting" often seemed to be around those aspects of my life – finances, status and all the intangibles that constitute my experience of class' (2009: 439). Such perception of upper-class/middle-class resistance to hearing working-class pain, even by those most concerned to 'understand' the other, illustrates the defensiveness with which privilege can be embodied. Reay (2000: 153) argues that the 'complicated self-hoods of working-class children . . . have not adequately informed either psychological or psychoanalytic theorising' and that a much more sophisticated understanding is needed of 'social jealousy, fear, denial, longing and envy'. These, like Steedman's 'proper envy', should not be pathologised but should be seen as 'the rightful inheritance of the poor'. One aspect of psychoanalysis opening itself up more to considerations of class would be to follow these suggestions.

E said: '*It sounds omnipotent but I had to put a lot of it together myself . . . in making those links between class and say my shame . . . there was an inadequacy in my particular therapists although I felt helped by them.*' A said that one therapist would '*individualise and pathologise*' the difficulties he described. B described himself as having '*to make some transitions in relation to my therapist who didn't have to move so radically or make jumps*'. D felt that in her group analysis it was a 'no-go' area.

Corpt (2013) vividly describes how, despite her experiences of the 'injuries of class' and its accompanying shame, she seldom talked about this in ten years of a training analysis with an analyst she perceived to be from a higher social class. She describes her confusion about feeling like a 'have-not' despite ostensibly leading a middle-class life, and how she worked hard at passing, including buying the same expensive clothes as her analyst. At no point could she address the 'real shame and feelings of loss about actually deep down being a "have-not"' (2013: 64). Corpt considers whether this impasse was an accommodation on her part, protecting her connection with her analyst, and also herself from painful feelings of humiliation. However, she also argues that she needed her analyst to be able to see class 'as a psychologically complex part of me' and to have a kind of 'realness', something she feels was foreclosed by the theoretical approach and neutrality embedded in the institution. She argues that such disavowal of class and money can lead to premature foreclosure of issues of indebtedness, shame and gratitude. Her 'class shame' became a central aspect of a second analysis; it no longer needed to be a 'disavowed aspect' of her identity as an analyst. Subsequently she was surprised to learn from her first analyst that she maintained an air of superiority that had made it difficult for the analyst to reach her – an example of a defence covering up socially induced painful feelings of inferiority.

Others from working-class and lower middle-class backgrounds had more positive experiences in relation to class. H felt that she was aware, mainly through how he spoke, of her therapist coming from a '*higher social class*' than herself, and doubted whether he could understand her. However, she said she liked him and it ceased to be a problem. G recounted how she had had quite a chequered history with different therapists, but with her main therapist she did feel she could talk about her class experiences and feelings.

The therapists from middle-class and upper middle-class backgrounds had varied experiences of being understood in their class concerns. N said that none of her analysts had been able to help her with her class background. She felt that they all '*bought into the mystique*' surrounding her family, and were too fascinated and excited by the social charisma to be able to help her with the shame and isolation she had felt. One thought it was right that N should feel shame, which stimulated her defensiveness. Such an unanalytic response chimes with reflections from analysts with high-status or wealthy patients. For example, Altman (1995/2010) acknowledges his sense of gratification and Glick (2012) describes the analytic potential for narcissistic identifications with such patients. Moral superiority on the part of the analyst in the face of great wealth is also identified by Glick as a potential analytic trap, and also recounted by Bodnar (2004). None, N said, understood the hatred connected with the UK class structure. There was no acknowledgement of the '*realities of the psychology of the class system*', something she thought would have helped her see how her fears had a basis in reality as well as enabling her to explore them intra-psychically. Subsequently these limitations were evident in the shortcomings she identified in her own clinical work (see p. 125). Such analytic blind spots illustrate what happens when class is not adequately recognised and thought about, as both social reality and intra-psychically.

Another middle-class therapist, K, said that class had never been part of any dialogue with her therapists whom she took to be middle class. '*It hasn't been something that I've noticed or thought about.*' As the interview progressed it became apparent that there were some quite striking class experiences in her background (see p. 106). She expressed surprise that the class differences had emerged as such a big feature in the interview: '*It was completely unpredicted by me and I hadn't thought about it at all before.*'

Other middle-class therapists felt more heard and understood in their concerns about class. J had had lifelong huge anxiety about snobbish attitudes towards working-class people. She had been persistently concerned for the disadvantaged. She felt her '*complicated inversion*' had been well understood by her analyst, and that her unconscious identification with the '*do-gooder*' and marked guilt had been effectively analysed. It was still though an issue that had enormous resonance for her (see p. 123), illustrating what Sennett calls 'the perverse seductive power of inequality' (Sennett, 2003). P also felt that during his analysis differences of 'race', skin colour and class were well explored. He said: '*I was lucky enough to have an analyst who didn't see everything as just in the mind, it was slightly more broad based. Recognition of reality, so to speak.'* Here there is a reference to 'reality' to include the social, as if this was outside the usual psychoanalytic dialogue. This is a recurrent theme, usually signifying some kind of felt impasse (see Chapter 7).

This chapter illustrates the often difficult journeys that therapists from non-white and non-middle-class backgrounds had through the institutions of psychoanalysis. The accounts of this chapter underline the sense that class is everywhere and nowhere. It is everywhere in the fabric of the setting of psychoanalysis, its unacknowledged institutional and economic framework, yet it is nowhere in its explicit discourse. It concurs with Walkerdine et al.'s (2001) argument that the prevailing ideology of the production and reproduction of selves is one in which it is as if class is absent, yet played out against stark inequalities. The enduring effects of class on the psyche are vividly shown through the vicissitudes of social mobility, which provide much useful information about how class forms people. The lack of much psychoanalytic interest in class, combined with an ideology of presumed equality, means that important differences and useful understandings of the psychic landscapes of class are neglected. The reflections of many of these therapists could provide starting points for critical psychoanalytic reflection on the operation of class within the profession.

Notes

1 In workshops and talks on this subject I have found that simply asking people to identify and share their social class of origin and their present status generates intense and complex discussion.
2 Reading Corpt's account made me remember my awkward attempts to form friendships with schoolmates from working-class homes, which never developed into anything enduring. A recent study of cross-class friendships (Pellandini-Simanyi, 2015) identifies the many strategies that people employ to bridge income gaps within friendships, and the frequent weakening and dissolution of these.
3 In a discussion at a community psychotherapy centre, where the funding Labour council was concerned about the small proportion of disadvantaged and non-white clients, a supervisor argued that if you need help, it doesn't matter what colour you are. This kind of psychoanalytic liberalism is contradictory in its effects – an assertion of possibly progressive universalism that denies important differences.

References

Altman, N. (1995/2010) *The Analyst in the Inner City: Race, Class, and Culture through a Psychoanalytic Lens.* New York: Routledge.

Axelrod, S. (2012) 'The division 39 practice survey', *Division/Review* 5: 28–31.
Blackwell, D. (1998) 'Class, status and conflict in mind and society', *Group Analysis* 31: 16–120.
Blackwell, D. (2002) 'Out of their class', *Group Analysis* 35: 367–38.
Bodnar, S. (2004) 'Remember where you come from: Dissociative process in multicultural individuals', *Psychoanalytic Dialogues* 14: 581–603.
Botticelli, S. (2007) 'The return of the repressed: Class in psychoanalytic process'. In Suchet, M., Harris, A. and Aron, L. (eds) *Relational Psychoanalysis: Vol. 3 New Voices*. New Jersey: Analytic Press.
Bourdieu, P. (1984) *Distinction: A Social Critique of the Judgement of Taste*. London: Routledge.
Bourdieu, P. (1999) *The Weight of the World*. Cambridge: Polity Press.
Bourdieu, P. (2000) *Pascalian Meditations*. Cambridge: Polity Press.
Ciclitira, K. and Foster, N. (2012) 'Attention to culture and diversity in psychoanalytic trainings', *British Journal of Psychotherapy* 28: 353–73.
Cooper, A. (2010) 'Institutional racism: Can psychotherapy change?', *British Journal of Psychotherapy* 26: 486–501.
Corpt, E. (2013) 'Peasant in the analyst's chair: Reflections, personal and otherwise, on class and the forming of an analytic identity', *International Journal of Self-Psychology* 8: 52–69.
Eribon, D. (2013) *Returning to Reims*. Los Angeles: Semiotext(e).
Friedman, S. (2015) 'Habitus clivé and the emotional impact of social mobility', *The Sociological Review* 63: 1–19.
Glick, R. (2012) 'The rich are different'. In Berger, B. and Newman, S. (eds) *Money Talks*. London: Routledge.
Hoggart, R. (1957/2009) *The Uses of Literacy*. London: Penguin.
Kuhn, A. (1995) *Family Secrets: Acts of Memory and Imagination*. London: Verso.
Maher, F. (1999) 'Coming out'. In Zmroczek, C. and Mahony, P. (eds) *Women and Social Class – International Perspectives*. London: Taylor and Francis.
Mahony, P. and Zmroczek, C. (1997) *Class Matters: 'Working-Class' Women's Perspectives on Social Class*. Basingstoke: Taylor and Francis.
Orbach, S. (2011) 'Bringing history to mind: Discussion of "interpellations"'. In Dimen, M. (ed) *With Culture in Mind*. London: Routledge.
Pellandini-Simanyi, L. (2015) 'How do friends manage income differences?' *Sociology* 1–16. Available at: https://doi.org/10.1177/0038038515594975. Accessed January 2016.
Raymond, J. (1999) 'Class matters – yes, it does'. In Zmroczek, C. and Mahony, P. (eds) *Women and Social Class – International Perspectives*. London: Taylor and Francis.
Reay, D. (2000) 'Children's urban landscapes'. In Brewer, S. (ed) *Cultural Studies and the Working Class*. London: Cassell.
Reay, D. (2013) 'Social mobility, a panacea for austere times', *British Journal of Sociology of Education* 34: 660–77.
Reay, D., Crozier, G. and James, D. (2013) *White Middle-Class Identities and Urban Schooling*. Basingstoke: Palgrave Macmillan.
Ryan, J. (2006/2013) '"Class is in you": An exploration of some social class issues in psychotherapeutic work', *British Journal of Psychotherapy* 23: 49–63. Reprinted with postscript in F. Lowe (ed), *Thinking Space: Promoting Thinking about Race, Culture and Diversity in Psychotherapy and Beyond*. London: Karnac.

Sennett, R. (2003) *Respect: The Formation of Character in an Age of Inequality*. London: Allen Lane.
Skeggs, B. (2004) *Class, Self, Culture*. London: Routledge.
Steedman, C. (1986) *Landscape for a Good Woman*. London: Virago.
Walkerdine, V., Lucey, H. and Melody, J. (2001) *Growing Up Girl*. London: Routledge.
Whitman-Raymond, L. (2009) 'The influence of class in the therapeutic dyad', *Contemporary Psychoanalysis* 45: 429–43.

7
CLASS WITHIN THERAPY RELATIONSHIPS

Here I explore how the dynamics of therapy relationships may be inflected by class, based on my own research and the contemporary writings of others. Dimen argues that class has powerful unconscious resonances such that: 'The fault lines of class and other hierarchies show up systematically in transference and countertransference' (Dimen, 1994: 79). Whitman-Raymond describes how fraught with anxiety the elucidation of class in clinical work can be. She asks: 'How can clinicians begin to talk about the pain of our class limitations and class exploitation as they are experienced, and at times replicated, in the clinical setting?' (Whitman-Raymond, 2009: 440). This chapter provides many diverse examples of how therapists do often do this, within various class permutations, and sometimes fail to do so. I show how different therapists conceptualise and work with class issues, and the barriers to this.

I asked the therapists in my study (Ryan, 2006/2013) to describe in some detail their clinical work with two patients, one working class, and one middle class, as this was perceived by the therapist and/or in accordance with patients' self-ascriptions where these were present. They were asked to select cases where they were aware there were class issues, either for their patients or for themselves in relation to these patients, or both. It became apparent that prior preparation for this part of the interview was advantageous, and I sent guidelines to all subsequent interviewees outlining possible topic areas and questions. This is unusual in qualitative research but reflects the reality that to ask therapists to talk in detail about their clinical work does entail thought and preparation. They were asked to provide some general background to their descriptions of their work with each patient, their understandings of class issues for that patient, and any class-related aspects of the transference–countertransference that they perceived. I would at times ask for more elaboration, or sometimes suggest links to other parts of the interview, if appropriate. The interviews were psychoanalytically informed, in the sense that all parties were experienced in psychoanalytic modes of self-reflection and thinking, and the topic was clinical work.

Most therapists readily located examples of work where they felt class was an issue of some kind. The exception was K, who said of her NHS work: '*I did obviously have working-class patients there, but I don't think class is what I was thinking about, and I don't think I'd have mentioned it in an assessment.*'

Many of the interviews were highly charged, and it was as if we had embarked on unusual discussions. The therapists' accounts were a mixture of what they were felt were class issues for particular patients, and also of how they felt class played out in the interface between the two of them. B asked: '*Does the social class appear in the transference and how would the analyst hear it?*' – a highly pertinent question that puts the onus as much on the therapist as on the patient. Here I illustrate some class-related transferences and how these therapists heard and responded to them.

In what follows, the data from the interviewees from lower middle-class backgrounds is combined with the data from those from working-class backgrounds, as much of their material, both biographical and professional, contained similar concerns and was distinctively different from that of the middle-class interviewees. This generated four possible pairings of therapist and patient as regards class: two with a class difference and two with a similarity. I did not start out with any assumption about dividing the research material up in this dichotomised way, but the subsequent analysis of the transcripts did suggest that with the two possible pairings with class differences there were distinctive themes, and there was almost no overlap between these. That talk about class can readily default to the binaries of working class and middle class, the 'haves' and 'have-nots', or 'us' and 'them', indicates the intensity of emotion and projection at play and the powerfulness of social divisions and inequality, even if this does not always correspond to more complex or differentiated realities. Class issues of many different kinds were reported in all combinations. Here I have selected some detailed accounts and described others more briefly.

Working-class and lower middle-class therapists with middle-class patients

There were several accounts of middle-class patients' apparent contempt, disparagement and arrogance, '*being put in your place*', which either overtly were, or were felt to be, class-related. Attacks and negative transferences can happen in any therapy, focused on many seeming issues, but it is striking that, when questions are asked about class, this was only described in this combination and not in any of the other pairings. The following example illustrates these themes.

H said of her patient, whose mother owned a very successful business in the ex-colonial country she had come from: '*She was part of the elite, she spoke in this incredibly posh way, and was very, very aware of class. I started to feel uncomfortable with her early on, and I was aware of it being all my stuff about class, and she said to me in the second or third session: "I don't know, I have to say this because it's bothering me, I'm wondering if you are going to be any good, because you sound quite working-class." It was awful, it felt like she's got right under my skin. . . . It set off these feeling of am I good enough? . . . Can I be a good therapist because I don't speak in the right way? and a sort of anger towards her. I thought, who does she think she is? I'm very very aware of all that, and that I mustn't retaliate, but what I felt then was: I've got to work harder to show her I'm good, I've got to see behind all this and not get caught up in my own stuff and see what it's about for her. . . . Which I was able to do, but only by going back into therapy myself . . . because nobody had actually said that to me before . . . and it confirmed my worst fears. . . . I managed with her to turn it around, so I was able to get her to see that she was projecting onto me her own feelings of inadequacy, that although she was posh, she was still black, and . . . she still felt she didn't belong . . . and we did some very good work . . . based on that she was always trying so hard to prove herself.*'

This illustrates one of the many intersections of 'race' and class that surfaced in other accounts. Further exploration suggested what 'working class' signified for this patient: '*It meant for her to be black, very black, both metaphorically and in reality. . . . To be working class was to have no culture. . . . The rejected . . . she was desperately trying to be the kind of person her mother had said she should be but all the time she actually felt like the disparaged people that her mother would talk about, those ordinary black people, "not like us", so it's all sort of mixed up there with race.*'

Asked how she addressed this, H said: '*It was a real struggle because it all could have failed because I could have got very retaliatory . . . or/and I could actually have become totally inadequate and become the useless working-class therapist that* she thought I was going to be. . . . I'm aware of it when I see other patients . . . and again it's always the accent I go for, and I feel I have to prove myself a little bit more, because I don't speak the same way as them, and that they will pick this up and think, "Well, is she any good, is she educated?"' Here, the explicitly class-related attacks had the potential to re-traumatise the therapist, to evoke old class wounds, illustrating the powerfully injurious impact of earlier class experience, and the considerable psychic work required to retain an analytic position.

The potential for feelings of class-related inferiority to be stimulated is also illustrated by A, working with a rich woman with a high professional status: '*I felt instantly crushingly inadequate. . . . She placed me instantly, she knew exactly like Henry Higgins just where I came from, what my wealth was . . . this came out later. She complained about the chairs, wrote to the manager about the smell in the room, we moved to a different room. This was a measure of the command she felt she had.*'

Other therapists also experienced being the target of contempt. F said: '*It was in her attitude and some acting out she did, it wasn't just contempt, it related to class.*' Asked about how she approached this: '*I think I have struggled with my own prejudices . . . it's probably my own values and beliefs about human beings and equality that ground me when I'm struggling with how little she's been paying for years and years and how much she's now earning now she's going. . . . I have to challenge these things in myself . . . partly you realise through the work everybody whatever their class is human . . . her family was just hell, that modifies all those fantasies about how wealth would just make life easier.*'

F's statement about human equality occurs alongside her acute awareness of the significance of class difference, keeping them both in productive tension. It differs from the more usual class-blind assumption of the equality of individuals, for which F had previously criticised her analyst (see p. 112). F used her belief that wealth cannot buy happiness to overcome her feelings of envy and resentment. A also felt huge envy of his patient's wealth and reflected how he had had to live quite a long time to understand that money cannot buy love: '*I felt genuinely valued but as someone from below stairs . . . just the sadness about divisions between people that she genuinely felt.*'

Several therapists described what they saw as middle-class bluff and bluster, a false confidence, which '*gets them through some situations*'. B said: '*Middle-class people sometimes seem a bit naïve, take things for granted easily, which seems a bit silly. . . . I take it that confidence is on the side of the ego some place and it can be strangely oddly very fragile . . . it seems self-confident but not as clever as it seems.*'

Class contempt as an aspect of transference exposes what is often kept politely or defensively hidden: attributions of inferiority and superiority according to class. It illustrates the middle-class use of class as a defence, to create an illusion of superiority and confidence, or to exert power. It shows the powerfulness of the social world in the construction of classed psyches such that working-class or lower middle-class past experiences and fears of inferiority and humiliation render them vulnerable to middle-class disdain or arrogance.

The impact of class and wealth in the transference–countertransference matrix is also evident in Bodnar's (2004) work with a rich upper-class woman, which she prefaces by an account of her own upwardly mobile trajectory. Bodnar observes how initially boundaries were drawn around her working-class and the patient's upper-class identifications, such that she found herself deferential to the patient's fear of exploitation or being without means, a contract that she suggests has long characterised tensions between the working classes and the upper middle classes. She only began to question her own complicity in this, in not charging the patient adequate fees, when the patient purchased an expensive apartment and repeatedly emphasised the cost of unwanted gifts from her mother with whom she had an antagonistic relationship. Bodnar expressed astonishment at the lavish spending, and questioned the patient's portrayal of her mother (as the rich-bitch) that she had previously gone along with. The patient's furious and contemptuous response of 'How dare you?', revealed previously unaddressed aspects of the transference: coming to therapy was 'slumming it'; her unspoken awareness of the analyst's class background made it exotic; the analyst was like the nearly invisible household servants of her childhood, who silently witnessed her exaggerated entitlement, akin to the hired help who neglected her own needs.

Bodnar questions her own sense of moral superiority over such lavish spending, as part of her hidden but enacted working-class identifications, which meant she didn't 'stoop' to charge the patient a full fee. She describes an 'untouchable contempt', the defensive disdain between herself and the patient, held in place by a class hierarchy that allowed a disconnection from the underlying emotions. It was through enactments, in not charging the patient an appropriate fee and then in expressing astonishment at lavish spending, that aspects of class were first hidden and then revealed. The subsequent deconstruction of the class issues in their relationship revealed the role of intergenerational transmission of unspoken trauma and loss in the patient's family.

These accounts illustrate how the intensity of the analytic encounter can reveal class-based anxieties and projections, and exposes the viciousness at the heart of class, much of it described in psychosocial work. The rawness and forcefulness of these denigrating projections were intensified by the injurious legacies of these therapists' own class experiences. Most therapists found ways of surmounting and working reflectively with such projections, and also with their own envy, but the personal demands of this were often great. They drew on their own values, their understandings of class forged through experience, and their professional skills, to meet these challenges. They successfully crossed 'the boundaries of inequality' (Sennett, 2003), despite the lack of wider psychoanalytic recognition of these significant conjunctures.

Middle-class therapists and working-class patients

The potential for contempt in the transference, previously described, finds an echo in a fear of being denigrating that some of the middle-class therapists with working-class patients expressed. Several also described being stuck when they encountered class-related anger, which they felt unable to sufficiently take up or explore.

J, working in a low-fee organisation, described a man in a skilled manual occupation from a working-class family, referred because of an apparently psychosomatic complaint. She felt that she had helped him put into words his angry feelings: '. . . *all related to his bosses who earn lots of money, had big cars and used him as a skivvy. You could see he resented being in the position he was, violently . . . he was in a sort of conflict situation with them, which of course repeated some of his earlier experience, and also repeated something in the therapy with me, because there I was, middle class, with a little warm consulting room, with the loo at the back. . . . I think it was very difficult for him to articulate anything about my position. I couldn't help him do that . . . I mean, it was there in the transference, obviously, but you wondered whether with this man you should be trying to pursue or open this up. It might have been because there was a very violent part to him and in the countertransference I think I knew that. . . . I never did feel fear with him . . . it's possible that there was more around than I was able to deal with, he was talking all about these men with big cars, and mine isn't a big car, but that must have been there.*' Earlier J had spoken about her class embarrassment at having a fairly posh car, which sometimes she hid from her clients, suggesting a subliminal level of fear about envy.

J said overall the therapy was successful although she was still left with a sense of untouchable areas: '*He had a grievance about his upbringing, but he wanted to hang on to that. . . . There was so much grievance because it had all been so bad . . . there was so much reality factor that it was difficult to go into it, there was very little to work on. . . . I don't know if there was a countertransference that made me feel nervous of doing that, because of what might have been an outcome. . . . I felt there was something a bit untouchable.'* Here there is an appeal to 'reality factor' as contrasted with the assumed concerns of analytic work – a recurrent theme but one used to limit the work, as if exploring the 'reality' factors was somehow intrinsically unanalytic. This further constrains analysts' ability to think about and work with patients who come from backgrounds of social and economic deprivation.

M also felt inhibited in taking up some aspects of the transference with a working-class upwardly mobile patient: *'There is clearly a very ingrained sort of class issue for him and power differential and things like that. . . . There's a sense that anybody in the upper class has more power and can afford to be ill, and I'm sure that includes me in the transference.'* M wondered whether his hesitation in exploring this further was to do with his perception of the patient's paranoia and having to be especially careful of what he said to him, or whether it was: *'a class thing, a kind of reversed snobbery. . . . It is difficult to challenge him, because of the sense that he would perceive it as dismissing his realities. . . . I suppose in the countertransference, I'd like to challenge him. . . . I don't think it's all about class, but you could see him stuck in that sort of grudge, he's very much stuck there.'*

The references to 'grudges' and 'grievances' is a significant use of language that suggests the complexities of this conjuncture between social circumstances and unconscious processes, and of the emotional politics of class, to use Skeggs' term. The relevance of this to wider political concerns is suggested by the psychosocial work of Paul Hoggett and others. The authors identify the centrality of grievance, resentment and stuck victim positions to conditions of divisive social policies and political disempowerment, in the absence of political movements giving voice to real injustices. They suggest a structure of feeling whereby: '*ressentiment* occurs where grievances become blocked and turn in on themselves, leading to something more socially toxic' (Hoggett et al., 2013: 5), providing 'the affective basis' for antagonisms between people. Such a perspective might enable the framing of 'grudges' and 'grievances' in wider terms.

In the present study, the language reflects therapists' sense of frustration at what they felt they could not work further with, and maybe their own sense of powerlessness as regards the inequalities of social circumstance. They found it difficult to make further use of their probably correct perception of how self-defeating this angry stuckness had become. This pinpoints the difficult line that therapists may have to tread between the recognition of justifiable anger at social circumstances and the ascription of personal agency, something which can run the risk of appearing not to think the anger is warranted. Some therapists (see p. 127) did find ways of negotiating this. It is also a complex clinical judgement as to how and when to address rage without incurring undue destabilisation or fragmentation. Nonetheless it is striking that class-inflected anger of the kinds described could induce a kind of retreat or drawing back on the part of some therapists.

Another therapist, N, in work with a patient from a working-class background, had many struggles with the perceived differences between them, and the transference–countertransference dynamic. N felt guilt, and fear of being denigrating: '*She immediately made me feel guilty about my privilege, not only my privilege but also my friends' privilege.*' N felt, unlike with other issues, she could not '*see the projections as well as own the reality . . . it has been difficult for me to speak about her family of origin . . . the work has been about unconsciously separating from them, as well as consciously. My guilt has meant that I am constantly aware of not wanting to denigrate them, even now I hesitate to describe them as a disturbed family. . . . I do think the class difference has been there, all through the work.*' She linked her difficulties with this patient to her early acute awareness of class differences (see p. 114), which she felt had not been helpfully addressed in her own analyses.

These excerpts illustrate Sennett's description of what happens when the 'boundary of inequality' is not crossed, namely, silence, caution and fear of giving offence (Sennett, 2003). It shows the powerfulness of class in creating distance and withdrawal. Such anxious awareness of the potential for denigration of the working-class other suggests how deeply the culture-wide valuations of class permeate the psyche, whatever the conscious beliefs otherwise. My own experiences, as a middle-class therapist with many upwardly mobile patients, resonates with many of these descriptions, and was part of the spur to these investigations. With some, I felt acutely the discrepancies in our socioeconomic circumstances, especially as regards childhood, but often found myself unable to think when the work demanded that I explore the particular meanings of class, especially within the dynamics of the relationship. My anxiety and fear of anger and envy inhibited me in taking up any transference that touched upon my relatively privileged status.

Some therapists cast the impasses they felt in terms of 'reality factors', and the assumed opposition between the exploration of these and an analytic stance. P however did not use the language of grudges and grievances in describing his work with a working-class man '*who was defiant and proud about it but who was carrying a lot of hatred and envy*'. Coming from a very economically and emotionally deprived background, the patient described himself as a football hooligan. He had, P said, '*a terrible anger*', and a determination never to be so impoverished. P was seen both as the '*toff*' and as the immigrant who had made good and who tried to conceal himself with his accent. P described a threat of violence at times during the analysis, which he managed to contain. He also described the patient's huge hatred against 'the system' that led him into extensive fraud: '*All his endeavours had been to get at somebody.*' P said that at the end of a long intensive analysis: '*He was still as angry and emotional but the language had changed, he had an ability to look at things that would worry him.*' He had also made many positive changes in his material and professional circumstances, an example of how it is possible to move out of repetitive stuck positions but not lose very justifiable anger at social circumstances, something which many people fear therapy will lead to.

The interview data suggests that P's ability to work productively with this working-class white patient was linked to P's experiences of being subject to racism, and also having felt well understood in his own analysis in relation to issues of 'race' and class (see p. 114). P's account does not suggest fear or guilt in the face of intense class-related anger. He was able to work with the intertwinings of social realities with intra-psychic issues, rather than seeing them as opposed. Previously P had criticised the notion of 'reality factors' being used to limit psychoanalytic interest. This suggests how much can be learned psychoanalytically from those subject to social oppressions and discriminations of various kinds, as the following examples from working-class therapists also show.

Similarities of class

Janine Puget, in her re-theorising of the psychoanalytic representation of social reality, observes that one barrier to recognising how the social field has its effects is that analyst and patient often live in the same social and cultural world. She suggests that 'the unconscious link' with the social field is easier to recognise when something alien is experienced (Puget, 1991). My research corroborates this in that there was greater wealth of clinical detail evident with class differences than with similarities. However, with working-class pairings some salient aspects of class were reported, as the next examples show.

Working-class and lower middle-class therapists with working-class patients

Anger, feelings of inferiority, shame and envy within a class context were identified in clinical work with working-class patients, as well as the complexities of blame and responsibility. F described a woman who had huge conflict about the professional training she was pursuing, in that she felt she had to become middle class to do it: '*She had so much anti-feeling about being middle class, she was really really ambivalent about it and we worked quite a lot on whether she could be black and working class and a professional* (my substitution here), *and make it her own and that was a very powerful issue in the therapy.... It was a real eye-opener to her that she could own the material she was developing ... it didn't belong to the middle class and she didn't have to become one of them, she could actually take these things that she had learned and use them in her own way.*' In this passage, fundamental questions about the dominant culture and the social ownership of skills and ideas are touched upon, and led to F commenting: '*Well, the middle class don't own psychoanalysis, they don't own course materials.*'

F described some of the psychic fragilities and defences she felt this patient was struggling with in relation to her social circumstances: '*For this woman to own that she had anything valuable ... of having something good inside her ... that counteracts feelings of envy, but I think if there's a narcissistic wound that's being defended against, then it's very hard to think you've got anything at all. And when everything externally is reinforcing that, then it's really hard to challenge that and find a place where you can take responsibility for what you haven't got. If you feel resentful, not having had it for external reasons, then to take responsibility for your own deprivation in order to do something about it, whether internally or externally.... If you take responsibility ... are you letting people you do blame off the hook? ... But are you going to remain in this victimised place where you can't take any responsibility because you are a victim? And it was very complicated with this woman because she was a fighter ... she was doing extraordinarily well but at enormous cost, it was just unbelievable, and for her to do that in a different way, from a place of confidence rather than defensiveness, was just extraordinarily difficult.... The shame she felt about revealing her vulnerability ... she had to be so defended against any emotional vulnerability.*'

This passage suggests how F trod the ethical and therapeutic tightrope of addressing stuck and self-sabotaging anger that had a formative basis in stark inequalities. It brings out the immense psychic, as well as other forms of, labour that someone from a working-class background of economic deprivation and also subject to racism has to undertake to exist and succeed without unsustainable conflict in a middle-class environment.

F had been seen by this patient as middle class within the transference, which she had found difficult: '*It touches on my prejudices about "them".*' Because she was quite confident she was not middle class, she could take up this powerful transference: '*and be the middle-class illusion*'.

Other therapists felt they used their own class experiences to understand their working-class patients, although all were aware of the dangers of over-identification. C commented that some working-class patients may be ashamed of feelings of inferiority in a supposedly egalitarian society. He described his sense of identification with how his patient's background *'tended to be glossed over, a romantic notion of it being presented at first'*. He continued: *'I felt angry on his behalf, the way he had been intimidated by people of a different class, and sometimes made to feel ashamed of his background, his shame was very buried. . . . I identified with that a lot, not having a voice and finding it.'*

This was echoed by E who described how, with a patient from a different working-class background from her, nonetheless she felt that she could understand something about the *'poverty and basic things about class, how to speak in a public arena . . . I think my class background has enabled me to make links with her, I'm not saying a middle-class therapist wouldn't have been able to . . . It wasn't an easy fit, more I had a kind of trajectory or understanding of where she might be able to get to. . . . I had to wait for her to find her voice.'* E had earlier emphasised her own feeling of not being entitled to speak or have a voice, part of the low self-esteem she felt was connected to class.

H described a working-class patient from an extremely deprived background who felt huge shame and humiliation about her childhood. H could identify with *'wanting to hold your own in a world where everyone appears to be more privileged than you, that sense of shame'*. Whitman-Raymond (2009) describes using her identification with a working-class patient over a matter of hygiene that was felt as deeply shameful, and the consequent enriching of the clinical work. In my own clinical work, I learned how resistant class-related shame can be, in extensively stalling or making exceedingly painful the exploration of adverse childhood circumstances. The imperative earlier in life to hide family circumstances and dynamics felt as hugely shameful, and the precariousness of such a defence, means that subsequent exploration in therapy can be feared as unsurvivable exposure, to both the assumed gaze of the other (the therapist) and to buried, often unverbalisable and overwhelming emotions. Holmes is one of the few analysts (see Chapter 8) to address the traumatic aspects of class. In the final chapter, I explore the centrality of shame to class experience.

A however described disidentification and lack of empathy, at times amounting to hostility, towards a patient he saw as *'lumpen proletariat'*. She was, he said, always complaining and blaming everyone for her circumstances. He became quite confrontational which he said was not successful. He related this to how: *'I used to have a phobia of the really poor, of slipping* back into the id, my family has always worked, clawing themselves out of the grime and poverty of the East End.' A had ironically described himself as a poacher turned gamekeeper, suggesting the need of those who feel only precariously different from the (despised) underclasses to radically distinguish themselves. A did not feel any fear of giving offence but rather enacted some class-based contempt.

The implicitly middle-class culture and frameworks of psychoanalytic therapy were cited by H as causing difficulties for work with some working-class patients, as did the writers about psychotherapeutic work in poor urban communities (see Chapter 4). She raised the question of impulsiveness within a class context, something Reich in his work in the free clinics had observed. H thought that delaying gratification was an attribute engendered by middle-class upbringing, the belief *'that if you work hard you will get rewards later . . . it must be quite hard to have that if you really don't think there'll be any rewards later . . . so if something good comes your way you grab it now'*. She saw this as reflecting the very different employment options for working- and middle-class people. I asked her about the clinical implications of this. H said: '*I was aware I had to prove myself to them from the very first meeting, which probably meant I was working in a less analytic way, more like counselling, more immediate. . . . I would talk more . . . it was very important to establish the empathy because I would feel they wouldn't expect me to understand and therefore I had to work much harder in showing them I could understand. . . . It was absolutely crucial I could get that across quite early on . . . it's obviously important with all patients, but I was more aware of it.*' Such flexibility in approach has been argued for by many other writers on psychoanalytic work in poor communities.

These therapists' capacities to work with class issues were not only matters of identification, understanding and empathy. Rather, they mostly appeared able to take up and work with stuck positions of victimhood and blame, and the accompanying entrenched powerlessness. Such ability came not from any wishful denial of social reality but rather the reverse, a huge understanding of what that could mean and also a commitment to what therapy could do. Their understandings of poverty and class, while born of their own experiences, is something that could be available to other therapists, from the sociological, psychosocial and autobiographical literature, should they so wish (see Chapter 5). The skilfulness of these therapists is also testimony to the psychic work that they themselves had done in their own upwardly mobile paths, addressing the impacts and insidious internalisations of class that affected them, to reach the thoughtful positions they were able to articulate and use.

Middle-class therapists with middle-class patients

Unsurprisingly the class issues in these dyads were less salient. The economic, social and cultural resources that make psychoanalysis accessible and attractive mean that assumptions of shared class status, values or lifestyles may go unquestioned. N described a strong sense of identification and engagement with a patient with similar social circumstances. While aware of the dangers of over-identification, she also acknowledged her relief to be working with someone from a similar background, having previously described the difficulties she had felt with a patient from a working-class background: '*I feel a good therapist with her at a superficial level . . . it's much less demanding superficially than working with someone from another class background . . . (it's) an enormous trap, collusion in the symbiotic sense.*' She also felt money and fees were easier to address. M also mentioned that with a middle-class patient he had a sense of ease relating to her educational and social background: '*It doesn't get in the way.*' However he emphasised how relatively unimportant this was compared to the psychotic aspects of her disturbance.

In some instances downward mobility was also encountered. P said he was aware of patients who attacked their privilege and wealth, sometimes self-destructively. He described a patient, unable to sustain his very successful career, who was very ashamed of his upper middle-class background. He had had a breakdown, during which time '*he was wandering around with a suitcase and two cardboard boxes*' wanting to shed all his social attributes and identifying strongly with the dispossessed. P described how the patient's acute sense of shame was located in early experiences of his poorer peers being barred from his family's exclusive enclosed property, and from forming friendships with him. This created an enormous sense of betrayal that he felt he had to make up for, and a strong but troubled identification with the excluded. P, at times, felt the temptations of the demand from this patient to label his upper middle-class privileges as utterly wrong. The patient saw P's education and training as having enabled P to think, whereas his had only been to produce, a comment perhaps of the drive of the privileged to reproduce their class status through their children. The patient eventually found a viable compromise for himself, in work that used his professional skills in ways he found morally acceptable and not too demanding.

K described a patient who pursued fame and celebrity status, but with feelings of inauthenticity: '*He's got enormous social confidence, and it makes him utterly miserable how good he is at it, because he feels it is just a complete sham.*' K acknowledged her own feelings of fascination and envy. The issue of therapist fascination with rich or famous patients, which N reported she experienced with her own analysts, also occurs in writings about money and psychoanalysis (see Chapter 9). It reflects the social power imbued in elite status, that can be unreflectingly enacted by therapists of lesser means, for example in feeling important or gratified by having a rich patient, as Altman, in the next chapter, describes. Or it can create no-go areas as N's experiences illustrate, and Bodnar (earlier) describes.

The thoughts of these therapists and also those writers cited indicate the many kinds of concerns that surface when class within clinical work becomes an explicit topic of discussion. Their testimonies suggest that class issues may be especially salient or cause most unease where there are differences between patient and therapist (as apprehended or imputed); nonetheless they can and do operate where there is seeming similarity. This is an important corrective to the common trope that it is only where there are differences that social and cultural issues need to be thought about. Similarities of middle-class status may obscure class issues, reflecting the cultural hegemony of middle-class mores within the profession and also the unconsciousness with which privilege may be lived or enacted.

The transference–countertransference issues often bore a strong relationship to the class background of the therapist, in combination with the (putative) class of the patient. They bring out what is often kept hidden or felt to be unacceptable in relation to the class other, especially the judgements, fantasies and projections of inferiority and superiority that are embedded in the psychic living of class. That the influence of biographical factors was so salient raises important questions in a professional setting. It seems that here the influence of trainings was minimal. The previously reported absence of discussion about class on trainings or in most post-qualification contexts meant that therapists fell back on their own experiences, formulations and values in their clinical work, with varying effects. This gap in psychoanalytic education is also suggested by the references to 'reality factors', invoked as imposing limitations to the therapy with these particular working class patients. Such a notion was not used in relation to middle-class patients, nor within the working-class dyads. The implication is that 'reality' could not be thought about psychoanalytically, nor incorporated into clinical work with the patient. This in effect fences off the impact of aspects of social experiences into a no-go area. It indicates how most psychoanalytic education and discussion does not embrace contemporary writings on working psychoanalytically in poor communities, for example those cited in Chapter 4. It illustrates the wariness that Puget and Sanville (2000) argue psychoanalysis has towards social reality. Thus are understandings of inequality and class within psychoanalysis marginalised, to the potential detriment of clinical work.

One therapist, B, in asking *how* the analyst would hear class in the transference, implicitly raises the question of whether anything different is needed from ordinary analytic listening. Many of the present accounts indicate how class issues can be facilitators of transference, leading on to further productive work, if adequately taken up. In opening up the idea of transference beyond that of individuals or families to include more socially based attributes, we might ask if this widens the more usual understanding of transference, or whether it represents a more fundamental change. None of the therapists interviewed here suggested that radically new approaches or entities were needed. Laurence Spurling (2016) discusses whether incorporations of the social world into therapeutic discourse are to be seen as enlargements of the frame of the therapy, or as enactments. His review of the wider clinical literature that includes explicit references to social or political issues, often initiated by therapists, suggests, as might be expected, every possibility at play in this respect. If there were enactments involved in the work reported here, they were rather failures to adequately pursue and understand class concerns and dynamics that were being expressed, seeing them as 'too much reality', beyond the scope of the therapy. Bodnar (2004) however does see her displacement of her moral disdain about wealth into undercharging her rich patient, and also her subsequent introduction of money and class into the clinical dialogue, as enactments, albeit ultimately fruitful ones. Those interviewees who did productively integrate their understandings of class into the therapeutic dialogue did not suggest these were any kind of enactment, apart from one, A, who acknowledged that he had enacted some class hostility. Rather, their accounts suggest that ordinary analytic listening amplified by reflective sociocultural understandings, an ability to work with class in the transference, to maintain the tension between social and intra-psychic considerations without closing down either, and also a flexibility of approach, are all required.

References

Bodnar, S. (2004) 'Remember where you come from: Dissociative processes in multicultural individuals', *Psychoanalytic Dialogues* 14: 581–603.

Dimen, M. (1994) 'Money, love, and hate: Contradiction and paradox in psychoanalysis', *Psychoanalytic Dialogues* 4: 69–100.

Hoggett, P., Wilkinson, H. and Beedell, P. (2013) 'Fairness and the politics of resentment', *Journal of Social Policy* 42: 1–19.

Puget, J. (1991) 'The social context: Searching for an hypothesis', *Free Associations* 2: 21–33.

Puget, J. and Sanville, J. (2000) 'Social reality', *International Journal of Psycho-Analysis* 81: 998–1000.

Ryan, J. (2006/2013) '"Class is in you": An exploration of some social class issues in psychotherapeutic work', *British Journal of Psychotherapy* 23: 49–63. Reprinted in F. Lowe (ed), *Thinking Space: Promoting Thinking about Race, Culture and Diversity in Psychotherapy and Beyond*. London: Karnac.

Sennett, R. (2003) *Respect*. London: Allen Lane.

Spurling, L. (2016) 'Transference and the psychosocial'. Unpublished paper presented to the Psychoanalysis Working Group, Birkbeck, University of London.

Whitman-Raymond, L. (2009) 'The influence of class in the therapeutic dyad', *Contemporary Psychoanalysis* 45: 429–43.

8
CONTEMPORARY PSYCHOANALYTIC WRITINGS ON CLASS IN THE CLINIC

The last chapter showed how class can become activated in conscious and unconscious ways in the intensity of therapeutic encounters. This chapter addresses the clinical writings of contemporary psychoanalytic psychotherapists where class explicitly features; my explorations of the literature found many more sources than I had expected. Ricardo Ainslie, in his considerations of class and immigration, remarks on how class and other social configurations are often harder to address in therapy than familial and parental ones (Ainslie, 2009, 2011), underlining the importance of exploring the clinical work that does do this. Here I gather together these scattered clinical writings involving class, something not done before, to identify the approaches taken by different psychoanalytic writers. The focus is on the substantive contents of the clinical material and also on how different authors perceive and theorise class as having its effects. Such attention to how any one writer brings the social more into their clinical work shows the many challenges of doing this.

Relational psychoanalysis represents the most developed recent clinical thinking about class, with several writers claiming they are breaking new ground theoretically and clinically. Different writers within this school of thought vary considerably in how they mark out a psychoanalytic space for the social world. Here I consider the reflection/projection model put forward by Altman and then address Layton's elaboration of this, with her concept of normative unconscious processes and critique of unlinking. Such relational work, portraying classed identities as constituted via processes of splitting, disavowal and projection and based on difference, has been very fertile in addressing the dynamics of clinical work, but it has limitations that I outline. Stephen Hartman introduces a valuable perspective on class as transmitted through parental work and bodies, proposing a 'class unconscious'. He also extends the relational schema by using Laplanchian ideas, which I argue have much to contribute to a reorientation of psychoanalysis towards a greater incorporation of the social world. Other authors rely more on existing theory, as in Ruth Fallenbaum's powerful account of the traumatic effects of exploitation and damage at work. Dorothy Holmes also sees class as a source of trauma and makes use of the Freudian super-ego. In many of these writings class intersects with 'race', gender and sexuality and such multiple identifications and configurations are illustrated by other authors.

Altman: a reflection/projection model

Altman's title, *The Analyst in the Inner City* (Altman, 1995/2010), underlines the relatively unusual recognition of psychoanalytic work in such contexts, and his book has become a much cited and taught work on class and 'race' in the clinic. Some of the factors specific to work in such public spheres were addressed in Chapter 4. Here the concern is more with the clinical material and theorising emerging from Altman's work, in which he advocates two- and three-person models. Throughout, Altman, like most relational authors, makes extensive use of his own responses and feelings to understand the dynamics of the relationships between himself and his patients. How a patient's concerns are read off from the analyst's subjectivity and self-awareness is an important point of debate in case material of this kind.

Altman begins his chapter on class with a vignette about his encounter in private practice with a well-off man from a prominent family whose care as a child was delegated to servants, a familiar upper-class scenario, as we have seen (Chapter 3). Altman highlights his sudden heightened awareness of his humble office, its simple furnishings and his own somewhat shabby appearance, illustrating the visceral, instant and embodied ways in which class operates. He felt gratified at having a 'high status' patient, something writers on the role of money also observe (see Chapter 9), and realised he was envying the patient, and denigrating himself. Altman observed how, unusually, he initially felt no empathy for the patient's experiences of emotional neglect. The patient's wish to delegate paying the fees to an accountant left Altman feeling disregarded, as he then surmised the patient had felt neglected by his parents. This is an example of the use of a mirroring response to infer the feelings of the other; only subsequent clinical work can indicate whether this is a correct or useful insight, or whether it says more about the analyst than the patient. Altman however argues that when he was the one with relative status and money, with inner-city patients 'the hierarchy' was reversed.

Altman, in his main example of Ms B from a working-class family who dropped out of her prestigious university, describes many issues familiar from writings on social mobility (see Chapter 6 especially), although he does not reference these. Subsequently Ms B quit her 'good' job and went onto welfare. Altman writes of her 'powerfully self-defeating tendencies, based on her conflict about succeeding in life, which would mean surpassing her parents and the rest of her family' (1995/2010: 84), and of 'her tremendous destructiveness in such an undermining of self, as well as our work together' (Altman, 1995/2010: 85). As the work continued, he realised how succeeding professionally made Ms B feel isolated and that she felt she couldn't connect with him or her family unless she was 'down and out'. This perception modified his previous attribution of self-destructiveness, a realisation that is often overlooked in clinical work where class transitions are at issue. He became aware of his own inclinations to focus on her vulnerabilities, as this confirmed in him a sense of being useful – also a recognisable therapist problematic. Altman also acknowledges how he had previously felt gratified by Ms B's socioeconomic success, an indication of the traps involved in equating therapeutic success with upward class mobility, something Layton (2014a) names as therapeutic collusion with neo-liberal values. Such collusion risks minimising or disregarding the losses and conflicts upward mobility may give rise to and inappropriately interpreting seeming self-sabotage as inner destructiveness rather than a relational issue.

Altman argues that what he calls a one-person psychology, or drive theory approach, cannot adequately address class since, in his view, this is an inherently relational phenomenon. Rather, he maintains, such approaches wrongly reduce conflicts that derive from the social world to intra-psychic or familial dynamics. Instead he proposes two- and three-person models. There is undoubted truth in the accusation of psychic reductionism in some psychoanalysis, especially as regards the way social envy is seen. Carolyn Steedman, in her now classic autobiographical interrogation of class and psychoanalysis, *Landscape for a Good Woman*, sees Freud's account in 'Family romances' as 'the most extraordinary and transparent political paternalism' (Steedman, 1986: 12). There Freud describes how when a child apprehends the social category to which his or her parents belong, envy leads to replacing them in daydreams with parents of 'higher social standing' (Freud, 1909).

Freud interprets these fantasies as concealing erotic aims and Oedipal wishes, not also as social envy or desire for a better quality of life. However, Altman's statements are unduly caricaturing of what he calls drive theory. They also invalidate the ways in which earlier left Freudians addressed class issues, as we have seen, with complex understandings of the intertwining of the intra-psychic and the social. Holmes strongly criticises Altman for what she considers his 'ill-informed' approach, for abandoning all aspects of classical theory, and for championing the needs of the poor by valorising one approach and 'vilifying' others (Holmes, 1997).

There is though much to agree with in aspects of Altman's model, in which the actual social status of patient and therapist, their relationships to the social context in which their work takes place, and the various perceptions, projections, identifications and desires at play between them are all seen as part of the therapeutic relationship. Chapter 7 illustrated the possibilities for many kinds of projective processes, for identifications and disidentifications, between patient and therapist in the terrain of class, and the utility of being able to address and deconstruct these. Bodnar also suggests there is 'a broad continuum of dissociative processes where self meets culture' and that to decontextualise individual personality from cultural reality is to compromise analytic work (Bodnar, 2004: 581). However, the ways in which Altman theorises the relationship of the social and the psychic is more problematic. He proposes an essentially reflective relationship: 'What exists on the social level *cannot but find reflection* in the individual psyche, and vice versa' (Altman, 1995/2010: 89, my italics). Social structure, the structure of a public clinic, what takes place within therapeutic dyads in such a clinic and within individuals, all are assumed to reflect one another – another form of reductionism. The problem here is with the inevitability and simplicity that Altman attributes to such correspondence, not with the possibility that this can sometimes or often happen. Assumptions of parallel and mirroring processes are rife in the therapeutic world; while often having considerable interpretive power, they can also be dangerously misused. Too much similarity can be assumed, and this can block further exploration, deny complexity and difference, and leave no room for non-conformity.

Furthermore, this leads to a too-mechanistic parallelism in which interpersonal projective processes are seen as each party disowning and projecting something that 'really' belongs to the self. Altman describes how Ms B's low social class position contributed to him seeing her as 'helpless and needy', which he says made him less aware of such unwanted qualities and feelings in himself, confirming him in his competence. Ms B became the needy one, wanting caring and nurturance: 'What we each disowned in ourselves, the flip-side of our conscious self-images, reappeared in the transference in the sense that Ms B felt she was taking care of me by being helpless. . . . Our roles were reversed' (Altman, 1995/2010: 92).

While in many cases such a process is recognisable, this model does not allow for the possibility that someone might perceive or misperceive a socially disadvantaged person as helpless and needy, without this being a disowning or disavowal of those very same qualities in themselves. It might be a result of identification, prejudice or misinformation, or indeed be accurate. Many writers, including Bourdieu, have described working-class circumstances as rendering people closer to necessity, as having fewer choices and options. In Altman's case, there is a failure to distinguish between perception (of possible social realities) and projection, in a model in which all perceptions are only constructions of the perceiver's mind, and therefore projections. The paradox here is that Altman, with the best of intentions, is trying not to make strange or to other people less well off than himself, to understand their experiences as part of a common humanity; but, in doing so, he risks misrecognising and obliterating important specificities by his conviction of an inevitable intra-psychic correspondence between patient and therapist. The dynamics of similarity and difference are at play here and, as with all important social divisions between people, both have to be kept in productive tension, rather than resorting to a dichotomised position.

While we may appreciate his honesty, Altman's somewhat repetitious statement of his own privilege and guilt, a more than recognisable trope, has the effect of distancing the disadvantaged clientele. Adrienne Harris (2009) has drawn an important distinction between guilt and guiltiness in sociopolitical matters; the latter involves a form of anxiety, a defensive shame-laden stance, lacking possibilities for 'mature remorse' or effective reparation. This she regards as an unstable basis for either theory or politics.

A further theoretical problem is Altman's reliance on a model whereby the powerfulness and unconscious nature of what may transpire between two people of differing social class is mistaken for the entirety of class itself. Thus: 'projective-introjective processes, when deployed rigidly and defensively, form the basis of classism, not valid understanding across class lines' (Altman, 1995/2010: 93). Although clearly aware of the actual material and economic circumstances of his inner-city clientele, his model, by focusing only on the dynamic interpersonal, runs the risk of collapsing class into psychological processes, despite all Altman's intentions otherwise. His model fails to adequately include the force of extensive material privileges and disadvantages inherent in a class system, whereby, however concerned a well-off person may be to 'understand' and respect the less well-off other, this does not mean that they would cede their power, wealth or status, become less class-defined, nor that substantial class differences would not still operate. It might, though, make for some better cross-class relationships, although that cannot be assumed.

This problem derives from his assumption that: 'In a sense, racism, classism, and ethnocentrism (as well as sexism and homophobia) have a common deep structure. . . . On one level these categories are interchangeable, simply different surface manifestations of the process whereby a denigrated or simply disowned "other" is created, even as "race", social class and culture each have their own histories and contexts, defining characteristics, and dynamics' (Altman, 1995/2010: 81).

Altman's unification of the psychological processes involved in all these phenomena collapses all questions of history, difference, inequality and injustice into common psychological processes. These processes, especially the misrecognition involved in hostile projections, are indeed very important components of many social and interpersonal situations, which psychoanalysis is well placed to address. However, what sets them in play historically and socially, structures them and maintains them, may be very different in each specific case. For example, the bases of the hostilities involved in homophobia are not necessarily the same as those involved in racism, even if both can involve similar processes of disavowal and projection. The social histories, determinants and felt threats are different, and the various hostilities can involve distinct psychological processes as Elisabeth Young-Bruehl's (1998) psychoanalytic study of prejudices suggests.

There are two problems here – one is the elevation of *categories* of social class to become social class itself, encompassing all its manifestations. The second is that, whereas of course social class categories and people's perceptions of these do come to serve psychic functions, this is not therefore the source of their existence, nor the sum total of how class has its effects. Social divisions in society are created and driven largely by economic and political forces, although they are lived, sustained, and shaped by how they come to serve psychic functions as well, and by how they cause psychic distress. It may be that much relational psychoanalysis is influenced by American functional sociology. The nearest Altman comes to explicit use of social theory is in his statement: 'Social class categories, then, are constructed on a social level, serving social functions. They are also constructed on a personal psychological level to serve psychic functions' (Altman, 1995/2010: 91).

This maintains an absolute distinction between what is social and what is psychological, rather than the imbrication and interrelatedness that other writers have argued for.

Layton: distinction and normative unconscious processes

Layton's extensive writings on class avoid some of these problems, partly because from the outset she incorporates other aspects of psychosocial, sociological and political thought into her clinical thinking. She situates what she observes in the clinic within her understanding of neo-liberal ideologies and practices. Such interdisciplinarity is essential for a more productive engagement between class and psychoanalysis, and it is instructive to consider the use Layton makes of social theory as well as her understanding of how class is manifested and reproduced in the clinic. Layton has been foremost in demonstrating and critiquing 'unlinking', the 'unconscious pull' to divorce individuals from their social context, which she regards as a dominant norm (Layton, 2006a). To even speak of these terms as separate is, she suggests, a distortion, except in as far as this reflects the 'truth' of society's dominant culture, appearing to us as obvious or common sense, an argument similar to Adorno's (1967). Her use of unlinking, with its reference to Bion's ideas on the fragmentation of thought and emotion that follows from failures and denials of linking, is important in underlining how widely and fundamentally this common divorce operates. It also implies how seeing the social world as only an overlay to the intra-psychic world, as superficial compared to the latter, is not only mistaken, but derives from an untheorised position, in which it becomes psychoanalytic 'common sense'.

However, Layton suggests that those in subordinate cultures are less likely to 'buy into the unlinking norm', being especially and painfully aware of the links between social forces and their individual struggles. This echoes Fanon's statement to the effect that since the racial drama is played out in the open 'the black man' has no time to make it unconscious, something Gurney (2009) applies to 'class drama'. Such perceptions of the links between social and personal struggles can form the basis of resistance and political activity, but they also can coexist with or be replaced by symptoms of many kinds, and convictions of individual responsibility and self-blame, where the link with the social world becomes lost or repressed. Layton's suggestion of 'normative unconscious processes' captures this well: 'Because cultural hierarchies split and categorize human attributes and capacities, subjectivity is marked by unceasing conflict between those unconscious processes that seek to maintain the splits and those that refuse them. I call the ones that seek to maintain the splits "normative unconscious processes"' (Layton, 2008: 67).

Layton (2006b) cites Bourdieu as arguing that many of the processes and markers of class distinction take place below the level of consciousness and language, although she also criticises him for not being attentive enough to emotion, for presupposing only a narcissistic subject and leaving no place for the possibility of caring about different others. She highlights the passages in Bourdieu's work where he describes the ways in which social relations are objectified in things and in people, and 'impress' themselves through often unconscious bodily experiences. These objects, practices and tastes become markers of class distinction. Such unconscious internalisation can lead to the instant, automatic and visceral perception of class difference or similarity that commonly occurs.

Layton argues that the child's relational world is the basis for an always conflictual internalisation of class, and the grounds for haunting anxiety. She links this to her theory of the normative unconscious: '. . . that part of the unconscious that is produced by social hierarchies of various kinds and that, in turn, works to reproduce and secure a hierarchical *status quo*' (Layton, 2006b: 53). This is a more complex version of the reflective model in which social divisions are seen as reproduced in the unconscious, producing internal conflict.

Layton, similarly to Altman, claims: '. . . class identities are formed via a defensive splitting off of parts of self too closely associated with anything felt to characterize other, especially lower- but also upper-class fractions' (Layton, 2006b: 53). In a later work, she uses a vignette to illustrate the role of fantasy, defences, unconscious collusions and resistances against social norms, which she claims show ways in which children '. . . struggle their way into and negotiate class positions that are simultaneously gendered, raced and sexed' (Layton, 2014b: 5). Here, the attainment of classed identity is seen entirely in terms of the parts of the self that are repudiated and projected. Thus, the child '(O)nly becomes a white, middle-class girl by racializing parts of herself as black and lower class. Ambivalently attached to these repudiated and projected parts of self, she demands that the "Other" live out his or her assigned role. Indeed, when those parts are too anxiety provoking to be owned and integrated, they appear not as intrapsychic conflict but rather as interpersonal conflict that is played out in relationships – over and over and over' (Layton, 2014b: 6).

There is a resonance here with some of the class-related projections in the interview material of Chapters 6 and 7, and also with the psychosocial work, such as Reay's, which shows how class fears and hostilities may become expressed in terms of assumed characteristics of others, repudiated by the self. What is underplayed here is the part that class similarity, identification with the white middle-class parents and peer group, the materiality and experiences of class privilege, may all play in the intergenerational formation of such a classed identity. What is also questionable is whether they are built only on difference and not on similarity. Much of the psychosocial work shows how identities are based on particular conditions of life and ways of living, as well as perceptions of different others. Such perceptions can reflect different material realities and cannot always be characterised as repudiation and rejection, even though anxieties of various kinds may involve this, defaulting to an 'us' and 'them' dynamic. Nor can the totality of class be captured by the notion of identities.

However, what Layton does provide is a rich phenomenology of anxieties concerning class, as well as a framing of these within an understanding of contemporary neo-liberal demands and pressures. This is especially important in bringing class into the psychoanalytic frame. She explores the uncharted emotional and psychodynamic dimensions of Bourdieu's work via evocative anecdotes of the feelings and anxieties aroused by shopping, a prime point of class distinction, in stores of very different economic and class status (Layton, 2006b). This leads Layton to make several suggestions about how she sees emotions 'sustaining' class identifications and distinctions, and how what is repudiated can return in states of anxiety and phobias, especially in unfamiliar classed locations.

Her first observation is the disgust and discomfort felt by an upper middle-class[1] friend in a lower-class store, and her own shame and anxiety in an upper-class one, her fear of committing some social gaffe, her sense of not belonging. Layton notes how she can defensively render this as moral disdain (like Bodnar, 2004) hiding any envy she might feel for the upper class's access to goods she does consider better. She argues that the anxieties that make her stick to cheaper stores '. . . legitimize(s) the upper-class's right to have more, to have better, and to dominate' (Layton, 2006b: 54). Here we can see the role of anxiety in reinforcing and perpetuating class inequality. Whereas the shame and anxiety she feels is conscious, what structures the unconscious is 'the taboo on having a proprietary relation to culture and knowledge' (Layton, 2006b: 54), ceding that entitlement to the better-off. She illustrates this by Bourdieu's statement that 'objective' limits become 'a sense of limits'. Disempowerment and lack of entitlement can come to seem fitting or natural; to want more, forbidden, dangerous or pointless, as in the often-reported injunctions in first-person accounts of working-class childhoods to 'know your place' or 'don't get above yourself'. A 'propriety relation to knowledge and culture' can also be embedded in enactments of class privilege that presume the superiority or universality of particular cultural forms.

An informal survey allows Layton to explore further how emotions sustain class identifications and differentiations. In particular, she identifies upper-class abhorrence of poor, working-class shops and goods as involving a fear of contagion, of being too close to need and dependence. In this way distinction is sustained by a fear of falling into a state of necessity, a familiar middle-class trope, amply illustrated in some of the research cited in Chapter 5. The identification of working-class status with unwanted need, dependence and vulnerability is a theme running through much of Layton's work, and she subsequently relates this to how prevailing neo-liberal economic and social agendas demonise interdependence and promote the notion of self-sufficient entrepreneurial individuals (Layton, 2014a). Here she proposes that upper-class status is 'attained and maintained' by disdaining what is connected to the lower classes, thus implying that emotions and behaviour create class status. Here again the relational position is in danger of substituting the emotional and the psychological for the whole of class, which is not to invalidate Layton's depiction of how dynamic emotional processes are involved in living, sustaining, and reinforcing classed identities. Rather it is to point out the necessity for an approach that can incorporate and move between all the aspects of class.

Layton also notes the sadness and concern felt by some upper-class subjects in her survey at the poor quality of goods, the noises, smells, and crowdedness in lower-class stores. Bourdieu argues that such pity is just another guise of how distinction operates – allowing the dominant classes to impose their values on the lower classes, to create distance from necessity, without any recognition of how this is not objective. Layton, however, argues that such concern opens up a political space for alliance and struggle.

Layton's account of how class inequalities can be reproduced in the clinic, and the ways clinicians may unconsciously collude with these, is, as previous chapters showed, a central part of understanding class in relation to psychoanalysis (Layton, 2014a). These reproductions she sees as enactments of normative unconscious processes. She frames her accounts in terms of how current neo-liberal pressures may promote specific kinds of enactments and performances of class distinction. She describes how the desire for, and the conflicts of, social mobility were experienced by two different patients, with varying degrees of disdain and ambivalence.

Layton's first case concerns a woman who rose socially from her working-class/blue-collar background by working very hard to become a highly paid professional. In love with a man from a working-class background, she repeatedly filled the sessions with mocking contempt for his supposedly working-class ways, with which he himself appeared comfortable. Layton, struggling with her own difficulty in bearing the patient's class contempt, pointed out to her how much she seemed to need to have close to her a working-class 'other' that she could denigrate. The patient's panicky reaction to this interpretation, at the recognition of her defensive use of class mockery and the fear of this defence not being any longer available, led to much productive work on what Layton named as class grandiosity. She and the patient came to understand how this related to a need to dislike and disown her own vulnerability, to disidentify from her working-class mother for whom her socially aspirant father had great disdain. Layton sees this grandiosity as a defence against the patient realising how much her sought-after father's love was contingent on her achievements and upward mobility, contributing to a fragile, insecure sense of specialness. Layton understands this as the patient's defending herself against falling back into the lower classes as represented by her mother, disavowing her love for her mother, longing for her father's love, identifying with his disparagement, and retaliating against her mother's difficulty in giving love to her upwardly mobile daughter.

This example illustrates well the inevitable entanglement of class matters with the particular dynamic formations of love and desire in any one family, something Holmes from a different theoretical position also depicts (see p. 151). As Layton describes it, the conditional class-inflected nature of the father's love led to great cynicism about love and to sadomasochistic ways of relating, in which dependency and need were denied. Layton sums this up as the patient having 'become the kind of non-relational maximizer of self-opportunity described as exemplary in neoliberal literature' (Layton, 2014a: 11).

Layton's second example is a man from a working-class family, with a history of previous trade union activism, who was the recipient of somewhat conflictual parental wishes that he rise in class. Although professionally successful, this very success involved great ambivalence and, it transpired, rage, so that he repeatedly got fired from jobs. He loved his work, but his rage at his parents who were felt as unloving and tyrannical, as well as at other authoritarian figures, led to continual self-sabotage. He was much occupied by many protests against abuses of authority, and also by what he saw as the underdog world of patients in the face of analytic authority. Becoming middle class represented to him a loss of integrity. Layton remarks how at times she fell into the trap of unduly pathologising his repeated protests against injustice, unconsciously enacting her own class arrogance, 'the defensively grandiose aspects of my analytic stance' (Layton, 2014a: 14). This is another way in which class gets reproduced in the transference–countertransference matrix.

Both these examples are characterised by parental demands for upward mobility, and it is the contingency of their love that Layton sees as the intergenerationally transmitted wounds of being lower class. The consequences are 'split states of grandiosity/pride and self-hatred/shame', mediated by the specifics of libidinal investments. All these can determine how class is negotiated, whether with conformity, pride, challenge, shame, ambivalence, resignation or rage. Layton's first patient identified with upper-class authority and denigrated those lower, the second alternated between deference, rage and panic. Current neo-liberal ideologies and pressures may create such parental demands in which love becomes contingent on social success, one of the pernicious effects of class.

Much contemporary writing suggests that the children of first-generation immigrants may also find themselves trying to fulfil parental wishes for upward mobility, leaving little recognition of their own desires, with the resulting internal and external conflicts. However, there are many families who, while desirous of social advancement, do not make their love so drastically contingent on it. Further, in other instances the upward social mobility of the child may be primarily brought about through his or her own desires and talents, nurtured outside the family, rather than through parental pressure, as in Hanley's (2016) account. This can engender aspirations that conflict with the family subculture, or the family may be supportive, but because of the huge distance between social classes, painful losses and separations are still experienced, as Chapter 6 has illustrated.

I am familiar from my own clinical practice with how the virulence of the UK educational class system,[2] combined with the child's own talents and interests, can lead to often traumatic experiences of estrangement from the family of origin. In several instances this resulted in considerable fragility and instability, whereby present-day achievements are repeatedly undermined by unconscious self-sabotage, initially hard to recognise as such. This can be accompanied by a confused sense of longing for aspects of the family that is also disdained or that feels too distant, guilt and loss at not remaining close by, combined with hostile ambivalence or lack of confidence towards present-day professional success or values. Thus are social divisions lived out in symptoms that may bring people to therapy. Hanley provides a first-person account of achieving a positive accommodation with this, where she can enjoy her hard-won middle-class position and way of life without losing her accent or her connection to her family (Hanley, 2016).

In Altman's and Layton's examples there is very little space, either internally or externally, for a positive sense of being working class. This is portrayed through the perceptions of Layton's survey and clinical subjects as evidence only of personal failure, weakness and need, to be disdained, pitied and avoided. Whereas there may be much clinical purchase to be had from understanding of middle- and upper-class contempt for the working classes as based on horror of need and dependency, there is a problem with making what are the perceptions, emotions and defences of these class fractions into a theory of class itself, or as an accurate portrayal of being working class now. What we do not hear enough of are the voices of anyone currently working class, or of anyone for whom this is a source of positive identity, self-respect and integrity – something harder to achieve now than ever, perhaps. This is a general shortcoming in the psychoanalytic and psychodynamic literature. Nor do we hear much of strategies of resistance to prevailing ideologies of upward mobility, or of different kinds of accommodations to these.

Work, injury and the 'class unconscious'

Hartman's boldly entitled article 'Class unconscious: from dialectical materialism to relational material' (Hartman, 2007) is unusual and thought-provoking in bringing work into psychoanalytic discourse as part of how class is known about and embodied. His article is distinguished by the range of theoretical frameworks he invokes to illuminate the relationship of class and psychoanalysis which incorporate and go beyond relational psychoanalysis.

Hartman notes, quite appositely, that within psychoanalysis contemporary usage of 'class' tends to be descriptive for lack of theoretical development. Class background is sometimes mentioned as part of an initial description, but its engagement with dynamic matters is seldom included. Hartman is concerned 'to give material relations a place of primacy in the unconscious and in the development of our sense of self and other' (2007: 210). In order to explore how the material world 'engages' the psychic world, he proposes a 'third place' which he names the class unconscious. This is the 'unformulated experience of class in unconscious territory' (2007: 210), a promising depiction, even if the postulation of a new unconscious entity is more problematic. What he calls the 'class third' is a material Other: a set of 'bodily material practices that are only known to us . . . through work' (2007: 211) which 'interpellates' the worker according to its own logic.

Hartman further proposes that 'a child receives early knowledge about class through an unconscious communication from his parents about work'

(2007: 211). For the child, such messages may be enigmatic and undecipherable, received as uncontested facts of life that cannot be reflected upon, so that much of class experience remains unavailable to consciousness. In its reified state, he says, the class unconscious cannot be mentalised as a third point of view, otherwise we would be more conscious of the conditions of work and its history.³

Hartman's estrangement from his working-class father frames his article: 'Ours is a struggle that bears the strains and injuries of class' (Hartman, 2007: 209). He discovered the power of his class unconscious 'by accident', realising that he had come to an unsatisfactory arrangement with an upper-class, well-off patient. This left him anxiously waiting by the phone in the early mornings, waiting to hear whether the busy patient would be available for a session, before he could leave for his office. Hartman made a link between the dread he felt waiting for his patient's call, and memories of his father, a roofer, who would pace around in the dark winter mornings, waiting for the phone to ring to hear whether he had any work that day, a scene charged with anxiety and resentment. Knowledge of class was formed as his anxious, beaten-down father, unable to be both parent and worker, waited for the union dispatcher's call, which mostly did not come. Hartman conveys his sense of his father's aching body, injured and scarred from industrial accidents. He was, he says, interpellated by the scars on his father's arms – a useful way of describing the impress not just of his father's wounds but also of the whole history of class domination and exploitation that led up to this.⁴

Hartman argues that for his upper-class white patient implicit awareness of class and 'race' accrued when his mother placed the fretful baby in the black nanny's hands. This is an important recognition of work in a domestic setting, and of how the bodily communication of class can be conceived of as starting from the earliest moments within a structure of delegated class- and 'race'-inflected childcare, as I also argued in Chapter 3.

Hartman's second clinical example concerns a man whose father was a factory foreman, and for whom his parents' love was compromised by their hard and unrelenting work. They provided food and shelter, but couldn't show affection with their bodies. Nor could they show any recognition or appreciation of their son's sensitivities, aspirations and achievements, a lack that upward mobility can bring. No expression of weakness was tolerated by a father for whom work could signify something deadly. His parents enjoined him to 'know his place', as he imagines his present-day clients would, were he to charge more for his highly skilled, much sought-after work, rather than living close to financial collapse. Hartman elaborates on how this man's desire for recognition from the father, whose love was so compromised by work, played out in the transference, around the constraints of analytic work and love.

Hartman's article is important for his introduction of work as a force shaping the transmission of class within families, something relatively unusual in psychoanalysis. The notion that for a child there is something enigmatic, mystifying and unknowable about parental work, something experienced through his or her parents' bodies, affects and attitudes, is an interesting use of the Laplanchian idea of enigmatic signifiers. Like Hartman I suggest that Laplanchian theory, with the emphasis on the primacy of the other, has much to offer in understanding how the often unspoken world of parents' work and class experience may be bodily communicated – implanted or intromitted, to use Laplanche's terms. I take up the relevance of Laplanche further on and in Chapter 10, especially as regards how it could be the vehicle for resolving the historic split in psychoanalysis between those theories which prioritise drive and desire, and see these as determined primarily internally and intra-psychically, and those which, taking a more cultural and social perspective, dispense with drive theory and one-person psychologies, as Altman (earlier) and much relational psychoanalysis does.

Hartman however uses the notions of enigmatic signifiers and interpellation alongside an approach which does position the psyche as in some sense independent of the material world. Thus, he maintains that the material world does not *structure* the psychic world, but rather that it *engages* it (my italics). Hartman's notion of the class unconscious is where these interact and psychoanalysis, in his view, lacks but needs a theory of 'how class works on the body, on the psyche and between psyches . . . of how the State penetrates the psyche' (Hartman, 2007: 217). Here Hartman is clearly positing a psyche and a body originally outside history, outside power, not already constituted by these. However, the rest of his writing illustrates the intimate and fundamental structuring of mind and body by class, and indeed he argues convincingly against those who assume too great a degree of autonomy of mental processes from the material world. Hartman seems to prefer a theoretical position that assumes an autonomous originating psyche, in tune with the general position of much psychoanalysis, but it does sit oddly with his creative use of Laplanche and (implicitly) Althusser, an indication of the general theoretical slipperiness of this area.

The injurious nature of work and its relation to class is taken up in a different way by Ruth Fallenbaum in an account of injured workers and the Kafkaesque virulence and inequities of compensation schemes (Fallenbaum,

2003). This powerful article is, as Harris (2003) says, overwhelming at first reading, indicative of the traumatic nature of the workers' experiences, and the quality of the writing. Fallenbaum describes her psychotherapeutic work with nine federal employees whose workplace psychological and physical injuries entitled them to forms of compensation. In her emphasis on the particular conditions of employment she also supplies a material analysis. All were ethnic-minority women, in mainly manual or blue-collar clerical jobs, whose incomes were vital for the well-being of their families. The injuries they suffered included physical ones, the psychological sequelae of these, harassment, bullying and sexual abuse, leading to diagnoses of depression and PTSD. Access to therapy services took place through the US Institute of Labor and Mental Health, which was founded in 1977 to educate therapists about the realities of class, racism and power in the workplace, as well as providing individual and group therapy to workers.[5]

Fallenbaum records the workers' persistence with their jobs despite being at breaking point, their difficulties in recognising that their workplace was so destructive to their well-being and the devastating consequences of not being able to earn. The trauma of this was increased hugely by the hostile, protracted and disrespectful nature of the claims process, often amounting to re-traumatisation, something we see now with the humiliating and punitive ways in which disability and unemployment benefits are administered. Fallenbaum writes how: 'The shame, diminished self-esteem and blow to the worker's narcissism that results from being unable to function at work is thus mirrored and reinforced by the . . . bureaucracy, the examining doctors, and ultimately the workers' community' (Fallenbaum, 2003: 79).

Fallenbaum realised that much of what she was hearing clinically echoed some of the literature on trauma, the ways in which destructive external events can affect the inner world and a person's fundamental sense of safety. She depicts a situation of working-class disempowerment and vulnerability to ruthless employment practices, amounting to class trauma. Many of her patients repeatedly wondered whether what had happened to them was their fault. Fallenbaum observes how extremely painful it was for the workers to acknowledge that the people and institutions they had relied on really were malign, unfair and irrational, leading to loss of any trust in the benign functioning of society. She notes how this disillusionment destroyed belief in the predictability of the world, leaving people feeling vulnerable and powerless, which may partly explain why those in oppressive conditions so readily blame themselves. Her therapeutic approach emphasises the importance of a prolonged process of bearing witness to each worker's individual stories of ill-treatment, something often emphasised in relation to other extreme situations, as a first step in establishing and validating the reality of their perceptions. In this way enough trust in the therapeutic process and therapist could be established to work further on their grief, alienation and self-blame.

Fallenbaum's article brings into the psychoanalytic arena a range of experiences and a social context that are too often missing from most psychotherapeutic work. It brings out how both psychoanalytic and social understandings are needed to work well clinically, and it is relevant that her work emerged from a political process of establishing a Section on Social Responsibility within Division 39 of the American Psychological Association (which has psychoanalytic sections). Furthermore she poses the conundrum that faces many therapists working with people in adverse social circumstances, of whether or how to make extra-therapeutic interventions, such as advocacy on behalf of the patient, as well as preserving the frame of the therapy.

Dimen in her comments on Fallenbaum's paper, asks why it is so difficult for analysts to keep in mind the ways in which: 'Alienation *is* the psychology of class' (Dimen, 2003: 93). She relates this to the white-collar status of analysts, who are relatively more empowered than many blue-collar workers, in doing work that can provide personal enhancement and some control over their time. Yet, as she pointed out (Dimen, 1994), such autonomy is fragile, insecure and always compromised by the need to earn. Professional coyness and anxiety about status can lead to resistances to recognising possible similarities as workers in a capitalist system. This can block identification with or understanding of the plight of blue-collar workers, resulting in analytic blind spots as regards the impact of such realities. Fallenbaum's article is an important counter to this.

Class as trauma

Class is also seen as a source of trauma by Holmes, yet 'analysts shy away from comprehensive analysis of the influence of race and class' (Holmes, 2006: 232). Here, the trauma is the accumulation of early destructive experiences, and of the chronic effects of living and working in poverty and insecurity. Writing from an ego psychology perspective, she explores some of the dynamics of 'success neurosis' in relation to racism and classism. She combines a Freudian explanation of this in terms of guilt at Oedipal rivalry and Oedipal victory, with the notion of the internalisation of negative societal 'messages', where the damage to the self leads to entrenched and fundamental doubting of one's own abilities, and consequent self-sabotage. This internalisation she sees as operating pre-Oedipally, set down very early, and involving primal wishes to be loved and accepted. This is akin to Layton's 'normative unconscious', although theorised differently: 'If one is not in the right racial grouping or social class, one is extremely negatively valued, and this valuation often becomes a highly malignant, introjected reality' (Holmes, 2006: 219).[6] This she sees as like the effects of trauma in causing lasting interference with ego functions, even where ego capacities may be intact. Such early internalisation[7] can render the desire for and achieving of success as taboo and dangerous, not 'knowing your place'. Success becomes a conflictful state of affairs, often vulnerable to forms of self-destructiveness, in which one abandons a beloved primary object. Holmes' use of introjection is valuable in underlining the deep and harmful psychic effects of social forces, creating an inner state of unprocessable harm and suggesting how aspects of class can remain unsymbolised, as Hartman also does.

Holmes uses the Freudian super-ego, whereby what she calls 'societal opposing forces' are internalised (similar to Skeggs' dialogic other, see Chapter 5) to understand the ways in which people can anticipate punishment for achievements considered out of their class, as well as punish themselves. In one clinical example, that of a black professor from a very impoverished background, Holmes understands the patient's repeated dreams of dead loved family members as illustrating 'the distortions formed in the patient's super-ego relating to her lower-class standing, which was represented in her as deadening internal objects that kept her aspirations for success at bay' (2006: 224). Holmes notes how resolution of these conflicts and greater professional satisfaction were achieved both by work on libidinal issues, sibling rivalry and guilt, and also by a lessening of the severity of her internal representations of 'structured, institutional racist proscriptions against her success'.

Another clinical example concerns a white woman from an impoverished background who, while academically successful, was experiencing great difficulty in completing an advanced qualification or finding work. The patient felt she didn't have her mother's permission to be successful: '[T]o succeed is to risk being criticised and rejected by them. So I say, "Don't worry – see, I'm a failure too. No threat"' (2006: 230). The patient had a recurring memory of how she had been frequently and hurtfully ostracised at school for acting 'snooty', to which her mother's agitated rejoinder had been to assert repeatedly that they were not 'poor white trash'. This added to the complexity of her struggle between what Holmes calls a devalued and a more positive view of herself. Holmes links this struggle to the patient's self-defeating need to return to an impoverished state in order not to experience the 'disorganized grandiose excitement, narcissistic self-sufficiency, and manic exhibitionism' (Holmes, 2006: 231) that achievement could bring. This latter description captures well the fragile, conflictful and disconnected states sometimes involved in upward social mobility and success, and also accords with some of Layton's descriptions of grandiosity in a class context.

Holmes' clinical examples are notable for the intertwining of class and 'race', and for the integration of Oedipal and erotic dynamics with these. Her work also brings the fundamentally damaging or traumatic effects of class and racism in individual histories into clinical purview, similarly to the writings of Fallenbaum, discussed earlier, and Trevithick and other authors (see Chapter 4). Such work provides psychoanalytic elaborations of the 'hidden injuries of class' (Sennett and Cobb, 1972). It begins to rectify the paucity of working-class voices and life experiences within psychoanalysis, and is an important reminder of the necessity to address the materiality of class in each history as well as the interpersonal dynamics and relationality that this may give rise to.

Displacements and class

It is no surprise that much clinical writing on class concerns the psychic complexities of upward mobility, since one of the barriers to private therapy may be removed by higher incomes. Further, the displacements and conflicts of upward mobility, which previous chapters have illustrated, may also propel someone towards therapy. The displacements of emigration into different cultural contexts can also bring previously unaddressed class issues to consciousness, and/or result in changed class status, as Ainslie's work illustrates. Downward mobility is much less studied, but as an example in Chapter 7 (p. 130) suggests, it may stem from a conscious rejection of the values and status of well-off parents, combined in some cases with oedipal issues, or, as the psychiatric literature indicates, be seen as a sign or consequence of mental illness.[8] These displacements in time and social space suggest both the persistent effects of earlier class identifications and also the ways that these can be modified. As Harris says: 'We might think of class as having layers of conscious and unconscious meaning, living as encrypted or secret identifications long after the material conditions that shaped them have altered' (Harris, 2003: 111). And also, I would add, lived in new material conditions, whether those of aspiration and success, or of the loss and insecurity that deindustrialisation and precarity have brought about. This brings out the multiply configured aspects of class, as something lived both consciously and unconsciously, linked to past, present and future, and entwined with many other factors. These multiple identifications provide the ground for various displacements, for example, from 'race' to class or vice versa, sometimes reducing one to the other, at other times holding the multiplicity involved. Displacements can also involve gender and sexuality, as other writings (e.g. Layton, 2004b; Maguire, 2004; Botticelli, 2007), beyond the scope of this book, suggest. Eribon's memoir is valuable in exploring in detail how his sexuality and his class origins (as working class) played out against and alongside each other (Eribon, 2013).

Ainslie, basing himself on Layton's ideas of normative unconscious processes, argues that powerful psychological processes are mobilised in relation to those who may be perceived as below or above oneself in the social hierarchy, involving both class and skin colour (Ainslie, 2009). He examines in many clinical examples how such processes are at play in the experiences of immigration, where pre-existing class experiences, often 'deeply encoded' and significantly unconscious, are activated by contact with new social circumstances. For one man, from a lower working-class background with significant early losses, his experiences of class prejudice and rejection carried over unconsciously into the immigrant context with its many narcissistic injuries. Ainslie writes how 'his immersion . . . in American culture and his financial success served to counter the desperation of his class origins . . . but he could not erase their lingering self-representational implications' (Ainslie, 2009: 9). He remained intensely ambivalent and distrustful of his family's acculturation. However, the impact of the many injuries attendant upon immigration lessened through therapy work on the links between his experiences of social marginalisation and familial rejection. Ainslie (2011) provides further examples of how immigrants travel with their social class, whether upwardly or downwardly mobile. In one, a woman moved from a lower-class milieu in America into an upper-class one in another country where her white skin colour was highly valued. Despite the social gratification she obtained which, according to Ainslie, she clung to defensively, this left her with extreme underlying vulnerability and anxiety, and led to devaluing those 'below' her. For another woman, immigration brought downward mobility, which resulted in rage and prejudice against fellow immigrants who came from a lower social class in her country of origin, from whom she now felt less socially distant. This, Ainslie says, created regressive anxieties and intra-psychic tensions, which had been held in check by the previous social structure in which her family had lived. Altogether, Ainslie concludes, class identifications are more important and more charged than usually thought, such that changes in class position, even if desired, may feel threatening and lead to regressive responses.

Keith Armitage (2009) provides a clinical account in which he views class as figuring as a site of displacement for other unspeakable anxieties and historic traumas. He argues that too often class is understood not in terms of the conflict inherent in our systems of capitalist production and economic life, but rather is abstracted, understood merely as difference, located in terms only of personal narrative and 'heritage'. Structural class antagonisms and conflicts of interest are depoliticised, which reaffirms the necessity for accounts that go beyond difference.

Armitage sees the clinical consequences of this as that when class is spoken about it is often to indicate some unlocalisable, unspeakable failure, as an inability to fulfil some norm or ideal. His example concerns a mixed-'race' young man with a white, originally well-off father who had fallen on hard economic times, and a black mother who had given up her work to have children. He was privately educated at a school where he was bullied and isolated because, he said, there were no other children like him, by which he meant 'lower middle class'. At other times when he was talking about perceived inadequacies on his part or experienced injustices, he would also refer this to class. When Armitage suggested that perhaps 'race' was also involved, he was taken aback and alarmed. As the therapy progressed, and with the emergence of a preoccupation with a significant black figure, the patient began gradually to be able to speak about 'race' and racism, the silences about this in his own family, and the difficulty of being the black son of a white, now dead, father, whereas Armitage says: 'The dynamics of identification across "race" could never be spoken of' (Armitage, 2009: 61), to be displaced instead into class issues, in this case the downward mobility of the family.

Armitage's account also illustrates the importance in a psychoanalytic context of being able to move between the material and the fantasised status of these categories, the social and the intra-psychic. Different intersections of class and race with each other have been threaded through many of the clinical examples of this book. This is not to suggest that they act similarly in the formations of psyches or socially, despite the many entwinements. It is important to maintain the specificity of the historical processes that create and sustain racism and those that perpetuate class systems, not conflate them, at the same time as recognising their conjunctures and intersections.

Intergenerational transmission and forms of resistance also take different, if sometimes, allied forms.

What kind of theory?

This chapter has delineated a multiplicity of psychoanalytic approaches where class has a presence in clinical work. Relational writings have much to offer in understanding how therapy relationships may be structured by social hierarchies and inequality, and by the processes of splitting, projection and disavowal that may ensue. These, if not simply enacted, can offer important understandings about how class structures and pervades relationships, consciously and unconsciously. I have argued however that, important and productive as this has been, it is limited by the (unintended) tendency to re-psychologise social forces, and by its focus mainly on difference. As Layton herself writes: 'Whilst relational psychoanalysis makes more space for integrating the psychic and the social than perhaps any other version of contemporary psychoanalysis . . . much of it still participates in the same depoliticizing and decontextualizing that pervade most dominant American discourses' (Layton, 2004a: 243). Clinical work, rather, needs to be better informed by social and political understandings (as much of Layton's in fact is) in order to adequately take account of the ways in which the material and social world impinges on and forms people, in particular the many far-reaching inequalities it creates and reinforces. Class, in other words, should not be seen only as difference, however powerfully these differences become psychologically elaborated and operative, as so much literature attests they do. The materiality and the embodiments of class, and the historical legacies at work, all need to find a place in psychoanalytic thinking. The clinical and psychosocial work addressed here and in previous chapters, on the traumatic effects of early and current class experiences, serve as useful indicators of this.

Furthermore, relational psychoanalysis is founded on a rejection and discarding of much classical psychoanalysis, characterised by its writers as drive theory or one-person psychologies. I take this problematic up further in the final chapter. It is clear however that any greater incorporation of the social world into psychoanalysis does require a form of theory that can address how this world impinges upon and constitutes us, a reorientation towards what precedes us and what shapes our subjecthood. Hartman (see p. 148) suggests that Laplanche's concept of 'enigmatic messages' – the unconsciousness of the other, and their otherness to themselves – could illuminate how class, as conveyed through his father's anxiety and wounded body, was transmitted enigmatically to him. In taking this suggestion further, I propose that Laplanche's reorientation of psychoanalysis can, at least schematically, provide the basis of a greater incorporation of the social world into psychoanalysis. Laplanche throughout criticises the recentring or ipso-centredness that he sees Freudian theory slipping into, despite its foundational impetus in decentring the subject. Rather, he proposes, through detailed critique and extensive rewriting of much of Freud's work, a reorientation towards the primacy and the agency of the other as a fully constituted subject. We saw an example of this in Chapter 3 (see p. 41) in Laplanche's critique of Freud's scotomisation of a working-class figure, part of my argument about how class became extruded. This reorientation creates a theoretical space, as I elaborate further in Chapter 10, which could be taken up to understand in psychoanalytic terms the forces of the social world, although Laplanche himself does not suggest this. Part of Laplanche's reorientation of psychoanalysis is also to propose that drives are not primary, and do not come only from internal sources, but are shaped by what impinges on us, and our responses to that. In doing so he provides a way of not having to discard drive theory in order to accommodate the social world, and also suggests detailed ways in which that world can be seen as shaping us, as Chapter 10 pursues further.

Notes

1 The different class categories are not spelled out here (nor do they need to be) but Layton's use of 'upper' class may relate more to the US context than the UK one. Whatever the precise definitions, the import of class distinction, especially in relation to poor and working-class people, is clear.
2 Whereby until the advent of comprehensives, and in many places afterwards, children were segregated by a selective examination at age eleven.
3 Which may be the case in some families, see for example Chapter 6, p. 110.
4 'Interpellation' is a term taken from Althusser to capture the ways ideology, embodied in major social and political institutions, constitutes the nature of individual subjects' identities.
5 One can now only be impressed at the existence of such an organisation, founded at a time of considerable left-wing activity and administered through various unions.
6 Laplanche and Pontalis define introjection as: 'In phantasy, the subject transposes objects and their inherent qualities from the "outside" to the "inside" of himself' (Laplanche and Pontalis, 1973). The authors point out that while akin to identification it is also close in meaning to incorporation with its bodily model, underlining the unmentalised nature of introjects.
7 Defined as the process whereby intersubjective relations are transformed into intrasubjective ones. Often used interchangeably with introjection, it is also distinct in referring only to a relationship that is transposed, rather than an imago.
8 However, at the present time, with the impact of the global crisis and of austerity politics, many younger people are now unable to acquire the standard of living of the

previous generation, however modest, and are effectively downwardly mobile. It will be interesting to see what these experiences bring to therapy – if they can afford it.

References

Adorno, T. (1967) 'Sociology and psychology (Part II)', *New Left Review* 1(47): 79–97.
Ainslie, R. (2009) 'Social class and its reproduction in immigrants' construction of self', *Psychoanalysis, Culture and Society* 14: 213–24.
Ainslie, R. (2011) 'Immigration and the psychodynamics of class', *Psychoanalytic Psychology* 28: 560–8.
Altman, N. (1995/2010) *The Analyst in the Inner City: Race, Class, and Culture through a Psychoanalytic Lens*. New York: Routledge.
Armitage, K. (2009) 'Young, lower middle class and black', *Sitegeist* 3: 51–64.
Bodnar, S. (2004) 'Remember where you come from: Dissociative process in multicultural individuals', *Psychoanalytic Dialogues* 14: 581–603.
Botticelli, S. (2007) 'The return of the repressed: Class in psychoanalytic process'. In Suchet, M., Harris, A. and Aron, L. (eds) *Relational Psychoanalysis: Vol. 3 New Voices*. Hillsdale: Analytic Press.
Dimen, M. (1994) 'Money, love, and hate: Contradiction and paradox in psychoanalysis', *Psychoanalytic Dialogues* 4(1): 69–100.
Dimen, M. (2003) 'Keep on keepin' on: Alienation and trauma', *Studies in Gender and Sexuality* 4: 93–103.
Eribon, D. (2013) *Returning to Reims*. Los Angeles: Semiotext(e).
Fallenbaum, R. (2003) 'The injured worker', *Studies in Gender and Sexuality* 4: 72–92.
Freud, S. (1909) 'Family romances'. In Strachey, J. (ed) (1955) *The Standard Edition of the Complete Psychological Works of Sigmund Freud*, vol. 9: 237–41, London: Hogarth.
Gurney, P. (2009) 'The ac(ci)dental tourist', *Sitegeist: A Journal of Psychoanalysis and Philosophy* 3: 41–50.
Hanley, L. (2016) *Respectable: The Experience of Class*. London: Allen Lane.
Harris, A. (2003) 'Working in the trenches: Commentary on Ruth Fallenbaum's paper', *Studies in Gender and Sexuality* 4: 104–12.
Harris, A. (2009) 'The socio-political recruitment of identities', *Psychoanalytic Dialogues* 19(2): 138–47.
Hartman, S. (2007) 'Class unconscious: From dialectical materialism to relational material'. In Suchet, M., Harris, A. and Aron, L. (eds) *Relational Psychoanalysis: Vol. 3 New Voices*. Hillsdale: Analytic Press.
Holmes, D. (1997) 'The analyst in the inner city', *Journal of the American Psychoanalytic Association* 45: 644–8.
Holmes, D. (2006) 'The wrecking effects of race and social class on self and success', *Psychoanalytic Quarterly* 75: 215–35.
Laplanche, J. and Pontalis, J. B. (1973) *The Language of Psychoanalysis*. London: Hogarth.
Layton, L. (2004a) 'Dreams of America/American dreams', *Psychoanalytic Dialogues* 14: 233–54.
Layton, L. (2004b) 'Relational no more: Defensive autonomy in middle class women', *Annual of Psychoanalysis* 32: 29–42.
Layton, L. (2006a) 'Attacks on linking'. In Layton, L., Hollander, N. and Gutwill, S. (eds) *Psychoanalysis, Class and Politics: Encounters in the Clinical Setting*. London: Routledge.

Layton, L. (2006b) 'That place gives me the Heebie Jeebies'. In Layton, L., Hollander, N. and Gutwill, S. (eds) *Psychoanalysis, Class and Politics: Encounters in the Clinical Setting*. London: Routledge.

Layton, L. (2008) 'What divides the subject? Psychoanalytic reflection on subjectivity, subjection and resistance', *Subjectivity* 22: 60–72.

Layton, L. (2014a) 'Grandiosity, neoliberalism and neoconservatism', *Psychoanalytic Inquiry* 34: 463–74.

Layton, L. (2014b) 'Performing Class, Enacting Distinction'. Unpublished paper.

Maguire, M. (2004) *Men, Women, Passion and Power*. London: Routledge.

Sennett, R. and Cobb, J. (1972) *The Hidden Injuries of Class*. New York: Knopf.

Steedman, C. (1986) *Landscape for a Good Women*. London: Virago.

Young-Bruehl, E. (1998) *The Anatomy of Prejudices*. Cambridge, MA: Harvard University Press.

9

MONEY AND SOME POLITICAL ECONOMIES OF PSYCHOANALYTIC WORK

Class and money have an obvious and fundamental intertwining: lack of money is a powerful aspect of class exclusion from psychoanalysis, for intending therapists as well as for patients. To a large extent, it structures the whole field. Several of the therapists in my study from working-class backgrounds mentioned the costs of their training, and the difficulties of doing this alongside others who were much better off. One, for example, said: '*I was just struggling to pay for my training . . . and I tried to bring it up, but I don't think it was really worked with. . . . I think it was interpreted . . . it was perceived not as a reality but as just my own way of seeing myself.*' Money is also an increasingly significant financial issue for many from middle-class backgrounds within the psychoanalytic field, with the downward trends in middle-class incomes.

The symbolic meanings of money and of the payment of fees are areas of rich and extensive psychoanalytic exploration within clinical work. However, the status of self-employed practitioners as sole traders in a competitive field, the acts of monetary exchange that psychoanalysis involves and the class aspects are all much less examined. This represents another disavowal of the material bases of psychoanalysis, which I attempt to rectify here. How we are formed and perceive ourselves (or not) as workers in a psychoanalytic economy, with different identifications and material circumstances, merits thought, especially given present economic pressures.

Private practice, Michael Rustin (2001) argues, has always been and still is the 'positive condition' for the development and survival of psychoanalysis. It is undeniably also the source of professional satisfaction and creativity for many practitioners. However, it is also an important source of the limited popularity of psychoanalysis, and something that does cause dissonance for many of its practitioners. Money, like class, has been named the last taboo (Krueger, 1986), something more shameful to talk about than sex, a dirty secret. The situation is, as would be expected, highly contradictory. Fenichel (1938), whose article on money still remains relevant, points out that discussion about money is often regarded as 'indelicate', both because of the (assumed) unconscious equivalence of money with faeces and also because this attribution of 'indelicacy' helps perpetuate conventional social ideology and illusions about money. His invocation of delicacy and shame recalls Elias' naming of these emotions as key aspects of class distinction. As Dimen (1994) persuasively argues, there is reluctance and coyness surrounding the subject. Crick (2007), in a review of low-fee issues, also notes how reluctant analysts are generally to explore financial realities, and how the 'awkward' matter of fees can become a blind spot. Many writings do however bemoan the falling incomes of analysts, the increased difficulty of securing patients and a reliable living and the growing competition from other therapies. There is the beginning of a discourse around the political economies of psychoanalytic work, and what the exchange of money in psychoanalytic work signifies, as some therapists have addressed the felt contradictions of their positions in a market economy. Here I consider the terms in which such discourses are framed, drawing on both the more abstract literature and the experiences of therapists at work.

Psychoanalytic political economies

Michael Schneider addresses the economy of psychoanalysis in class terms. He refers to the 'ambivalent class situation of the analyst', the ways in which psychoanalysis can be both subversive of normative social orders and also a force for conformity and adaptation (Schneider, 1973/1975). Both these aspects are evident within the history of psychoanalysis. Schneider sees the initial social marginality of psychoanalysis as necessitating its institutionalisation in psychoanalytic organisations and official trainings. This created pressure for conformity and patronage within the organisations, and a diminution of their radical or critical nature, all familiar phenomena, widely commented on. Psychoanalytic organisations embody a concentration of social capital in networks of affiliation, which, with the power to confer acceptance and work, have important effects on the livelihoods of practitioners.

Schneider underlines the dependence of most analysts for their livelihood on high-fee patients, and their exposure to the laws of supply and demand of this marketplace. This increases their investments in the status quo. Alexander Mitscherlich, in discussing the relationship between sociology and psychoanalysis, describes the 'naïve identification, on the part of many analysts, with their privileged status, instead of a reflective attention to the conditions of their society' (Mitscherlich, 1970: 34), something still recognisable now. What these authors do not address, however, is the consciousness many practitioners do have of their situation and its class and other contradictions. Rather, practitioners are simply portrayed as unwitting subjects in the face of overall economic and ideological forces. However, it is probably true that each practitioner rather privately finds their own accommodation with the often contradictory demands of their need to make a living, their ethics and political commitments, their enjoyment of their work and the circumstances of their patients. Very few discuss their fee-charging practices openly, and there is little collective framework for discussion about money, which some recent writers have tried to remedy.

Bennett argues that the disciplinary disconnection of psychoanalysis from political economy means that many practitioners find it hard to reconcile their therapeutic with their economic selves, by 'owning up to being at once rational and self-interested subjects' (Bennett, 2012: 21). He describes how Freudo-Marxist psychoanalytic writers, such as Reich or Fromm, who theorised as one and the same subject what Bennett calls economic man (sic) and psychoanalytic man, have for the most part been excommunicated or sidelined from the mainstream of the psychoanalytic profession. He also argues that the disconnection between radical social thought and psychoanalysis that grew greatly from the mid-twentieth century left a vacuum of thinking regarding the political economies of psychoanalysis. Bennett suggests that the grip of neo-liberalism today is such that:

> [I]t is hard to imagine any professional analyst today insisting, as Fenichel insisted in 1938, that the 'correct' application of psychoanalysis to social issues is that of investigating how the dominant ideology of exploitative class-society is reproduced in the psychology of all classes.
> (Bennett, 2012: 21)

Current practitioners, Bennett avers, do not readily see themselves as inevitably working within the context of neo-liberalism, even those who hold other values. Psychoanalysts, he claims, are 'more comfortable discussing their patients' unconscious attitudes to money as a transferential object than discussing the relationship between the economics and the ideology of their own profession' (2012: 21). However, while there is much to agree with in this general sentiment, Bennett ignores all those contemporary analysts and therapists who are indeed viewing their clinical experiences through the prism of current neo-liberalism, and critically reflecting on the many ways in which this pervades their clients' lives and inner worlds (see especially Chapters 4 and 8).

Different approaches to examining the tensions, contradictions and ambivalences surrounding money matters are illustrated by the following writers. Although much of it floats strangely free of class considerations, I have tried to identify important class resonances.

Psychoanalysis and the exchange of money

Viewing psychoanalysis as a financial transaction does raise the question: what is being exchanged? Adam Phillips (1997) points to the paradoxical nature of money within psychoanalytic practice when he describes the patient as, in his view, agreeing to buy something that no one can describe in advance. This makes the transaction a different sort of contract from that usually obtaining. Dany Nobus (2013), in his ambivalently ironic consideration of Lacan's pecuniary arrangements and ostensible greed, also argues how different buying psychoanalysis is from other commercial transactions. There is no specifiable product or customer satisfaction that can be measured, and no money-back guarantee.[1] The analysand pays to do work on him- or herself. Money, according to Nobus, ensures the presence of the analyst, not as a passive listener, but as 'an open depository' where the analysand can 'store' his or her conflicts without fear of being rejected. Rustin (2001) suggests that analysands are paying for a kind of work by the analyst that can only be done in this very particular way, centrally involving transference.

Nobus goes on to ask, why does the patient have to pay such a high fee? He answers it in terms of the necessity to avoid the analysand experiencing the analytic presence as a gift of love, or of feeling indebted to the analyst, seeing money as a neutralising signifier. This is an old, much disputed argument that Freud himself came to discount, in favour of acknowledging the analyst's need for a living. As many have repeatedly pointed out, whatever is felt about either paid or free therapy can always itself be material for analysis, and there are many other aspects of the analytic situation that can disrupt such idealising attributions. Crick (2007) also suggests that the higher the fee, the less likely it is to be analysed, an instance of how this is regarded as the taken-for-granted normality. Giving figures for fees in London in 2013,[2] Nobus argues that the cost of psychoanalysis depends much more on the presumed prestige of the analyst than on anything to do with the degree of complexity or difficulty of the work undertaken – that is, with the analyst's accumulated social and cultural capital, rather than the work itself. Rustin argues that few analysts or therapists in the UK charge excessively, relatively speaking, but there is an absence of data here.

Frosh (2012) also argues that recognition of how money and trade are centrally involved punctuates the 'imaginary' situation in which it is possible for both analyst and patient to pretend that the relationship is one of love and care, separate from the material base of this relationship in a capitalist economy. This may counteract the more self-idealising aspects of psychoanalysis, but it does not adequately encompass the contradictions depicted by other writers, nor the very real emotional, ethical and professional investments analysts may have in their work, alongside the desire and necessity to earn money. Rustin (2001) depicts the contradiction as one in which the intimacy and emotions evoked by the analytic situation are felt to pertain to the kinds of relationships which are widely held *not* to be able to be bought or sold, and which are particular to the individuals concerned, not subject to the abstractions of the exchange of money.

Dimen, in her incisive, widely quoted and reproduced article, is exemplary in how she addresses the political economy of private practice (Dimen, 1994). She depicts the material basis of psychoanalysis as lying in commerce: 'We sell our services to make our living . . . analysts engage in trade. Without money, then, there's no psychoanalysis at all. But with it comes an unavoidable anxiety . . .' (Dimen, 1994: 83). Psychoanalytic labour is seen as a commodity like any other work. Addressing the role of the analyst in a class-structured society, she argues that the economic insecurity experienced by analysts as self-employed practitioners has increased as middle-class incomes have decreased and as competition from other therapies has increased. A recent survey of American psychoanalysts showed how dissatisfied most of the respondents were with their earnings (Axelrod, 2012). Such a situation, Dimen argues, has created an 'anxious elite', in possession of a status that may confer some authority and influence, but which forms of capital depend on the acquisition of knowledge and skill. This constantly needs renewal through hard work and discipline, it cannot be readily bequeathed, and co-exists with fear of loss of income and status. Dimen depicts the alienation and estrangement that the exchange of money and services can create, such that the analyst, paid by the hour, may feel he/she is doing piece work, and the personal satisfaction and benefit of the work can seem compromised.

Dimen attributes the implicit taboos and coyness about any discussion of money, fees and hours to several factors. These are: the anxiety about economic insecurity, the conflicts of analysts' altruism and professional ethics versus their need and/or greed and the felt specialness of psychoanalysis versus basic material demands. To which we might also add any fears about reputation and status. The popularity of her insightful article is testimony to a great hunger for such discussion.

Dimen also argues that the confluence of money and love within the analytic relationship is a living contradiction that cannot be resolved, only addressed and transcended through analytic work. This *contradiction* of love and money needs transforming into the *paradox* of love and hate, for useful work to be done. This requires the acknowledgement and acceptance of hate. Such hatred might be stimulated by a perception, true or otherwise, of the analyst's wealth as indicated by the environment of their consulting room,[3] by the very act of paying for something so personal and individual as analytic work, or by the feeling that analysis is in some ways 'just a job' for the analyst. Hatred and confusion are stimulated by the contradiction that money is an abstract medium of exchange in a market economy, but nevertheless it is what engenders and makes possible analytic commitment and engagement, and the personal and intimate space of a therapeutic relationship, with its evocation of transferences.

Hatred, I suggest, can also be aroused by the common practice of requiring payment for sessions that are missed by the patient. This practice reflects the analyst's desire not to be paid on zero hours contracts, as well as the maintenance of the integrity of the analytic space and frame. These factors are not unrelated, in that the continuity and consistency that is facilitated by this are part of therapeutic efficacy, but the analyst's own needs for predictable payment are seldom overtly acknowledged. Orbach (2014) argues that the needs or convenience of the therapist should not become a 'false god' of the therapy, and that financial arrangements should be negotiated more democratically and flexibly, taking into account both parties' constraints.

Money and clinical work

The psychoanalytic discourse around money contains many perspectives, but all comment on the need for much greater and franker discussion of it. One theme derives from Freud's various comments. In letters to Fliess, he wrote that his mood depended very strongly on his earnings: 'Money is laughing gas to me' (Freud, 1899/1985: 374). He recommended speaking frankly about money at the outset of a psychoanalytic relationship (Freud, 1913). He also wrote to Jung: 'I often appease my conscious mind by saying to myself: just give up wanting to cure; learn and make money, those are the most plausible conscious aims' (Freud, 1909: 136).

This latter aspect has been picked up most overtly in various Lacanian writings about money, especially those eschewing therapeutic improvement as a plausible aim. Lacan, in Nobus' account, can be seen as taking the pecuniary aspects of psychoanalysis to extremes, in the wealth he seemingly accumulated from very large numbers of patients seen for short sessions at high fees. Lacan's reputed refusal to give change for larger denomination notes, and to interpret such payment as an indication of the higher fee the patient unconsciously wanted to pay, and therefore should pay, is an extreme and unusual example of the exploitative potential of psychoanalytic relationships.[4] It underlines the wider ethical minefield, where what is being paid for involves a private transaction, with many hopes, vulnerabilities and dependencies involved, and with the symbolic power of interpretation invested in the analyst.

Freud's robustly self-interested perspective, while certainly present and necessary to some degree for all practitioners, negates the potential for contradiction and conflict, which many describe. His insistence that money was primarily a psychological problem for the patient but only a practical one for the analyst, has contributed to the neglect of these complexities. In conditions of austerity and scarcity this can be reversed; analysts may become afraid to offer especially challenging interpretations for fear of losing their patients, as Nobus and other writers suggest.

Many therapists, as well as Dimen, do exhibit an awareness of the contradictions they are caught up in. There appears to be an increasing analytic desire to discuss these, as witnessed in recent publications (e.g. Berger and Newman, 2012). From a Jungian perspective, Jane Haynes and Jan Wiener (1996) describe the widespread unease and silence about money, and the thinness of theoretical literature about it. Money, they argue, has an exceptional status in the analytic setting, being the only sustained concrete transaction that takes place, yet there is little or no training offered to trainees about this aspect of their work, and personal and collective 'shadow forces' inhibit realistic thinking. Theodore Jacobs describes this neglect as a collusive avoidance passed down intergenerationally from analyst to trainee (Jacobs, 2012).

For Haynes and Wiener, feelings about money are characterised by opposites, especially greed and altruism; and analysts are often unwilling to acknowledge their own dependence on patients' fees, instead focusing on the needs and vulnerabilities of the latter. Irwin Hirsch also argues that financial and professional ambition are often denied within the psychoanalytic field, and may even be projected onto 'bad' others in different professions (Hirsch, 2012). He also provides examples of the conflict when a patient may wish to end the analytic relationship but the analyst wants to prolong it for (unacknowledged) financial reasons.

Haynes and Wiener observe how it can be difficult to simultaneously hold in mind the idea of an analytic relationship with that of a financial contract; a different rendition from that of Bennett's (described earlier) about this dual aspect. They argue for a less shameful and less disavowed acknowledgement of analysts' needs to make a living.

Several articles explore further aspects of money, class and clinical work. Many comment on the sense of taboo or shame surrounding efforts to broach these issues. Lawrence Josephs (2004) underlines how what he calls 'normative standards of affluence' can function as a seductive ideal, often now unattainable by most analytic practitioners, but rendering them vulnerable to invidious comparisons and envy with wealthy patients, the latter something some of the therapists from working-class backgrounds in my study also mentioned. Kachina Myers (2008) asks how money 'got left behind' in the relational journey to intersubjectivity, with the analyst's monetary subjectivity remaining surprisingly unexamined: 'As the analyst's subjectivity gains respectability overall, the analyst's desire for money remains dirty, debased and disreputable' (Myers, 2008: 118). She sees the fee as being a real intrusion of the analyst's need into the therapeutic situation, and that this is the dilemma of the analyst's desire. In her view analysts frequently are unable to ask for and get their desired fees, even from those who could pay it: 'Fear of losing patients, fear of patients' rage, anxiety about having more, shame, guilt, and other apparently unbearable affects seem to prevent many analysts from getting their due' (Myers, 2008: 119). Analysts, she argues, should accept they are running a business. Perhaps the only surprise is why this needs to be asserted so strongly. Like Haynes and Wiener, Myers argues this is something women particularly struggle with, a discussion expanded on by Shanok (2012). She also suggests, as does Schonbar (1967), that such anxieties are especially acute for therapists from working-class backgrounds.

Class and the business aspects of trying to gain work after graduation are considered by Christopher Bandini who struggled in the immediate post-graduation years (something which I hear increasingly). He suggests that his analytic training did nothing to prepare him for the 'mundane and financial aspects' of the 'job' (Bandini, 2011). These were seen as superfluous, maintaining the illusion that psychoanalytic work was somehow above money, but leaving it a mystery to him how analysts did build practices. It is, he says, seldom acknowledged that analysts may need to market themselves 'aggressively', nor that an enormous commitment of time, resources and networking are required to run a practice. From a blue-collar background, Bandini originally saw becoming a psychoanalyst as a way to transcend class; for him, it has not brought 'upper-class affluence', and he doubts whether the old high-fee model is any longer viable. Bandini concludes that success as a psychoanalyst depends on entrepreneurial skill, class advantage and social expertise. He emphasises the importance of social capital in the form of patronage and social networks, well known but seldom acknowledged in its class significance. The 2012 survey (Axelrod, 2012) confirms that the strategies for obtaining work depend greatly on within-profession contacts, rather than other forms of self-promotion. Those from working-class, non-white or immigrant backgrounds may find it harder to acquire such social capital, whereas for those within indigenous middle- or upper-class networks it is more readily, if not effortlessly, possessed.

The necessity to carry out unpaid or very low-fee work during training and afterwards adds to class disadvantage in becoming a psychoanalytic therapist. All training organisations have requirements for how much clinical work is necessary for qualification; mostly this is fulfilled by trainees working in voluntary unpaid placements or working in their own organisation's low-fee clinics. Many continue with honorary placements and low-fee work after graduation. This is a source of accessible and affordable therapy for patients, albeit with less experienced clinicians, but like internships generally it privileges the already privileged. There is now the beginning of collective concern about this, with a 2016 conference organised by the Psychotherapy and Counselling Union, to campaign against unpaid and other inequitable conditions of work.

Low-fee or free psychotherapy

Some of the monetary concerns described earlier are abrogated in contexts in which psychoanalysts or therapists are paid by some third body for their work, which may be in effect free for the patient at the point of consumption. However, from the point of view of the patient, the therapist may still be seen as being paid to care, and thus the felt contradictions of money and psychoanalysis as 'just a job' are still present.

The circumstances for therapists are mostly similar. Many are contracted as self-employed practitioners. Salaried jobs for psychotherapists are very rare, apart from some in the NHS. Most work on arrangements (seldom real contracts) where, although a certain number of hours of work may be specified, and the therapist may be paid for no-shows, he or she will not be paid for sickness or holidays. The amount of work is often insecure and subject to the vagaries of funding or reorganisation. The fees for such work are relatively low, especially in the voluntary sector and far less than what is possible in private practice, yet many therapists do commit themselves to and value public sector work. Many therapists now also find short-term work through various funded schemes, such as employee assistance in the UK, or managed care in the USA, where they will be subjected to diverse bureaucratic demands without necessarily any guarantee of filled hours. As well, private insurance-based work is possible, with restricted conditions of frequency and length. Recent years have seen the growth of private psychotherapy group practices and agencies, charging relatively high fees where the psychotherapist may be effectively on a zero hours contract.

The sidelining of financial concerns within the frameworks of psychoanalytic trainings and organisations suggests a fantasmatic and disdainful relationship to these economic realities, a split-off state of affairs, another disavowal. It is as if these vital economic concerns, income and how work is obtained, were not of interest, and could somehow be managed without any discussion, which is then deemed not to be merited. Such an attitude was probably typical of the bohemian, upper middle classes, with their disdain for money matters, whose cultural milieu was inextricably involved in the early evolution of UK psychoanalysis. This may have once been tenable when the class basis of those entering the psychoanalytic profession was mainly upper middle class and well off, when there was a plentiful supply of patients and less competition. I often wonder whether trainees embarking on a training have ever researched or been provided with any information about the prospects for making a living. Some trainings are now taking steps to include the business aspects of setting up a psychoanalytic practice in their curricula. A further step would be to carry out a survey of actual psychotherapeutic work and incomes, as has been initiated in the USA. Such information would open out a necessary debate by addressing the social and economic realities of psychoanalytic practice, its monetary and class basis. It might defray some of the inhibitions around discussing money and fee-setting policies. It would lessen its divorce from social realities, however unwelcome these are, and address the dual aspect of psychoanalytic subjecthood.

The considerations of this chapter have foregrounded the necessarily embedded nature of psychoanalysis within contemporary market economies. The various debates have tended to assert the primacy of the therapist's need to earn, as a reaction to how this need has often been obscured or elided, considered in some way improper, embarrassing or too mundane to foreground, the legacy of a wider upper-class ethos of disdaining to talk about money, while having lots of it. It is true that many of the values and practices of psychoanalysis are countercultural to those of current neo-liberalism and the demands of a ruthless market economy. Its modus operandi of slow, detailed, reflective and open-ended thinking, of focus on the uniqueness of each individual, are often in conflict with a world in which time equals money, and in which most services are monetised and measured by their cost-effectiveness. Its value for its recipients cannot on the whole be measured in monetary terms, even if it can result in a more effective orientation to the rigours of reality. The temporary suspension of some of the demands of reality that is created by the frame of psychoanalytic sessions – where in principle anything can be said and felt – is essential to its efficacy. However, money is the one demand of reality that cannot, for the most part, be suspended for psychoanalysis to be possible. It is this nexus that seems to pose such difficulties; where the fault lines of psychoanalysis, as a discipline that radically separates material reality from psychic reality, are revealed.

Notes

1 Although clients are now required to complete a feedback form after *every* session in some IAPT services. And for many third-sector organisations, funding applications often require general client satisfaction ratings. While for many psychoanalysts such practices may be anathema, perhaps we should revisit the question of how patients can have a voice as to their satisfaction or otherwise with the therapy experiences. Despite all the evident complexities of this, why should it be so taboo?
2 Nobus quotes fees of between £30 and £300 per session. Generally, UK fees are considerably lower than US ones.
3 In which the patient described Dimen as 'The Landlady of Time'.
4 As Movahedi (2013) says, there is no evidence that Lacan would have lowered his fee if the patient 'unconsciously' paid less with a smaller note.

References

Axelrod, S. (2012) 'The division 39 practice survey', *Division/Review* 5: 28–31.
Bandini, C. (2011) 'The good job: Financial anxiety, class envy and drudgery in beginning a private practice', *Contemporary Psychoanalysis* 47: 101–17.

Bennett, D. (ed) (2012) *Loaded Subjects*. London: Lawrence and Wishart.
Berger, B. and Newman, S. (eds) (2012) *Money Talks*. New York: Routledge.
Crick, P. (2007) 'The impact of a low fee on an analysis'. Panel presentation, Vienna, European Psychoanalytic Federation Conference.
Dimen, M. (1994) 'Money, love, and hate: Contradiction and paradox in psychoanalysis', *Psychoanalytic Dialogues* 4: 69–100.
Fenichel, O. (1938) 'The drive to amass wealth', *Psychoanalytic Quarterly* 7: 69–95.
Freud, S. (1899) In Masson, J. (ed) (1985) *Complete Letters of Sigmund Freud to Wilhelm Fliess*. Cambridge: Harvard University Press.
Freud, S. (1909) In McGuire, W. (ed) (1974) *The Freud/Jung Letters*: 129F. Princeton: Princeton University Press. Paperback edition.
Freud, S. (1913) 'On beginning the treatment'. In Strachey, J. (ed) *Standard Edition*, vol. X11: 121–44, London: Hogarth.
Frosh, S. (2012) 'Psychoanalysis, money and the miser'. In Bennett, D. (ed) *Loaded Subjects*. London: Lawrence and Wishart.
Haynes, J. and Wiener, J. (1996) 'The analyst in the counting house: Money as symbol and reality in analysis', *British Journal of Psychotherapy* 13: 14–25.
Hirsch, I. (2012) 'It was a great month: None of my patients left'. In Berger, B. and Newman, S. (eds) *Money Talks*. New York: Routledge.
Jacobs, T. (2012) 'Money: Some reflections on its impact on psychoanalytic education and psychoanalytic practice'. In Berger, B. and Newman, S. (eds) *Money Talks*. New York: Routledge.
Josephs, L. (2004) 'Seduced by affluence: How material envy strains the analytic relationship', *Contemporary Psychoanalysis* 40: 389–408.
Krueger, D. (ed) (1986) *The Last Taboo*. New York: Brunner.
Mitscherlich, A. (1970) 'On psychoanalysis and sociology', *International Journal of Psychoanalysis* 51: 33–5.
Movahedi, S. (2013) 'Did you say bizarre?', *Modern Psychoanalysis* 38: 189–202.
Myers, K. (2008) 'Show me the money: (The problem) of the therapist's desire, subjectivity and relationship to the fee', *Contemporary Psychoanalysis* 44: 118–40.
Nobus, D. (2013) 'What are words worth? Lacan and the circulation of money in the psychoanalytic economy', *Modern Psychoanalysis* 38: 157–88.
Orbach, S. (2014) 'Democratizing psychoanalysis'. In Lowenthal, D. and Samuels, A. (eds) *Relational Psychotherapy, Psychoanalysis and Counselling*. London: Routledge.
Phillips, A. (1997) 'Foreword'. In Forrester, J. (ed) *Truth Games; Lies, Money and Psychoanalysis*. Cambridge: Harvard University Press.
Rustin, M. (2001) 'Facilitator or corruptor? The place of money in psychoanalytic practice'. In Rustin, M. (ed) *Reason and Unreason*. London: Continuum.
Schneider, M. (1973/1975) *Neurosis and Civilisation*. New York: Seabury Press.
Schonbar, R. (1967) 'The fee as a focus for transference and countertransference', *American Journal of Psychotherapy* 21: 275–85.
Shanok, A. (2012) 'Money and gender: Financial facts and fantasies for female and male therapists'. In Berger, B. and Newman, S. (eds) *Money Talks*. New York: Routledge.

10
SPEAKING CLASS TO PSYCHOANALYSIS

My explorations in this book have led me through many aspects of psychoanalysis, from its quotidian practices to questions of theory, from its institutional and social locations to the workings of the unconscious. I have attempted to encompass what considerations of class can throw up for psychoanalysis as a theoretical discipline and as a clinical practice, as well as how psychoanalysis can contribute to understanding the psychic embodiments of class. This involves addressing the lack of common concepts or a language in which matters of both class and psychoanalysis can be thought together, and shared across different discourses. Exploring very scattered work, I have delineated patchworks of linked themes which themselves raise further issues. Here I outline some implications of these themes, starting with economic and institutional matters, through considerations of psychoanalytic culture and values, to questions of clinical work and practice, and finally theory.

Money and access

Money, and the access it brings to psychoanalysis and its trainings, is a crucial reality that structures the psychoanalytic field. Psychoanalysis, in its longer-term and most intensive forms, continues to be effectively an expensive and exclusive good. This reality is largely not a collective concern of the profession as a whole, nor of its various representative bodies, despite many individual concerns and concerted actions that do seek to remedy this. In this way we do not allow the inherent injustice and inequality to really register with ourselves collectively, nor to be conveyed to trainees as an important part of the profession they are entering – a form of disavowal. Much more could be done to make this a central ethical concern in psychoanalytic education. Greater recognition of, and teaching about, clinical work in low-fee, third and public sector contexts would begin to address this professional neglect, and confer more status to such practices.

The role of money is thus seen in what is most valued professionally. The legacy of Freud's ambivalent distinction between the 'pure gold' of psychoanalysis and the 'copper alloy' of psychoanalytic psychotherapy (and now psychodynamic counselling) haunts us in ways that have riven the field and hampered thought across this divide, as well as devaluing what is now the most common and less expensive practice. The distinction between pure and applied clinical work is a class distinction, just as it is more widely in British society, but not adequately recognised as such, another disavowal.[1] Dropping these terms would be an important conceptual step to wider teachings across the whole range of psychoanalytic activity, including with disadvantaged or poorer populations, with lower-frequency work, and within the NHS. This would challenge the power of the symbolic capital inherent in the elite status of 'pure' psychoanalysis, capital that is underpinned by the economic and other assets needed to acquire it. This does not mean we should not nurture and value the kinds of practices and ideas that intensive long-term work makes possible, and that have long been the source of much innovation, in what has been called the 'laboratory' of psychoanalysis (Cooper and Lousada, 2010). However, it does suggest considerably broadening and diversifying what we mean by excellence, to include practices and ideas stemming from work in different circumstances.

The disregard of matters of inequality in access to psychoanalysis also contributes to the lack of professional thought on the classed nature of private practice and how, as Fereday (2015) says, its demographic does not reflect society. Greater recognition of the political economies of psychoanalysis, and the status of psychoanalytic practitioners as sole traders within a capitalist economy, would open up discussion on how this impacts on those from working-class backgrounds, and on clinical work more generally. Some organisations are beginning to address the material demands of building a career in psychoanalytic therapy; this also needs understandings of its political economies if it is to address the class factors involved and go beyond individual entrepreneurship. The class awareness of therapists is only just beginning to be explored, as the financial viability of high-fee, long-term private practice has decreased, and as the economic and other discriminations inherent in current training and post-qualification financial demands are increasingly voiced.

An open dialogue about money and work within psychoanalysis would disrupt secrecy and inhibition, and bring the economic facts into debate. It is not enough to leave the modest amounts of redistribution that do take place to the private activity of individual practitioners and their sliding scales. Imaginative ways of funding more people from working-class, ethnic minority or otherwise disadvantaged backgrounds as trainees and as patients need to be developed by organisations, as a few already do. The challenges now being mounted, for example, by the new Psychotherapists and Counsellors' Union, to the ubiquity of unpaid work in the development of therapy careers need to be supported more widely.

Furthermore, the viability and public acceptability of psychoanalysis as a whole would be enhanced by greater inclusivity towards and support for less expensive, more culturally aware forms of psychoanalytic work. The imperative that Freud and the early left psychoanalysts recognised, that the public acceptability of psychoanalysis depended on the availability of free and low-cost forms of therapy and of outreach work, applies even more urgently now. Those current psychoanalytic societies that have reversed their decline in numbers have often done so by broadening their scope to include psychoanalytic psychotherapy and associated practices hitherto considered not to be 'pure' psychoanalysis. It is also urgent to devise new forms of public communication and engagement with psychoanalysis. The popularity of writings that depict the intricacies and complexities of psychoanalytic work in accessible ways (e.g. the best-seller by psychoanalyst Stephen Grosz, 2013)[2] shows how great the interest is, but too often these efforts meet disdain or are given little recognition for what they achieve. Rather, they should be critically supported and consideration given to what makes such public communication of psychoanalysis effective – something that could also be taught, as it is in many sciences.

Inclusivity of practice

The desire for psychoanalytic clinical work to be more socially inclusive has resulted in many creative projects. I have outlined a few of these, but a much greater compendium and analysis is badly needed. This would not only help valorise such committed work but would also add to our understanding of psychoanalysis in greater contact with the wider world. Collective organisational and professional support for psychoanalytic work in these often challenging and complex environments is badly needed. A first step would be for more people who work in such projects to be supported to write up their clinical work, and their engagements with the conditions they work under. Further, these many forms of public and third-sector work need to be seen as central and not ancillary to the main business of psychoanalysis. The inevitable frustrations and tensions of engaging with bureaucracy and management in the public sector need not be seen only as tedious and demoralising (which they frequently are) and therefore withdrawn from, but also as something that can be taught and thought about psychoanalytically, as some writings illustrate. For example, the well entitled 'The Mole Leaves his Hole' provides an in-depth account of the exigencies of setting up a psychoanalytic service in the community and how these were overcome (Music, 2004). So also the psychodynamic and psychoanalytic counselling work carried out within the very difficult coal face of IAPT (Increasing Access to Psychological Therapies in the NHS) services needs to be addressed, and support given to those therapists, often younger, recently trained or on placement, who work in them. The recent detailed submission to Parliament by the umbrella organisations (UKCP and BPC) regarding IAPT, and about the support needed for psychoanalytic and psychodynamic work in the NHS, is an encouraging step from our representative organisations in taking political action.[3]

Many class-inclusive efforts have raised questions of whether psychoanalytic technique needs to be altered in different circumstances. The implication is often that any alteration to make psychoanalysis more comprehensible, more transparent, more culturally aware and inclusive, more flexible, is always a dilution or aberration rather than an enhancement, despite much evidence to the contrary. Fonagy (2006) has argued that the pervasive standardisation of psychoanalytic technique within the mainstream of the profession has led to a petrification which has hampered and devalued many inclusive and innovative clinical practices. This he contrasts to the creative proliferation of theories that has taken place. We know from various studies that psychoanalysts' actual clinical practices vary enormously, and may not conform to the explicit theories of their trainings, but instead rely more on pragmatic and implicit conceptual notions (e.g. Canestri, 2006). This increasingly explored aspect of the pluralism of contemporary clinical practice could allow more latitude and acceptance of innovative developments in projects at the cutting edge of inclusion and diversity.

The ways in which clinical work with disadvantaged groups or non-normative populations has actually contributed to psychoanalysis in issues of 'race', gender and sexuality as well as class needs to be given due recognition, which it does not currently get within mainstream bodies. So, too, the ways in which psychoanalytic skills can be used in combination with other psychological approaches (including even some forms of CBT) need to be taught and valued, as Taylor (2013), in his proposals for a revitalised profession, strongly recommends. Eschewing the discourses of purity and pollution, as Fereday (2015) also advocates, would help practitioners relate to the realities of modern mental health provision, and preserve spaces for psychodynamic and psychoanalytic work. Music (2004) argues that successful efforts such as he describes involve being prepared to compromise the 'purity of the strict psychoanalytic ideal', to earn the confidence of public sector staff through the 'soundedness' of psychoanalytic clinical judgement. This, he says, helped defray previous negative perceptions of psychoanalytic 'rigidity, inflexibility and elitism'. I do not underestimate the adverse powerful forces at play, and the strictures of limited funding, intrusive management and current ideologies, which some writings eloquently describe (e.g. Rizq, 2014), all of which can be undermining and depressing. I rather argue that a more vigorous, public and organised case be made for the contributions that different forms of psychoanalytic work and its various contemporary innovations can make within modern mental health provision, as is beginning to happen. This requires dropping some of the tribal passions and identifications embodied in the different organisations and schools of thought, and the defences of status and hierarchy, pure and applied. It involves stepping back from the narcissism of minor differences that is so destructively rife across the whole field, leading it to turn inward rather than outward towards the many contemporary challenges that psychoanalytic work faces.

Diversity and awareness

The experiences of therapists from working-class and non-white backgrounds entering the psychoanalytic field indicate how its implicit cultural mores can create dissonance and unease. More of these voices need to be heard and listened to. The reflections of such therapists provide useful insights into the variously transmitted ideologies and assumptions, especially the non-recognition of material and cultural differences. Their understandings of their own social mobility within the profession can also suggest much about the enduring effects and psychodynamics of class. All this could be an invaluable source of learning, as, in the case of 'race' and ethnicity, the powerful and much-viewed video, *Black Psychoanalysts Speak* (Winograd,

2014) has been. It could also be the means for collective support and action. The economic and structural disadvantages that trainees from working-class backgrounds face are further exacerbated by the role of social capital within psychoanalytic organisations. Networks of affiliation and patronage within psychoanalytic institutions are major factors in obtaining work and developing careers, but are seldom critically addressed. These also inhibit divergent and critical thought.

We have seen how psychoanalytic work in working-class and disadvantaged communities requires some understanding of the historical and present-day circumstances of such lives, and the respectful desire to explore these, given that nothing can be presumed in advance. It also requires analytic self-awareness of cultural assumptions and defences that may otherwise be unwittingly conveyed, some of which are exemplified in the psychosocial literature discussed previously. The question Gurney (2009) asks, whether one can be a psychoanalyst and *not* be symbolically middle class, could prompt self-reflection on how therapists may see themselves in relation to class, and how they may be seen within clinical work. Several psychoanalytic writers on 'race' and ethnicity have advocated the necessity for the history of colonial domination to be part of the self-awareness of therapists, extending the usual notions of transference/countertransference to include more cultural ones (e.g. Thomas, 2013). I suggest this should also be extended to histories of class domination, classification, exploitation and resistance, and the material and ideological aspects of class, as some clinical work is beginning to do.

Class within clinical work

The processes set in motion by any psychoanalytic encounter can provide a vehicle for understanding class as a psychologically complex aspect of a person. We have seen examples of how class can manifest itself clinically, including, but not limited to, the following: class within the transference–countertransference matrix; conscious and unconscious class-related identifications, imbued with many layers of meaning and affect; the traumatising effects of particular class experiences, often transmitted intergenerationally; and the unconsciousness with which privilege may be held and enacted.

Much clinical work reviewed concerns cross-class encounters and the difficulties that follow when the emotions aroused by these are neither recognised nor speakable. These various projections, disavowals and resistances are important in any one therapy. They underline the relationality of class as well as the insidious and harmful ways that it can operate on and between people. Such work, as well as illuminating the many ways class can come to constitute us, shows how it may become a vehicle for otherings of various kinds. The potential for such othering echoes some of the psychosocial work which suggests how 'us' and 'them' become expressions of unbridgeable difference, of conflicts of economic interests and cultures, and of intense, often hostile, emotion. 'Us' and 'them' is thus both a psychical default position in how class can come to be represented, and also a reflection of the economic and social divisions of a drastically unequal society. Such dichotomised thinking, often defensive, elitist, rigid and virulent in its consequences, can pose problems for a psychoanalysis that loses its connection to the social world. It can be seen as a form of paranoid thinking, in which despised characteristics are repudiated by the self and projected hostilely or enviously into the class other, with no recognition of similarities. But to see it only as that, without any recognition and understanding of the social chasm of inequality, power and circumstance that separates different classes, where one class profits from the exploitation of another, where indeed there are conflicts of interests and class struggle, is to perform the violence of misrecognition and to stymie useful clinical work. The clinical considerations of this book suggest how necessary and how difficult it sometimes is to hold the tension between these two perspectives, and not abandon one in favour of the other.

Powerful and ubiquitous as these othering emotions often are, I have argued that these alone cannot be an adequate account of how class has its effects on, in and through the psyche. Class identifications and identities, as built on processes of distinction and repudiation, and on circulating social imaginaries of various kinds, are only one aspect of how class operates, albeit a salient and prolific one. Rather we also need accounts of the formation of classed psyches in terms of the material circumstances and histories of different classes, and especially those of poverty, wealth and power; how class is embodied and transmitted in the earliest and continuing conditions of a child's social circumstances, and the kinds of class formations that follow from this. These material aspects have been much less explored psychoanalytically, apart from some of the sources addressed in Chapter 4, although there are rich autobiographical and wider psychosocial and sociological literatures to draw on.

Given the largely middle-class locations of psychoanalytic work, it is also important to generate psychoanalytic understanding of the inhibitions, defences, and disavowals of privilege that may be at play within therapy and outside, and which this book has gone some way to depicting. There may be understandable impatience or scorn for the attempts of middle- or upper-class therapists to understand the psychodynamics of their own privilege, but I have argued that this can be useful in several ways in addressing dominant mores. One is understanding and deconstructing the sheer unconsciousness with which middle-class capital of various kinds can be embodied and enacted, a kind of unconsciousness-raising exercise. This would make it less likely that middle-class cultural practices and values are seen as universal or unquestioningly superior, and leave more space for difference, understanding and respect. It would also allow greater awareness of how, within therapeutic dyads, any unconsciousness in this area can result in unhelpful enactments and limit therapeutic work. Analysis of the narcissistic dead-end of class guilt and of the ambivalences sometimes contained in well-meaning efforts towards greater inclusivity would also contribute to a less disavowed relation to privilege.

Further, some of the writings addressed here show how working-class figures may be installed in middle- and upper-class psyches in disavowed, foreclosed and melancholic ways. That is, a sense of class others may be embodied from childhood, with varying degrees and forms of unconsciousness, and then come to serve other psychic functions. This is one way, characteristic of a particular stratum, but central in the psychoanalytic literature, in which class comes to be represented internally. Here again it is not just class *difference* that forms identities built on privilege but also all the material and cultural resources and what these enable, within particular sets of relationships.

The clinical examples of this book have suggested how some therapists do integrate pertinent class issues into their work; these examples are necessarily diverse, and much more needs to be explored. Here, a desire and an ability to think psychosocially as this pertains to clinical work, to maintain a critical and culturally self-reflective approach to theory and practice, including to therapist subjectivity, seem essential. However, this does raise theoretical issues as to how the social world is represented psychoanalytically.

Shame and contempt

A less often articulated aspect of class is the way that the up/down dimensions of class hierarchies can be experienced, or be defended against, as matters of felt superiority and inferiority. I have suggested that this aspect of class is in many ways the most psychologically taboo; it offends any sense of respect and equality, yet it lurks under the surface in many encounters, and also in the enactments and resistances that abound in this territory. As

Chapter 3 showed, Freud did identify this up/down dimension of class as psychically powerful, only to discard it in favour of the putative primal scene, an unfortunate either/or move which has meant this aspect has received little psychoanalytic attention.

Shame and the associated feelings and defences repeatedly surface in work on the emotional aspects of class. Shame is often considered the most social of emotions, and along with the transformation of it into pride, it has a long political history in writings about subjugated lives and struggles against oppression. Shame and associated feelings are also prime mechanisms of class distinction, as Elias extensively shows. The subliminal elitism or subconscious superiority of the middle classes, described by several writers, and the more overt class contempt described by others, find their echoes in what Sayer (2005: 153) describes as 'the low-level shame, which shades into low self-esteem' as a product of subordinate class position.

Shame has many connections to the evaluative judgements, internalised or otherwise, which, as Chapter 5 suggested, are a ceaseless part of class. Lingering shame that was very hard to tackle was painfully described by some of the upwardly mobile therapists in my study. The way that class contempt can trigger feelings of class-related inferiority was illustrated in some of the therapists' accounts of clinical work. Helen Lewis argues that shame is especially hard to get rid of, because of the 'trapped' hostility towards the self that is involved and also because of attachments to the values of the supposedly shaming other, through whose gaze the self is seen (Lewis, 1971), as some of the sociological research has also shown. Shame also, as Sayer argues, can lead to *apparent* inarticulacy caused by a sense of lacking any authority to speak, especially in more formal contexts, something which Charlesworth's (2000) extensive work illustrates. This is very relevant to contesting the prejudices and biases as regards the suitability of working-class people for verbal forms of therapy. 'Finding a voice' was identified by several therapists from working-class backgrounds as part of their process of social mobility. Shame also undermines self-confidence, an attribute that the middle classes are seen as performing and possessing, however fragile that may be.

It is well recognised that therapy itself has the potential to be felt as a shaming experience. Foster identifies shame and its consequent anxiety as a key factor in relation to class and therapy: 'One of the least acknowledged barriers to treatment is . . . the emotional impact of class and the feelings of suspicion and shame that often characterize immigrant and oppressed cultures, and . . . feelings of superiority and guilt that characterize members of the dominant culture' (Foster et al., 1996: xiv). Trevithick (1988), describing the fear and antagonism towards therapy that many working-class women came with, notes how poverty intensifies feelings of shame and fear of humiliation. Class division is about more than economic deprivation or privilege: 'It's about constantly looking up or down to each other to see who is superior or inferior to us' (Trevithick, 1988: 73). Whitson (1996) also writes of the sense of class-related inferiority with which clients may come to therapy, in a society where simply being middle class is seen as a sign of psychological health. John Steiner (2015) argues that the inherent shame engendered by the analytic situation itself needs to be analysed.

Emotions in the register of shame, contempt and guilt, and the defences against them, are part of what make many discussions of class so inhibited and so charged, especially in a mixed-class context. Feelings of inferiority or superiority, and the associated displacements, projections and disavowals, are major aspects of class emotion.

Disavowal

My contention is that disavowal is a ubiquitous and powerful process involved in both the living and the representing of divisive social realities. We have seen how disavowal operates at a disciplinary level: how the theoretical extrusions and elisions that took place in the early formulations of psychoanalysis constitute a disciplinary disavowal that has limited and constrained the language and concepts with which to think psychoanalytically about class. This has, in combination with all the other factors considered in this book, contributed to the vacuum of psychoanalytic thought about class, and the relative lack of psychoanalytic interest in and understanding of working-class lives. In attempting to undo these various extrusions and disavowals, I have begun the process of reading class *into* psychoanalysis, something which could be taken much further. The valuable and extensive knowledge from related disciplines, of class as it is lived and felt about, could enhance efforts to extend the reach of psychoanalysis, both in more adequately understanding class concerns in any one therapy, and also in the committed engagements of psychoanalysis outside private practice.

Disavowal is also embedded in the living of class, its inequalities and destructive discriminations, in different ways for different class positions. Much of the sociological and psychosocial work reviewed substantiates the claim that in a culture dominated by middle-class values and economic power, working-class identities are commonly formed and lived through disavowal, and especially so in those institutions where working-class cultures, practices and allegiances are non-normative. Education is the prime example of this, with much of the most in-depth and psychoanalytically relevant psychosocial research on class taking place in this context of class confrontation, privilege and disempowerment. Disavowal can be a necessary protective and survival mechanism in the face of invasive and stigmatising social forces, a way of preserving some area of a valued self. Without it, as the work of Walls' (2006) on the double consciousness necessary as a shield to survive racism illustrates, breakdown may occur. There are, though, commonly psychic costs to such survival mechanisms, an area where psychoanalytic work has much to contribute.

Disavowals may also be anxiously embedded in upper- and middle-class ways of living class. Where there is a concerned or troubled perception of social injustice and a desire for inclusivity, there still may be othering, disdain, distancing, guilt and contempt at play, often unconsciously so, and paralysis of thought and feeling. This speaks to internal conflict and anxiety, and displacements of various kinds, which psychoanalysis is well placed to explore. In less consciously troubled perceptions, in what has been described as 'fortress mentalities', there may be foreclosures, a lack of recognition of the social realities of others, an unwillingness to acknowledge the implications of inequalities, in the interests of keeping undisturbed a privileged position and hermetic world view. Psychosocial writings have shown how this can result in the demonisation of working-class others. Psychoanalysis, in some manifestations of the discipline, has not been entirely free of this, in the labelling of sections of the working classes as too concrete in their thinking, too close to 'reality', less able to articulate emotion verbally, and therefore unsuitable for and excluded from analysis. These othering attributions are not only inappropriate and culture bound, but broadly fit with who can and can't pay for psychoanalysis. This is a problematic legacy that contemporary psychoanalysis could do more to disown.

Disavowals of social realities are also seen in current neo-liberal ideologies of self-sufficiency, and in denials of dependence and interdependence. This, Layton (2014: 473) argues, can be the source of the 'pathological narcissism and perverse states of disavowal' that she encounters in the clinic and perceives more widely.

Theory

Many theoretical issues have been thrown up by the explorations of this book, especially as regards the kinds of theoretical frameworks needed to more adequately encompass class and the impact of the social world within psychoanalysis.

I have argued that more weight needs to be given to how social forces and discourses impact on us and structure our psyches, whatever our class positioning. To do so can challenge the psychoanalytic assumptions of universal laws of the psyche outside of any social determination. Such universality was debated from early on and is still a dominant trope, if more qualified in recent debates. It is not, I suggest, a question that can be definitively settled empirically, despite sometimes being seen in this way; any 'findings' from cross-cultural clinical work are always open to contestation as to what they might mean. However, maintaining a questioning stance to this assumption is important as a signifier of openness to diversity and difference, and of a lessening of psychoanalytic hubris. It is also important in the debates about whether cultural and social factors are to be seen as relatively superficial, superimposed on supposedly fundamental psychic mechanisms, or whether they are to be treated as of equivalent (or greater) constitutive importance. I have argued that much greater space within psychoanalysis needs to be given to how we are constituted in and through the social world, in combination with the intra-psychic, and I have illustrated the problems that can arise in clinical practice when this is not done.

Positions in these debates predetermine what is seen and recognised in clinical work as important or intelligible, and how, if at all, class experience is explored and within what terms. The question is often framed as to whether a psyche outside power is conceived of, with power as external, to be internalised, identified with and/or resisted by an already existent subject, as much psychoanalysis implies; or whether we see ourselves as fundamentally constituted by these forms of power, dependent on pre-existing conditions and discourses which initiate our agency, the conditions of any subjecthood, as Butler (1997) argues. Adopting either of these positions is a strategic, philosophical and political decision but one which can have huge implications in what is then seen as possible, interesting and legitimate within the language and practices of psychoanalysis.

Positions which exclude or underestimate the foundational impress of social circumstance and history can be to the detriment of certain analysands, especially those who are in some way non-normative for psychoanalysis, as many examples have shown. Much is to be gained by an adequate inclusion and understanding of these conjunctures of personal and social circumstance, and the language used to represent them. Conversely, rather than neglect of social circumstances, the opposite response can occur, which is to see the force of social circumstance as so determining that little room is perceived for any intra-psychic investigation – a kind of psychoanalytic resignation. This is especially likely, as the considerations of Chapter 7 suggested, with non-white, non-middle-class analysands, commonly expressed as 'too much reality factor'. Here an unbridgeable opposition between 'reality' and the concerns of psychoanalysis is evoked, a consequence I suggest of the founding dualism of the psyche and the social. This blocks psychoanalytic exploration of what may be involved, takes 'reality' as self-evident, and neglects the constitutive relationship of each pole of this dualism.

Psychoanalysis, I have suggested, is typified by an ambivalence of class positions: as, on the one hand, a counter-normative, marginalised and subversive enterprise, but, on the other, one which can reinforce normative cultural values, adaptation to the status quo and organisational and theoretical compliance. These poles of possibility run through the whole history of psychoanalysis. Psychoanalysis is importantly counter-normative to many contemporary neo-liberal practices and ideologies in the mental health field, in its concern with the unconscious, with vulnerabilities, complexity, dependency and thoughtfulness, and, within some theoretical affiliations, its broadly humanistic values. It is also counter-normative in that psychoanalytic work is slow, takes time and does not offer quick solutions. However, in radically separating the psyche and the social, and privileging the former, it can unwittingly echo that aspect of neo-liberalism which also does that, which valorises the entrepreneurial self, free of any social context, where all mental health issues are seen only as matters of individual deficits, and the impact of social circumstance and policy are given no recognition. This makes it especially important that we find ways of integrating the social world more into our clinical and theoretical thinking.

Thus, the overall philosophical frameworks in which particular forms of psychoanalysis are embedded may facilitate or exclude the kinds of social considerations I have shown are important. Further questions arise about how the conceptual frameworks of psychoanalysis can embrace any such extensions, how we can more adequately embrace the social without losing the complexity, richness and specificity of what psychoanalysis can offer. This is an old question that first arose in the context of the historic free clinics. In contemporary times the relational position has productively carved out much more space for the social. However, it has done this through setting up an opposition with so-called drive theory, which is positioned as only a one-person approach, to be discarded in favour of two- or three-person psychologies. I argue that this opposition, like the dilemma Fenichel saw, is not a necessary one, stemming as it does from the presumption of the dualism of 'individual' and 'society' that, paradoxically, it also seeks to overcome. We saw how Reich, perhaps the arch drive theorist (and taken by him to problematic and homophobic extremes), also provided powerful and still relevant analyses of the social recruitment of unconscious drives and conflicts; this suggests that these are not necessary oppositions.

Rather, a form of theory is needed that encompasses the advantages of both the more socially orientated relational position and of modern classical psychoanalysis, with its languages of desire, drive and sexuality. Here I outline how, schematically at least, Laplanche's propositions might contribute to this. I have pointed out previously how Laplanche's theorisations led to him criticising Freud for scotomising the working-class figure of a nurse and her subjectivity. We also saw Hartman's innovative use of Laplanche's notion of enigmatic messages, as a conduit for the unconscious transmission of the exigencies of class, through the bodies and anxieties of the parents or caregiver. This important suggestion, if developed further, could create a theoretical space for the intergenerational transmission of class and class histories. There are many enigmatic and foreclosed aspects of class, in its dense imbrication of the personal, the sociocultural and the economic, and in the widespread unavailability of a language of class, especially in the worlds of therapy and psychology.

Contemporary trends in psychoanalytic and philosophical thought emphasise how as subjects we are always formed in alterity, under conditions we do not choose, and constituted through many forms of otherness. This means, to follow Laplanche, that the primacy of the other needs to find a central place in psychoanalytic theorising. This forms his critique of the ipso-centralising tendencies observable in Freudian theory, despite also its decentring of the subject. Laplanche argues that the other is primal in relation to the construction of human subjectivity and is always to some extent enigmatic. The enigma leads back to the 'otherness of the other', which is itself the other's response to his/her own unconscious, his/her otherness to their own self. He proposes a 'fundamental inversion' (Laplanche, 1999: 257) in which the individual's agency is seen as secondary to the founding moments of passivity or seduction, taking the latter in the most general (and not specifically abusive) sense of the term.

This 'fundamental inversion' has advantages compared to the postulation of two-person psychologies or concepts of intersubjectivity, which do not start from a position of constitutive alterity. Rather, in assuming two monads, they then try to explain the interconnectedness and interrelatedness of two individuals. Laplanche's emphasis on the role of the unconscious of the other in the transmission of enigmatic messages, and his reformulation of repression and drive in these terms, mean that his approach does not suffer from discarding core aspects of Freudian theory, which these other approaches are predicated upon. Laplanche proposes that drives are not primary but are constituted by impingements and incitements; and that the source of drives is the 'otherness of the other', as well as the body. Drives are thus seen as formed through the impingements and 'messages' of the adult world, as interiorisations of the enigmatic desires of others, carrying traces of these original external desires.

Laplanche's very detailed reformulations have only recently been applied by others to clinical work of varying kinds, and there are many unanswered questions as to how they can be put into practice clinically. Furthermore, his emphasis on otherness primarily involves other individuals and their unconscious, not social or cultural forces as such. John Fletcher (1992) and Butler (2014) however do extend Laplanche in this way, in the implications they draw for the status of Oedipal theory. Both argue that Laplanche's account of the origins of sexuality implies a significant departure from the universalising and restrictive assumptions of Oedipal theory. This chimes with my argument that to recognise the formative roles of non-parental figures, in the form of the hitherto disregarded working-class employees, in the early texts of psychoanalysis, does question the reductive and universalising assumptions at play.

Moreover, Laplanche's reformulations could also illuminate psychoanalytic perspectives on the intergenerational transmission of social history, an aspect of especial relevance to class, with its many forms of conscious and unconscious inheritance. Laplanche proposes implantation and intromission as processes that capture the ways we are subjected to and impinged upon by others. '[I]mplantation allows the individual to take things up actively, at once translating and repressing' (Laplanche, 1999: 136). It inaugurates the differentiation of psychic structures. Intromission is a more violent process, perhaps typical of many processes of racism or class exploitation, poverty and contempt. It blocks translation-repression, leads to foreclosures or repudiations, and creates elements that are resistant to any metabolising. Intromission can lead to psychosis, or to the unmetabolisable categorical imperatives of the super-ego. Laplanche thus provides us with the psychoanalytic underpinnings whereby individuals are subjected to the forces of the social world, through the enigmatic messages of adults, which are implanted or intromitted. These concepts are additions to the more familiar ones of internalisation, introjection and incorporation, which imply some kind of agency or activity of the subject, an 'I', not necessarily conscious. These, in Laplanche's account are secondary to and consequent upon these processes of implantation and intromission. In all these ways, Laplanchian theory can provide a framework, albeit one which leaves much to be worked out, for encompassing the impress of the social world and the workings of the psyche, how we are both subjected to and become subjects of class, thereby amplifying much of psychoanalysis. I am not here proposing his reorientation of psychoanalysis as any kind of an 'answer', but rather to show that it is possible to extend and enhance psychoanalysis to embrace our inextricable sociality, without discarding much of it.

Any such usage of theory also needs more historical, cultural and social frames of reference, as I have shown, and as the politically radical and other projects involved in transposing psychoanalysis into working-class contexts exemplify. Walkerdine (2015) also argues these understandings are needed to address the transmission of class in any one individual or in communities, and to avoid reductive and pathologising explanations in terms of supposedly inherent psychological characteristics. She sees the effects of complex histories of suffering across generations as a mixture of 'small' and 'large' histories, such that 'large histories are lived and mirrored in the small across haunted generations' (2015: 179).

Class does indeed haunt psychoanalysis: in the many disavowed and displaced forms that I have identified, in the limitations of theory, and in the recurrent concerns with the inequalities and discriminations of practice. There is much to be gained from a more adequate incorporation of class matters into the language and explicit discourses of psychoanalysis; in particular, it would allow a better recognition of all the psychoanalytic work that does take place outside private practice and lessen the condemnation of psychoanalysis as something only for the privileged. It would open up the whole area of how we are (differently) formed by class to the richness of psychoanalytic thinking. This would all contribute to psychoanalysis renewing itself and to better surviving contemporary ideologies, policies and financial strictures. But such a project does require the political will to do so: which returns us once more to the fundamental ethical and moral issues at stake in any consideration of class and inequality, and to the necessity for forms of collectivity that transcend purely individual concerns, important as these are.

Notes

1 'Applied' might be more appropriately used to designate non-clinical uses of psychoanalysis, when applied to other fields.

2 Other writers who popularise psychoanalysis include Susie Orbach, Darian Leader, Adam Phillips and Brett Kahr.
3 This evidence is available at bpc.org.uk, posted 15 June 2016.

References

Butler, J. (1997) *The Psychic Life of Power*. Stanford: Stanford University Press.
Butler, J. (2014) 'Seduction, gender and the drive'. In Fletcher, J. and Ray, N. (eds) *Seduction and Enigmas: Laplanche, Theory, Culture*. London: Lawrence and Wishart.
Canestri, J. (ed) (2006) *Psychoanalysis: From Practice to Theory*. Chichester: Wiley.
Charlesworth, S. (2000) *A Phenomenology of Working Class Experience*. Cambridge: Cambridge University Press.
Cooper, A. and Lousada, J. (2010) 'The shock of the real'. In Lemma, A. and Patrick, M. (eds) *Off the Couch: Contemporary Psychoanalytic Applications*. London: Routledge.
Fereday, G. (2015) 'Response to "a long-term strategy for the profession" by Nigel Burch', *British Journal of Psychotherapy* 31: 134–5.
Fletcher, J. (1992) 'The letter in the unconscious'. In Fletcher, J. and Stanton, M. (eds) *Jean Laplanche: Seduction, Translation and the Drives*. London: ICA.
Fonagy, P. (2006) 'The failure of practice to inform theory'. In Canestri, J. (ed) *Psychoanalysis: From Practice to Theory*. Chichester: Wiley.
Foster, R., Moskowitz, M. and Javier, R. (eds) (1996) *Reaching Across Boundaries of Culture and Class: Widening the Scope of Psychotherapy*. Lanham: Jason Aronson.
Grosz, S. (2013) *The Examined Life*. London: Random House.
Gurney, P. (2009) 'The ac(ci)dental tourist: Exploring the tribal areas between class and race', *Sitegeist: A Journal of Psychoanalysis and Philosophy* 3: 41–50.
Laplanche, J. (1999) *Essays on Otherness*. Abingdon: Routledge.
Layton, L. (2014) 'Grandiosity, neoliberalism and neoconservatism', *Psychoanalytic Inquiry* 34: 463–74.
Lewis, H. (1971) 'Shame and guilt in neurosis', *Psychoanalytic Review* 58: 419–38.
Music, G. (2004) 'A mole leaves his hole: An exploration of psychoanalytically-informed service development in the community', *Psychoanalytic Psychotherapy* 18: 285–304.
Rizq, R. (2014) 'Perversion, neoliberalism and therapy: The audit culture in mental health services', *Psychoanalysis, Culture & Society* 19: 209–18.
Sayer, A. (2005) *The Moral Significance of Class*. Cambridge: Cambridge University Press.
Steiner, J. (2015) 'Seeing and being seen: Shame in the clinical situation', *International Journal of Psycho-Analysis* 96: 1589–601.
Taylor, H. (2013) 'UK psychoanalysis: Mistaking the part for the whole', British Psychoanalytic Council discussion paper, June, 1–17.
Thomas, L. (2013) 'Empires of mind: Colonial history and implications for psychotherapy and counselling', *Psychodynamic Practice* 19. 117–28.
Trevithick, P. (1988) 'Unconsciousness raising with working class women'. In Krzworski, S. and Land, P. (eds) *In Our Experience*. London: Women's Press.
Walkerdine, V. (2015) 'Transmitting class across generations', *Theory and Psychology* 25: 167–83.
Walls, G. (2006) 'Racism, classism, psychosis and self-image in the analysis of a woman'. In Layton, L., Hollander, N. and Gutwill, S. (eds) *Psychoanalysis, Class and Politics: Encounters in the Clinical Setting*. London: Routledge.

Whitson, G. (1996) 'Working-class issues'. In Foster, R., Moskowitz, M. and Javier, R. (eds) *Reaching across Boundaries of Culture and Class: Widening the Scope of Psychotherapy*. Lanham: Jason Aronson.

Winograd, B. (2014) *Black Psychoanalysts Speak*. Psychoanalytic Electronic Publishing, Video Grants, 1:1.

INDEX

Abraham, K. 22, 24
Adorno, T. 15, 140
Ainslie, R. 134, 153–4
Altman, N. 67, 114, 135–40, 146
American Psychological Association 150
analysability 68
The Analyst in the Inner City (Altman) 135–40
anti-psychiatry movement 59
Argentinian Psychoanalytic Association 61
Armitage, K. 154
Aron, L. 74, 77
Association for Psychoanalytic Psychotherapy (APP) 57

BACC *see* Battersea Action and Counselling Centre (BACC)
Balint groups 78
Bandini, C. 166–7
Baraitser, L. 8, 14
Battersea Action and Counselling Centre (BACC) 63–5
Benjamin, J. 53
Bennett, D. 161–2
Berlin Poliklinik 21, 22–5; child analysis at 24; establishment of 20; founders of 22; funding for 22–3; lengths of treatment at 23
Berlin Psychoanalytic Society 23
Bernfeld, S. 21

'Beyond Consciousness? The Psychic Landscape of Social Class' (Reay) 91
Bibring-Lehner, G. 27
Big Flame 11
Black Psychoanalysts Speak (Winograd video) 175–6
Blackwell, D. 108
Bodnar, S. 108, 114, 122, 132, 137
Botticelli, S. 103
Bourdieu, P. 6, 91, 92, 107, 109, 141; psychoanalysis and 97–100; theorisations of class 84–5
British Association for Counselling and Psychotherapy (BACP) 4
British Psychoanalytic Council (BPC) 4
British Society 28
Butler, J. 15, 48, 182, 185

Calvo, L. 43, 46
Character Analysis (Reich) 27
Charlesworth, S. 63, 86, 179
Chavs: The Demonization of the Working Class (Jones) 96
Cherry, S. 77
child analysis at Berlin Poliklinik 24
The Civilising Process (Elias) 83–4
class: burden of 90; capital and 84–5; within clinical work 176–8; clinical writings of (*see* clinical writings on class, contemporary psychoanalytic psychotherapists); displacements and

152–5; education and 91; emotions and 1, 86–7; as exclusion 87–8; feminism and 91–2; gender and 2; hybridity and heterogeneity of 14; inequalities and 85–6; pluralistic approach to 12–14; politics and 6–9; processes and 82–3; psychoanalytic therapy and 5, 11–12; psychosocial thinking and 14–16; race and 2; Ryan and 9–11, 102–3, 118–19; and social mobility within psychoanalytic field (*see* psychoanalytic field, class/social mobility within); terms, use of 5–6; within therapy relationships (*see* therapy relationships, class within); as total figuration 83–4; as trauma 150–2; women and 87–8, 90–1
class, lived experiences of 82–100; ambivalences/ambiguities aroused by 87–9; Bourdieu and psychoanalysis of 97–100; evaluative judgements made as part of 89–93; middle classes and 93–7; overview of 82–3; sociological perspectives 83–7
class, psychoanalysis and 171–86; within clinical work 176–8; disavowal and 180–1; diversity/awareness and 175–6; inclusivity of practice and 173–5; money and 171–3; overview of 171; shame/contempt and 178–80; theory 181–6
Class, Self, Culture (Skeggs) 93
class decomposition 85
class difference, early awareness of 105–7
class drama 140
class mobility, psychic demands of 107–10
'Class Unconscious: From Dialectical Materialism to Relational Material' (Hartman) 146–50
clinical listening 70–1
clinical work, money and 164–7
clinical writings on class, contemporary psychoanalytic psychotherapists 134–56; Altman's reflection/projection model 135–40; displacements and class 152–5; Hartman's 'class unconscious' 146–50; Holmes's class as trauma 150–2; Layton's distinction/normative unconscious processes 140–6; overview of 134–5; theory types 155–6
Cobb, J. 54, 90, 99
cognitive behavioural therapy (CBT) 8
Coles, P. 48

Colombo, D. 42, 50
concreteness 68, 72
condescending alterations in technique 67
contempt 120–1, 178–80
Cooper, A. 59, 75, 89
Corpt, E. 103, 106, 109–10, 113
Crick, P. 160, 162–3
cross-class love/loss relationships 47–50; *see also* elision and disavowal of cross-class relationships; Freud, S.

Danto, E. 19, 20, 21, 23, 24, 25, 60
Davoine, F. 66
Deutsch, H. 26–7
Devine, F. 88
Dialectical Materialism and Psychoanalysis (Reich) 29
Dimen, M. 118, 150, 160, 163–4, 165
disavowal 180–1; class and 90; extrusion of class as 53–4
displacements, class and 152–5
Distinction (Bourdieu) 97–8
diversity, awareness and 175–6
dividedness, class and 90, 91
drive theory approach 136
Dynamic Interpersonal Therapy (DIT) 78

Eitingon, M. 22, 23, 24
Elias, N. 38, 83–4
elision and disavowal of cross-class relationships 36–54; abjected nurse and 37–40; love/loss and 47–50; Oedipus complex and 53–4; overview of 36–7; privilege and, identities built on 50–3; return of nurse and 40–3; Wolf Man case and 43–7
emotions, class and 86–7
Eribon, D. 99–100, 108, 153

Fairbairn, R. 65
Fallenbaum, R. 64, 135, 148–50, 152
Fanon, F. 67
Fenichel, O. 20, 21, 23, 31–4, 160; on capitalism 33; Children's Seminar group and 24–5; Freud and 31; *Rundbriefe* 25, 31
Fereday, G. 4, 172, 175
Fisher, D. 19
Fletcher, J. 185
Fletchman-Smith, B. 66
Fliess, W. 38
Fonagy, P. 174

Foster, R. 64, 67–8, 70–1, 179
Frankfurt Institute for Social Research and Critical Theory 25
Fraser, R. 9–10
free clinics *see* Berlin Poliklinik; Vienna Ambulatorium
free/low-cost clinics: accessibility to 60; BACC and 63–5; Freud's visionary speech about 57–8, 64; history of 58; innovations in 77–8; Langer on 61–3; political motivations/understandings and 61–6; White City project 66
Freiere, P. 65
Freud, E. 22
Freud, S. 21, 136–7; Colombo writings of 42; cross-class relationships and (*see* elision and disavowal of cross-class relationships); free/low-cost clinics and 57–8, 64; intention to debase notion of 43, 45, 47; Laplanche reworkings of 41–2; Miss Lucy R case 49–50; money and 164–5; Oedipus complex and 38–40; patients, disavowal of cross-class relationships in 53–4; on psychoanalysis *vs.* psychotherapy 73–4; seduction theory, abandonment of 39–40; Vienna Ambulatorium and 26; Wolf Man case 24, 43–7
Freud's Free Clinics: Psychoanalysis and Social Justice 1918–1938 (Danto) 19
Fromm, E. 25, 36
Frosh, S. 14, 58, 163
Fuechtner, V. 24

Gallop, J. 38
Gaudillière, J-M. 66
Gaztambide, D. 68, 73
Gherovici, P. 72
Glick, R. 114
Growing Up Girl (Walkerdine) 94–5
Gurney, P. 140, 176

Hanley, L. 2, 94, 145
Hardin, H. 48
Harris, A. 52–4, 138, 149, 152
Hartman, S. 135, 146–50, 155
Haynes, J. 165–6
Herron, W. 69
The Hidden Injuries of Class (Sennett and Cobb) 6, 90
Hill, S. 52
Hinshelwood, R. 53, 54

Hirsch, I. 166
Hitschmann, E. 26
Hoggart, R. 7
Hoggett, P. 63, 65, 124
Holland, R. 65
Holland, S. 61, 65–6
Holman, D. 63
Holmes, D. 135, 137, 150–2
Horney, K. 31

IAPT (Increasing Access to Psychological Therapies in the NHS) 174
identification with aggressor 32
identities, built on privilege 50–3
Imperial Leather (McClintock) 36
implantation processes 185
inequality 1; as identifier of class 5; of accesst to psychoanalytic therapy 73; and stratification 85–6; dieregard of 172
Institute of Labor and Mental Health 149
institutional frameworks, class discussion in 110–12
internal oppression 32
International Psychoanalytic Association 28
interpellation 32, 58–9, 148
The Interpretation of Dreams (Freud) 37
introjection 151, 185
intromission 185

Jacobs, T. 165
Jacoby, R. 19, 31
Javier, R. 69
Jimenez, L. 8
Jones, O. 96–7
Josephs, L. 166

Klein, M. 24

Lambeth Mental Health group 65
Landscape for a Good Woman (Steedman) 136
Langer, M. 61–3
Laplanche, J. 41–2, 148, 156, 184–6
Lawler, S. 96–7
Layton, L. 15, 96, 98, 136, 140–6, 155, 181
Lebeau, V. 50
Lewis, H. 179
Light, A. 10
'Lines of Advance in Psychoanalytic Psychotherapy' (Freud) 21

London Clinic 20, 28
Lousada, J. 59, 63, 65, 75
low-fee or free psychotherapy 167–9; and clinics 2, 19, 21f, 28, 58, 60f; *see also* money
low-level shame 179

Maher, F. 106–7
The Mass Psychology of Fascism (Reich) 30
McClintock, A. 36, 40, 47
melancholia 51
Mentalisation-based Therapy 78
middle classes 93–7; *see also* therapists; therapy relationships, class within; Lawler on 96–7; Reay on 91–2, 93, 95–6; Skeggs on 93; Walkerdine on 94–5
Mitscherlich, A. 161
Moketzie, D. 51
'The Mole Leaves his Hole' (Music) 174
money: access to psychoanalysis and 171–3; clinical work and 164–7; discussion about, as indelicate 160; low-fee/free psychotherapy and 167–9; open dialogue about 173; overview of 159–60; political economies and 160–2; private practice and 159–60; psychoanalysis and exchange of 162–4; psychoanalytic work and 159–60; role of 172; symbolic meanings of 159
Moskowitz, M. 58, 67
Mountain, I. 70, 71
Mulvena, T. 76
Music, G. 175
Myers, K. 166

National Health Service (NHS), UK 2, 7, 28, 57, 59
Nobus, D. 162–3, 165
normative unconscious processes 32, 134, 140–1, 143, 151, 153

Oedipus complex 38–40, 53–4
one-person psychology 136
Orbach, S. 111, 164
otherness of the other 185
over-identification 128, 130

Parent-Infant Psychotherapy (PIP) 78
'Peasant in the Analyst's Chair' (Corpt) 103
A Phenomenology of Working Class Experience (Charlesworth) 63

Phillips, A. 162
political contexts of psychoanalysis 20–2
political economies, psychoanalytic 160–2
practice, inclusivity of 173–5
private practice, money and 159–60
processes, class and 82–3; Bourdieu on 84–5; Elias on 83–4; emotions and 86–7; inequality and 85–6
psyche, defined 15–16
psychoanalysis: in America 74; challenges to 8–9; divisions within field of 73–8; excess hierarchy in field of 75; exchange of money and 162–4; exclusivity of 2; introduction to 1–16; organisations representing 4; perceptions of 2; *vs.* psychotherapy 73–6; in public sectors (*see* public sectors, psychoanalysis in); pure gold of 73, 172; in UK 74–5; working-class patients of 2–3
psychoanalysis history 19–34; Berlin Poliklinik and 22–5; Fenichel and 31–4; overview of 19–20; Reich and 28–31; social/political contexts of 20–2, 24–5; Vienna Ambulatorium and 25–8
psychoanalytic community 4
psychoanalytic consultations/supervision for mental health staff 78
psychoanalytic field, class/social mobility within 102–15; class difference, early awareness of 105–7; class mobility, psychic demands of 107–10; hybridity/ heterogeneity of 103–5; institutional frameworks and 110–12; overview of 102–3; therapists as patients and 112–15
Psychoanalytic Psychotherapy 59
psychoanalytic psychotherapy, copper alloy of 172
psychoanalytic therapy: defined 4; innovations in 77–8; overlap in field of 4–5
psychodynamic counselling 4, 172
psychosocial thinking, class and 14–16
psychotherapeutic culture and class 66–73
Psychotherapy and Counselling Union 167, 173
public sectors, psychoanalysis in 57–78; divisions within psychoanalytic field and 73–8; free/low-cost clinics and 60; overview of 57–9; political motivations/understandings and 61–6;

psychotherapeutic culture/class and 66–73
Puget, J. 126, 131

Racker, H. 61
Reay, D. 69, 91–2, 95–7, 99–100, 107–8, 110, 112
Red Therapy 11
reflection/projection model, Altman's 135–40
Reich, A. 21
Reich, W. 11, 21, 25, 28–31; clinical vs. political aspects of 28–9; Vienna Ambulatorium and 27
relational psychoanalysis privilege, identities built on 51–2
Rendon, M. 67
The Repression of Psychoanalysis (Jacoby) 19
Respect (Sennett) 1
Riviere, J. 37
Rosa, M. 70, 71
Rundbriefe (Fenichel) 25, 31
Rustin, M. 159, 162, 163
Ryan, J. 103, 118

Sales, S. 59
Sanville, J. 131
Savage, M. 85
Sayer, A. 86–7, 89, 179
Scheftel, S. 48–9
Schloss Tegel Sanatorium 24
Schneider, M. 160–1
Schonbar, R. 166
The Second Mother (Coles) 40
Sennett, R. 1, 48, 54, 90, 99, 114, 125
Sex-Pol 30
shame 84, 99, 178–80
Shanok, A. 166
Simmel, E. 22, 24, 31
Skeggs, B. 5, 10, 49, 63, 85–8, 90–2, 111
social class categories, elevation of 139
social contexts of psychoanalysis 20–2, 24–5
social marginalisation 70
social mobility *see* psychoanalytic field, class/social mobility within
Social Mobility and Child Poverty Commission 7
social psychoanalysis 97–8
societal opposing forces 151
Spurling, L. 132
Starr, K. 74, 77

Steedman, C. 136
Steiner, J. 180
Steinmetz, G. 97, 98
Strachey, A. 24
stratification, inequality and 85–6
subjectivity, defined 15
Suchet, M. 51–2
Swan, J. 38
symbolic violence 91

Taylor, H. 4, 58, 76–7, 78, 175
therapeutic collusion with neo-liberal values 136
therapists: middle-class, middle-class patients and 130–2; middle-class, working-class patients and 123–6; as patients 112–15; working and lower middle-class, middle-class patients and 120–3; working and lower middle-class, working-class patients and 126–9
therapy relationships, class within 118–32; middle-class patients and working/lower middle-class therapists 120–3; middle-class therapists and working-class patients 123–6; middle-class therapists with middle-class patients 130–2; overview of 118–19; similarities of 126–32; working-class patients and working/lower middle-class therapists 126–9
Trevithick, P. 70, 152, 179–80
Tyler, I. 5, 85, 86, 91

ungrievable lives 48
United Kingdom Council for Psychotherapy (UKCP) 4
'The Universal Tendency to the Debasement in the Sphere of Love' (Freud) 47
unlinking 15, 97, 134, 140

Vienna Ambulatorium 25–8; closing of 27; establishment of 20, 25; funding for 26; politics and 25–6; training institute and 26–7
Vienna Psychoanalytic Society 25, 26

Wachtel, P. 59
Walkerdine, V. 8, 66, 94–5, 115, 186
Walls, G. 54, 181
Walton, J. 37
Waters, M. 88

The Weight of the World (Bourdieu) 92
White City project 66
Whitman-Raymond, L. 69, 103, 112, 118, 128
Whitson, G. 71, 180
Wiener, J. 165–6
Winnicott, D. 51
Wolf Man case, class and 43–7; intention to debase notion and 43, 45, 47

working class: access to psychoanalytic therapy 21, 27, 60, 66f, 171–2; 'analysability' and 58, 68; bias against 2–3; disavowal and 180–1; women and 88, 90–1; *see also* class

Young-Bruehl, E. 139

Zajic, M. 38